How to Do *Everything* with

Microsoft® Office
Outlook® 2003

D1531003

Conversation

Hello!

Send

How to Do *Everything* with

Microsoft® Office
Outlook®
2003

Bill Mann

McGraw-Hill/Osborne

New York Chicago San Francisco Lisbon
London Madrid Mexico City Milan New Delhi
San Juan Seoul Singapore Sydney Toronto

The McGraw·Hill Companies

McGraw-Hill/Osborne
2100 Powell Street, 10th Floor
Emeryville, California 94608
U.S.A.

To arrange bulk purchase discounts for sales promotions, premiums, or fund-raisers, please contact **McGraw-Hill**/Osborne at the above address. For information on translations or book distributors outside the U.S.A., please see the International Contact Information page immediately following the index of this book.

How to Do Everything with Microsoft® Office Outlook® 2003

34567890 CUS CUS 01987654

ISBN 0-07-223070-3

Publisher:	Brandon A. Nordin
Vice President &	
Associate Publisher	Scott Rogers
Executive Editor	Jane Brownlow
Acquisitions Editor	Katie Conley
Project Editor	Elizabeth Seymour
Acquisitions Coordinator	Tana Allen
Technical Editor	Will Kelly
Copy Editors	Robert Campbell, Peter Weverka
Proofreader	John Gildersleeve
Composition	Carie Abrew, Tara A. Davis, John Patrus, Kelly Stanton-Scott
Illustrators	Kathleen Fay Edwards, Melinda Moore Lytle, Dick Schwartz, Lyssa Wald
Series Design	Mickey Galicia
Cover Series Design	Dodie Shoemaker
Cover Illustration	Eliot Bergman

This book was composed with Corel VENTURA™ Publisher.

Dedication

This book is dedicated to Patti and Jenn, who continue to tolerate my wacky writer's hours.

About the Authors

Bill Mann is the author of more than a dozen books, plus numerous technology articles for publications including *Internet World*, *TECH Edge*, *Palm Power*, and *Computer Bits*. Bill's past titles published by McGraw-Hill/Osborne include *How to Do Everything with Your Tablet PC*, *I Want My MP3! How to Download, Rip, & Play Digital Music*, and *Genealogy Online Special America Online Edition*. In addition to writing about Outlook, Bill develops and leads online courses in Outlook 2000, Outlook 2002, and Outlook 2003. When not working, Bill spends time with his family in Bedford, New Hampshire, and plays far too many computer games.

About the Technical Editor

Will Kelly is a long-time computer book technical editor who has worked on 30+ books about Microsoft Office, Outlook, HTML, Web development, and related topics. He currently works as a freelance technical writer and requirements analyst working on projects for the federal government as well as commercial clients. His articles frequently appear on CNET Builder.com and TechRepublic.com. He resides in the Washington, D.C. area where he gets away from work by hitting the gym and going to spinning classes.

Contents at a Glance

Contents

Acknowledgments

I want to thank everyone at McGraw-Hill/Osborne who was involved in this project and, in particular, Katie, Elizabeth, and Tana who made sure the project kept moving in the right direction.

Will, a big thank you for your insightful tech editing.

Bob and Peter, the same for your copy edits.

Finally, special thanks go to my agent, Margot. I really appreciate your efforts on my behalf.

Introduction

Microsoft Outlook has been a key part of the Microsoft Office suite since it made its first appearance. In the latest incarnation of Office, dubbed Microsoft Office System 2003 (sometimes also called Office 11), Outlook remains a key element. Perhaps reflecting this central position in Office, the latest version of Outlook (Microsoft Office Outlook 2003) is by far the most significantly redesigned (and improved) application in Office.

The greatest improvements in Outlook 2003 deal with e-mail. Some of the biggest e-mail related improvements are:

- A Reading Pane that shows far more of the contents of a message, in a much more readable form than in previous versions

- Search Folders that solve the old problem of figuring out where to put a message that deals with more than one topic

- A Navigation Pane that combines the old Outlook bar, the Folders List, and more into a compact, context-sensitive form

- Quick Flags that make marking a message for future action a one-click activity

- Intelligent grouping of messages, including a threaded conversation view

Other aspects of Outlook, while not changed as extensively, did undergo improvements, such as:

- The ability to view multiple Calendars side by side

- Tighter integration with Windows Messenger and Outlook Express

- Cached Exchange Mode, which shelters you from many network problems and allows you to keep working in Outlook on the run

This book is meant to be a practical guide to Outlook 2003. It isn't an encyclopedic reference guide that covers every possible way of doing anything you can do with Outlook 2003. This application is so flexible and capable, and does so much that I shudder to think how big such a book would be. Instead, *How to Do Everything with Microsoft Office Outlook 2003* is designed to be your guide to the key things that you'll need to do to set up, use, and maintain Outlook 2003. You'll find one good way to do each of the things you'll commonly need to do (along with a keyboard shortcut, if there is one, that does the same thing faster and easier).

The focus of this book is on Outlook 2003 as a stand-alone e-mail and personal information management (PIM) application. If you are using Outlook at home, and connect to e-mail from your Internet Service Provider (ISP) or a web-based service like HotMail, this book is targeted at you.

If you use Outlook 2003 at work, it is probably connected to a Microsoft Exchange server. In this case, Exchange manages Outlook's connections to the rest of the world. Almost everything in this book will still be applicable to you, although you should pay particular attention to Chapter 23, which talks about the major differences between using Outlook as a stand-alone application and when it is connected to Exchange.

The book is divided into five parts:

In Part I, "Get Acquainted with Outlook 2003," you'll do exactly that. From a quick tour of the significantly improved user interface, to the basics of keyboard shortcuts and the Outlook help systems, to installing and configuring Outlook 2003, this part gets you up and running.

In Part II, "Communicate Using Outlook 2003," you'll learn about using Outlook to interact with others. We're not talking only about sending and receiving e-mail here—Outlook 2003 can work with Windows Messenger (an instant messaging application) and Outlook Express (a newsgroup reader) to give you a complete online communication system. This section also covers many of the most important improvements to Outlook—features like intelligent message grouping, Quick Flags, and the long-awaited junk mail filter.

In Part III, "Manage Your Personal Information," you'll learn all about the PIM side of Outlook. With the Calendar, Contacts, Tasks, and Notes sections in Outlook, you'll be able to manage and find the personal information you need.

In Part IV, "Customize and Manage Outlook 2003," we look at the ways you can modify how Outlook works to better suit your needs. This is also the part of the book where we tackle more complex subjects like using Search Folders, managing and archiving your Outlook information, and attending to your online security.

In Part V, "Go Further with Outlook 2003," we delve into subjects that are important but don't fit in other parts of the book. This is where you learn to use the Research Library to conduct basic research without ever leaving the Outlook window, communicate with Outlook using handwriting and speech recognition, and work with Microsoft Exchange, Windows SharePoint Services, and other Microsoft Office System applications.

As I hope you can tell from this Introduction, I've written this book in a casual, easy-to-read style. It's designed so that, to the extent possible, each chapter stands alone. You can certainly read the book cover to cover, and I encourage you to at least read the introduction to each chapter. But if you're looking for specific information, you can skip around without worry. To make the book more useful to you, we've included certain helpful design elements. They are:

- **How To sidebars**   How To sidebars provide step-by-step instructions on completing a specific task. They can be particularly important tasks, or just tasks that are related to a subject we're discussing in the chapter.

- **Did You Know sidebars**   Did You Know sidebars contain extra information. They're usually background info like historical notes or other interesting tidbits.

- **Note icons**   Note icons provide helpful information related to the topic at hand. Be sure to read any Note you come across.

- **Tip icons**   Tip icons describe ways to make better use of an application or feature, as well as anything that might make things easier.

- **Shortcut icons**   Shortcut icons provide quicker and easier ways to do things. They're good to read if you want to make the best use of your Tablet PC.

- **Caution icons**   Caution icons flag items you need to be aware of. Always read these to avoid potential problems.

With that said, you're ready to learn how to do everything with Microsoft Office Outlook 2003. If you have any thoughts on the book, or about Outlook 2003 in general, I would love to hear them. You can reach me by e-mail at: books@techforyou.com

Part I

Get Acquainted with Microsoft Office Outlook 2003

Chapter 1

Welcome to Microsoft Office Outlook 2003

How to...

- Navigate the Redesigned Outlook Interface

- Use Other New Features and Capabilities

- Take Advantage of Some Common Keyboard Shortcuts

- Use the Help Systems

Microsoft Office Outlook 2003 is part of the Microsoft Office System 2003. Along with Word, Excel, and PowerPoint, Outlook has been part of the standard Microsoft Office suite for some time now. In Office System 2003, Outlook received a significant redesign that makes it more efficient and more powerful.

This chapter is a quick guide to the new and improved features of Outlook, as well as an introduction to the redesigned user interface and help systems.

Navigate the Redesigned Outlook Interface

The new Outlook user interface makes it easier to deal with the flood of messages and information flowing through your life. Figure 1-1 shows the Outlook user interface in the Mail view. While Outlook by its nature must present a lot of information on the screen, if you've used previous versions of the product, you'll probably notice that the new design is cleaner, with more room for actually reading message text.

Getting Around and Switching Sections

While Chapter 4 goes into detail on navigating the Mail view specifically, we can use this view to get a quick overview of the new user interface:

The bulk of the Outlook window is divided into two or more columns. The leftmost column (Figure 1-2) is the *Navigation pane*. The Navigation pane takes over the functions of the Outlook bar and the Folder list from previous versions. In addition, the Navigation pane displays folders and other information relevant to a specific view.

The content and even the title of the Navigation bar automatically change to match the view you're working in. The main Outlook sections—Mail, Calendar, Contacts, Tasks, Notes, and Journal—each have their own highly customizable view. Changing between sections is as easy as clicking the large buttons at the bottom of the Navigation pane, selecting a destination from the Go menu, or using simple keyboard shortcuts.

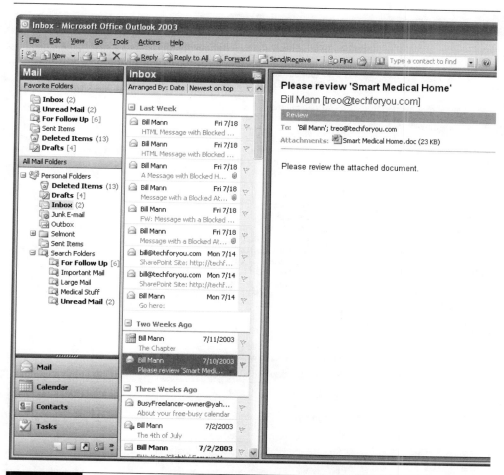

FIGURE 1-1   The new Outlook user interface is cleaner and provides more room for reading messages than old versions did.

An Improved E-Mail Reading Experience

Newspapers and magazine publishers have spent literally hundreds of years refining the ways that they present text to their readers. Microsoft has taken advantage of that work to transform the way Outlook 2003 presents your e-mail messages. The vertical column orientation you saw in Figure 1-1 is part of this, as is the *Reading pane*. The Reading pane (Figure 1-3) is vertically oriented, like a column in a newspaper or magazine, and allows you to see far more of a message without scrolling than the old design did. And it is plain easier on the eyes than the horizontal orientation of earlier versions.

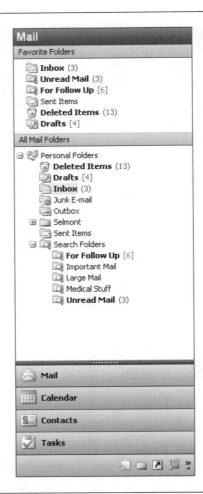

FIGURE 1-2 The Navigation pane integrates the old Outlook bar and Folder list with specific information on each view, freeing screen space and simplifying your work.

Chapter 4 provides complete information on Mail view, the Reading pane, and other interface enhancements that make working with your mail in Outlook 2003 a superior experience.

Use Other New Features and Capabilities

Aside from a new user interface, Outlook 2003 has numerous additional improvements and new features. Here are some of the major ones:

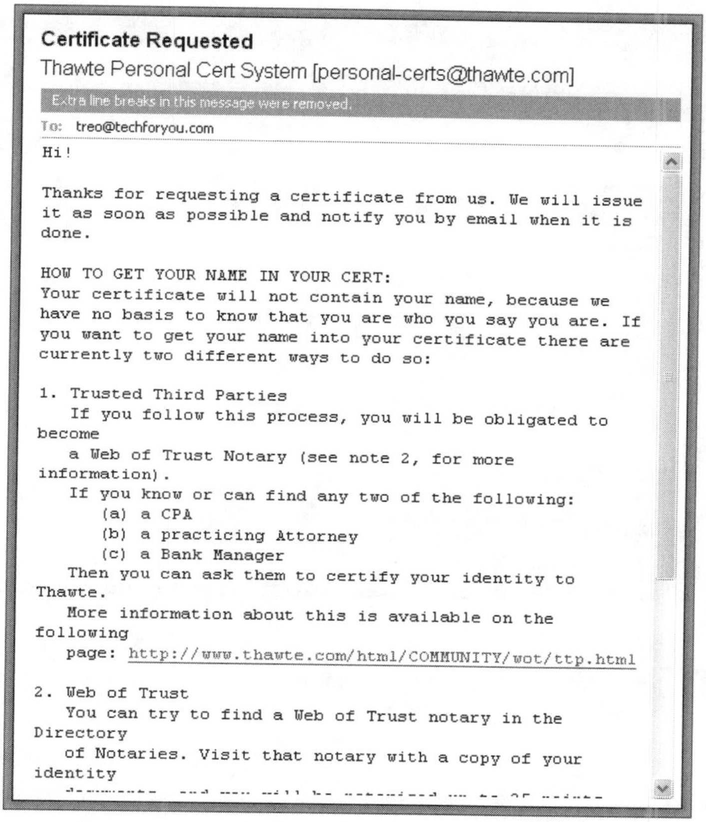

Certificate Requested
Thawte Personal Cert System [personal-certs@thawte.com]

Extra line breaks in this message were removed.

To: treo@techforyou.com

Hi!

Thanks for requesting a certificate from us. We will issue
it as soon as possible and notify you by email when it is
done.

HOW TO GET YOUR NAME IN YOUR CERT:
Your certificate will not contain your name, because we
have no basis to know that you are who you say you are. If
you want to get your name into your certificate there are
currently two different ways to do so:

1. Trusted Third Parties
    If you follow this process, you will be obligated to
become
    a Web of Trust Notary (see note 2, for more
information).
    If you know or can find any two of the following:
        (a) a CPA
        (b) a practicing Attorney
        (c) a Bank Manager
    Then you can ask them to certify your identity to
Thawte.
    More information about this is available on the
following
        page: http://www.thawte.com/html/COMMUNITY/wot/ttp.html

2. Web of Trust
    You can try to find a Web of Trust notary in the
Directory
    of Notaries. Visit that notary with a copy of your
identity

FIGURE 1-3   The Reading pane provides a larger, easier-to-view area for reading messages.

Search Folders (New)

Search folders are virtual folders that address the problem of what to do with messages that pertain to more than one subject. One message can appear in many search folders without your having to move or copy it. Outlook comes with four predefined search folders (For Follow Up, Important Mail, Large Mail, and Unread Mail), and you can create additional search folders that let you easily organize messages in ways that make sense to you. Figure 1-4 shows the four predefined search folders, as well as one, Medical Stuff, that I defined myself.

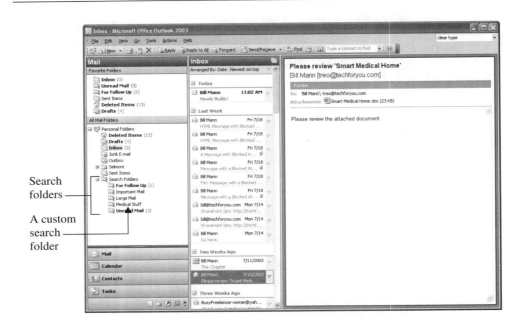

Search folders —

A custom search folder —

FIGURE 1-4 Predefined and custom search folders let you organize messages without moving and copying them.

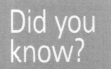
Outlook 2003 Works Particularly Well with a Tablet PC?

While Outlook 2003 is designed to meet the needs of the huge number of Microsoft Office users around the world, some of its new features prove to be particularly useful for Tablet PC owners. As I've worked on this book using Outlook 2003 on my Tablet PC, I've found these features to be particularly helpful:

■ **Ink support** Tablet PCs support digital ink and allow you to write on their screens with a special digital pen as if you were writing on a piece of paper. Outlook 2003 (and all the Office System 2003 applications) support digital ink. In Outlook, you can take advantage of the Tablet PC's built-in handwriting recognition, annotate Outlook items with ink, even send handwritten e-mail messages.

■ **Pen-friendly interface**   When you use a Tablet PC, you're usually using an electronic pen to tap buttons and icons instead of clicking them with a mouse. The large buttons in the Navigation pane are easy to tap with the pen. Similarly, you can select large, easily tapped icons for your toolbars. In addition, you can use a Tablet PC with its screen oriented vertically, as well as horizontally like on a regular PC. Outlook recognizes when the screen orientation changes and automatically reconfigures itself to make the most efficient use of screen space.

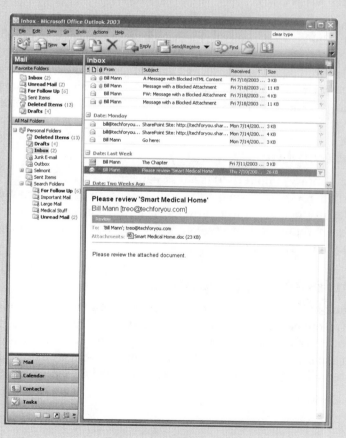

■ **Improved connection management**   Outlook 2003 is designed to allow you to work efficiently whether your computer is currently connected to Microsoft Exchange (Microsoft's messaging and collaboration server) through a corporate wired network, a wireless network, or a dial-up phone connection (or even if it is completely unconnected), automatically changing the way it works to match the available connection. This is perfect for Tablet PCs, which are designed to move from place to place with no warning and need to take advantage of whatever connection happens to be available at any time.

Quick Flags (New)

Quick Flags are color-coded flags that help you keep track of which messages need attention. Unlike when using the message flags in earlier versions of Outlook, you can set a Quick Flag with a single click, clear it with another, and change the color of the flag with two. Messages with Quick Flags set automatically end up in the For Follow Up search folder, guaranteeing that you can always find them. Figure 1-5 shows some e-mail messages in the For Follow Up search folder, with Quick Flags set.

The Research Library (New)

The Research Library (Figure 1-6) is a task pane that you can invoke from within Outlook (and other Office System 2003 applications) to do research without ever leaving Outlook or opening a web browser. The Reference Library can gather information from online sources, reference files stored on your computer, and resources on your corporate network.

Junk Mail Filtering (Improved)

Electronic junk mail, spam, has become a plague on e-mail users. Outlook 2003 incorporates a sophisticated junk mail filtering system that can greatly reduce the amount of unwanted, unbelievable, and obscene junk e-mail messages you receive. You can set the Junk E-mail Filter to store suspected spam in a separate folder for later inspection, or trust it to delete the junk with no intervention on your part.

FIGURE 1-5   Quick Flags make it easy to mark messages for follow-up.

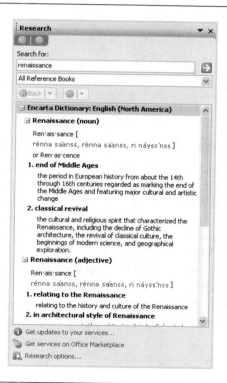

FIGURE 1-6   The Research Library lets you gather information without ever leaving the Outlook window.

To make the junk mail filtering system even more useful, you can define lists of safe and blocked senders and recipients, ensuring that messages from people you trust get through the filter and those you don't want to see always get blocked.

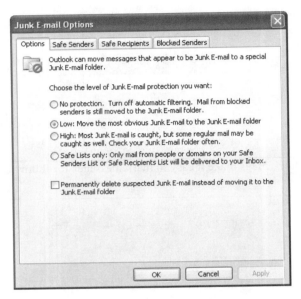

Enhanced Network Performance (Improved)

When connected to a Microsoft Exchange 2003 server, Outlook 2003 can communicate in more efficient ways, greatly reducing network message traffic. Of even more importance to you as an Outlook user, Outlook 2003 introduces Cached Exchange Mode, a completely new way of working with information from the Exchange server that helps insulate you from changes in your network connection. With Cached Exchange Mode, Outlook takes into account the bandwidth of the underlying connection to intelligently balance your need for the latest information with the connection's ability to deliver it. Thanks to Cached Exchange Mode, it is even possible to continue working with your e-mail messages and other Outlook items almost as if you had a good connection, even while you're not connected to Exchange at all.

Take Advantage of Some Common Keyboard Shortcuts

Keyboard shortcuts provide an easy way to navigate the Outlook interface. Keyboard shortcuts are combinations of keystrokes that perform some function that would otherwise require a mouse click, a series of clicks, or even navigating menus or dialog boxes. If you've never used keyboard shortcuts before, the "How to Use Keyboard Shortcuts" box provides detailed instructions.

Here are some common keyboard shortcuts you may find worth learning right away:

- **CTRL-1**   Opens the Mail view, regardless of the position in which the Mail button appears in the Navigation pane.
- **CTRL-2**   Opens the Calendar view, regardless of the position in which the Calendar button appears in the Navigation pane.
- **CTRL-3**   Opens the Contacts view, regardless of the position in which the Contacts button appears in the Navigation pane.
- **CTRL-4**   Opens the Tasks view, regardless of the position in which the Tasks button appears in the Navigation pane.
- **CTRL-5**   Opens the Notes view, regardless of the position in which the Notes button appears in the Navigation pane.
- **CTRL-6**   Opens the Folder list in the Navigation pane.
- **CTRL-7**   Opens the Shortcuts list in the Navigation pane.
- **CTRL-SHIFT-M**   Opens a new e-mail Message window.
- **CTRL-SHIFT-A**   Opens a new Appointment window.
- **CTRL-SHIFT-C**   Opens a new Contact window.
- **CTRL-SHIFT-K**   Creates a new Task.
- **CTRL-P**   Prints the selected item.
- **F3**   Opens the Search toolbar.
- **ALT-S**   Sends the current e-mail message.
- **F9**   Checks for new e-mail messages.
- **CTRL-R**   Opens a new e-mail message addressed as a Reply to the selected message.

How to ... Use Keyboard Shortcuts

Use a keyboard shortcut wherever it is faster or more convenient to use the keyboard than the mouse to accomplish a specific action. Wherever a keyboard shortcut appears in this book, it looks something like this: CTRL-SHIFT-M.

The three parts of this typical keyboard shortcut represent three keys on the keyboard. CTRL is the Control key (which on most keyboards is labeled "Ctrl"). SHIFT and M are the Shift key and the M key on the keyboard. When you see CTRL-SHIFT-M, it means to press M while holding down the CTRL and SHIFT keys. You can easily try this keyboard shortcut for yourself:

Open Outlook if it isn't already open. Now press CTRL-SHIFT-M. Outlook opens a new e-mail Message window.

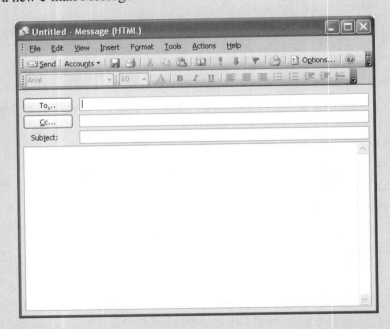

Now close the window and try creating a new e-mail Message window with the mouse:

1. Find the New button on the Standard toolbar.

2. Click the little down arrow to the right of the New button. This opens a menu of the kinds of new Outlook items you can create.

3. Click the Mail Message menu item to open the new e-mail Message window.

As you can see, using the keyboard shortcut can be a lot quicker than using the mouse. As they grow more experienced with Outlook, many people become heavy users of keyboard shortcuts, both for the time they save and for the convenience of not having to switch between the keyboard and the mouse so often.

You can find a much more extensive list of Outlook keyboard shortcuts in the Appendix. You will also find the keyboard shortcuts for specific actions listed where the action itself appears in the book.

Use the Help Systems

That's right. Help systems. Outlook 2003 has three help systems:

- There's the usual help that you expect to find when you click Help on the Outlook menu. This is the kind of help you found in older versions of Outlook, with a Table of Contents and a search capability. It looks a little different in this version of Outlook (see Figure 1-7) and includes lots of links to content on the Internet, but it is basically the same old help system.

- Then there's the Office Assistant, an animated cartoon character that provides you with tips as well as serving as a fun interface to the help system. You have a range of Office Assistants to choose from, with Clippit, the critter shown in Figure 1-8, as the default.

- Now there's also Microsoft Office Online, a web site containing the latest and greatest help information, along with lots of other resources you may find useful. As Figure 1-9 shows, Microsoft Office Online isn't confined to providing help for only Outlook. It serves as a central help and information resource for all the Microsoft Office System 2003 applications.

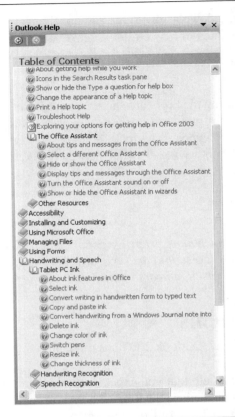

FIGURE 1-7 The traditional Outlook help system is still available, albeit dressed up and enhanced a bit.

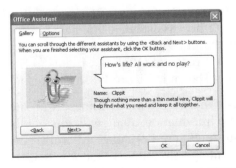

FIGURE 1-8 The Office Assistant can take many forms, including that of an animated paper clip.

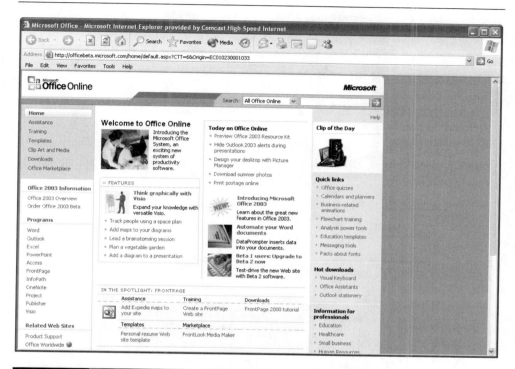

FIGURE 1-9   Get the latest help, tips, training, downloads, and information for Outlook
from the Microsoft Office Online web site.

The following sections provide guidance on when and how to use each of these
help systems.

Use the Outlook Help System or Microsoft Office Online

To get help from the Outlook help system or Microsoft Office Online, go to the
main Outlook window, then click Help | Microsoft Office Outlook Help. These
help systems share the Assistance task pane shown in Figure 1-10.

SHORTCUT   *You can also reach the Assistance task pane by pressing* F1.

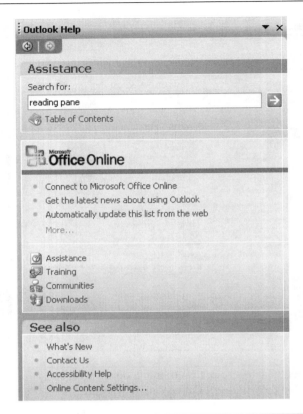

FIGURE 1-10 The Assistance task pane is a common location to find help in Outlook 2003.

You work with the Outlook help system in the top section of the Assistance task pane. You can enter a search term in the Search For text box and then click the arrow to the right of the box to search the help system for the term. Or you can click the Table Of Contents icon below the Search For text box to open the help system Table Of Contents you saw in Figure 1-7.

You work in the middle section of the task pane if you want to use Microsoft Office Online. You have options such as Connect To Microsoft Office Online and Get The Latest News About Using Outlook. If the Automatically Update This List From The Web option is visible, you can click that to have Outlook check for updates whenever you open the Assistance task pane.

Other features of Microsoft Office Online that you can connect to from this task pane include the Assistance page, a range of online Training courses for Office System products, the latest Downloads (templates and other products that work with Outlook, as well as updates to Outlook itself) and Communities, a collection of newsgroups related to Office System products. These newsgroups are places where you can ask questions of other Outlook users, as well as share your knowledge to help others. Figure 1-11 shows the microsoft.public.outlook newsgroup on Microsoft Office Online Communities.

Use the Office Assistant

The Office Assistant is an alternative way to get help in any Microsoft Office System application. Taking the form of an animated cartoon character, the Office

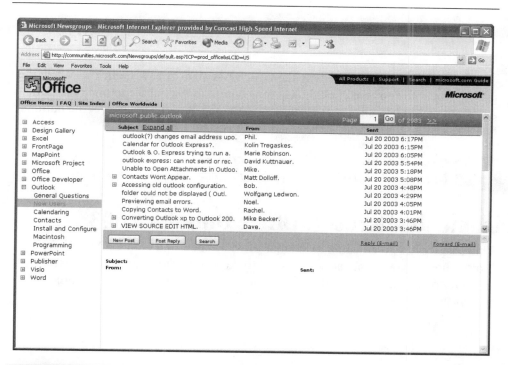

FIGURE 1-11   Microsoft Office Online Communities allow you to ask questions and share information with other Outlook users.

Assistant provides answers to questions (as if you had typed those questions into the Search For text box of the Outlook help system). It also offers you tips related to your current activities on the computer and displays system messages in little message bubbles instead of dialog boxes.

To activate the Office Assistant, click Show The Office Assistant in the Help menu. Once the Office Assistant appears, it will automatically offer suggestions whenever it sees the opportunity to do so. If you want to request help from the Office Assistant, click it. When you do, the Assistant displays a message bubble where you can enter a question or type the term you want to search for. Click Search to send the Assistant off looking for the information you requested.

If you want to change the way the Office Assistant behaves, click it. When the message bubble appears, click the Options button in the bubble to open the Office Assistant dialog box shown in Figure 1-12. On the Options tab, select the options that specify the things you want the Office Assistant to do.

 *If you don't want the Office Assistant to appear at all, you can clear the Use the Office Assistant check box to make the assistant go away.*

Welcome to Microsoft Office Outlook 2003

This chapter has given you a quick tour of what's new and cool in Outlook 2003. It also showed you some particularly useful keyboard shortcuts you can use with Outlook, and gave you the information you need to use Outlook's three help systems.

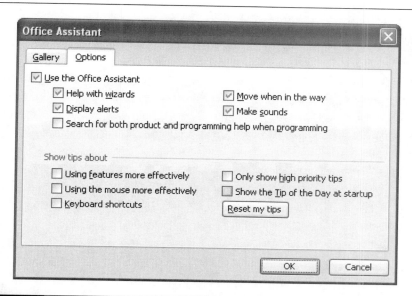

FIGURE 1-12   You can completely control the behavior of the Office Assistant from this dialog box.

It's almost time to really dig into specific aspects of Outlook 2003. But before you do, Chapter 2 helps you to be clear on the environment where you'll be using Outlook 2003, and shows you how to import information from an older version of Outlook if you've just upgraded to Office Outlook 2003.

Chapter 2

Get Ready to Dig In

How to...

- Understand Your Outlook Environment
- Avoid Upgrade Problems

Chapter 3 shows you how to install and configure Outlook 2003. But before you do that, it's worth spending a few minutes thinking about the environment in which you will use Outlook 2003. Outlook is still Outlook whether it is connected to a Microsoft Exchange server on a major corporate network or running as a stand-alone e-mail program on your home computer. But some aspects of installing and using Outlook do vary depending on the environment. The first part of this chapter describes the major environments you might use Outlook in, and points out any issues you should be aware of.

It's also worth spending some time learning about potential snags that can cause problems when you upgrade to Outlook 2003 from an earlier version of Outlook. The last part of the chapter addresses some possible problem areas.

Understand Your Outlook Environment

As I mentioned in the beginning of the chapter, some aspects of Outlook differ depending on the environment in which you use the program. While you can install Outlook and start using it without worrying about these differences, it can be useful to at least know about them, particularly if you are installing and maintaining Outlook yourself.

Outlook as a Stand-Alone Program

If you will be using Outlook at home, you will probably be using it as a stand-alone program. This means that Outlook 2003 connects directly to your Internet Service Provider for access to your e-mail. It also means that all your Outlook data will be stored on your PC, instead of on a central server that's backed up by someone else. Finally, using Outlook as a stand-alone program means that you'll likely have to set up your own e-mail accounts; attend to your own online security concerns; and manage, archive, and maintain your own Outlook data.

I wrote this book assuming that you are using Outlook as a stand-alone program. With the exception of Chapters 22 and 23, everything in the book is potentially relevant to you, and you should find Outlook working as described in these pages.

Outlook with Microsoft Exchange

If you will be using Outlook in a corporate setting, it will probably be connected to a Microsoft Exchange server on the corporate network. In this environment, the Exchange server interacts with the outside world. Outlook works as a client of Exchange, interacting with the rest of the world through Exchange.

You need to be aware of several things when you are using Outlook as a client of Exchange. The first and most important is that you need to talk to your network administrator before upgrading to or installing Outlook 2003. This is very important! Very few network administrators are comfortable having users installing major applications like Outlook 2003 without explicit permission and detailed instructions provided by the administrator.

Beyond this, there are several other things you should keep in mind. In most corporations today, by default, Exchange stores all your Outlook data on central servers, rather than on your computer. This is good in that your data will almost certainly be backed up for you. But it is bad in that if you lose the connection to Exchange (say the network fails), you won't be able to do much in Outlook.

However, if your network administrator authorizes you to use the new Cached Exchange Mode, Outlook maintains a continually updated copy of your data on your hard drive. In Cached Exchange Mode, Outlook becomes much less affected by the performance of the network. Within limits, you can work efficiently across slow or unreliable connections, and even work with your data while completely disconnected from the network (Outlook synchronizes everything for you the next time you have a connection).

> NOTE *Previous versions of Outlook used Offline Store Files to allow you to work while disconnected from the Exchange server. You might consider Cached Exchange Mode a highly evolved descendant of the Offline Store Files feature.*

The other important thing to know about using Outlook when connected to an Exchange server is that the network administrator can define policies that override your personal control of Outlook features. One example is a corporate retention policy, which limits how long you can store certain Outlook items.

Outlook with Windows SharePoint Services

Windows SharePoint Services allow you to connect Outlook to a shared team web site like the one in Figure 2-1. When you link Outlook to a shared team site, you

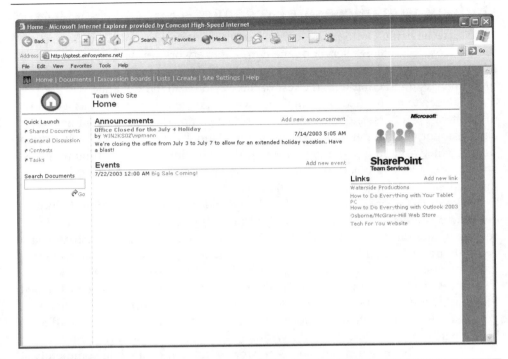

Outlook can integrate with SharePoint team web sites, simplifying online collaboration.

can view team events in the Outlook Calendar, view contacts from the team web site in the Outlook Calendar, and export some or all of your Contacts to the team web site.

If you use Windows SharePoint Services to connect Outlook to a team web site, you will probably do so in a corporate setting. The key thing to remember is that the SharePoint Team Site Contacts and Events you see in Outlook are just copies of the actual Team Site Contacts and Events on the team web site. You can't update the team site information from within Outlook, and whatever information you see only reflects the last time Outlook was able to update it.

Outlook with Business Contact Manager

Business Contact Manager is an Outlook 2003 add-on program that adds basic customer relationship management (CRM) tools to Outlook. Designed for

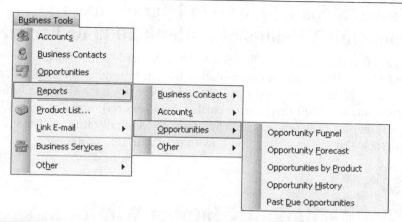

FIGURE 2-2   Business Contact Manager adds CRM capabilities and options to Outlook 2003.

individual sales professionals and very small companies, Outlook with Business Contact Manager adds new menus (like the one in Figure 2-2) and toolbars to Outlook that allow users to track business contacts, manage sales opportunities, generate reports, and more.

If you install Business Contact Manager, you'll still have all the regular capabilities of Outlook. The additional menus, toolbars, and folders related to Business Contact Manager will alter the appearance of Outlook slightly, but that's it. And of course, you gain all the sales and CRM capabilities of Business Contact Manager. These capabilities are described in Chapter 22.

Avoid Upgrade Problems

If you use an earlier version of Outlook right now and are preparing to upgrade to Outlook 2003, you should find that the upgrade goes smoothly in the majority of cases. However, there are a few situations where you might run into problems:

- Additional steps are required to upgrade from Internet-only versions of Outlook 2000 or earlier.

- Outlook 2003 does not coexist with earlier versions.

- Outlook is not fully compatible with old versions of Word.

Additional Steps Required to Upgrade from Internet-Only Versions of Outlook 2000 or Earlier

Outlook 2000 and earlier could be installed in Internet Mail Only (IMO) mode. This kind of installation supported e-mail delivered through Internet Service Providers instead of through Exchange server. If you are upgrading to Outlook 2003 from Outlook 2000 IMO (or an earlier IMO version), some of your Windows Address Book data may not appear. The "How to Manually Import Windows Address Book Data" box shows you how to deal with this problem.

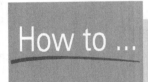

How to ... Manually Import Windows Address Book Data

Follow these steps to manually import data from your Windows Address Book when you have upgraded to Outlook 2003 from Outlook 2000 IMO or an earlier IMO version:

1. In the Outlook 2003 main window, click File | Import And Export. This opens the Import and Export Wizard.

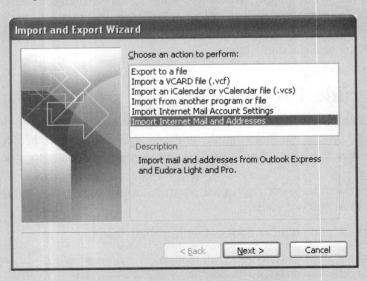

2. In the Choose An Action To Perform list, select Import Internet Mail And Addresses, then click Next. This opens the Outlook Import Tool.

3. In the Select The Internet Mail Application To Import From list, select Outlook Express 4.x, 5.x, 6.x.

4. Make sure that the Import Mail check box is cleared and the Import Address Book check box is selected, then click Next. This opens the Import Addresses screen.

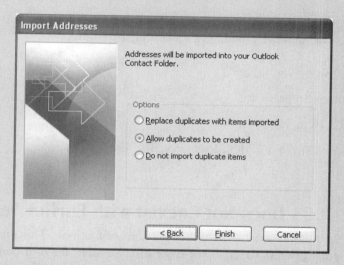

5. In the Options section of the screen, select the option you want Outlook to use when and if it encounters duplicate addresses, then click Finish to import the Address Book.

In addition to possible problems with the Windows Address Book, you may find some problems with rules when upgrading from an IMO version of Outlook to Outlook 2003. If you used multiple POP e-mail accounts with your IMO version of Outlook, and you created rules that use the Through The Specified Account option, those rules may not work in Outlook 2003.

The solution to this problem is to re-create the rules that don't work. Chapter 5 tells you how to create rules in Outlook 2003. If you create a new rule using the Start From A Blank Rule option, you will be able to create a new rule that uses the Through The Specified Account option and works properly in Outlook 2003.

Did you know?

You Can Upgrade to Outlook 2003 from Other Programs?

Upgrading to Outlook 2003 from an earlier version of Outlook is clearly the easiest and most efficient way to go. In this case, most of the work is done for you automatically. But if you've been using a different e-mail program and are moving to Outlook for the first time by installing Outlook 2003, you may still be in luck.

The Outlook 2003 installation program can upgrade you to Outlook 2003 from the following other e-mail and scheduling programs:

- Schedule+ 7.x, SC2
- Outlook Express 4.x, 5.x, 6.x
- MSN Explorer 8
- Eudora Pro and Eudora Light 2.x, 3.x, 4.x, 5.x

Outlook 2003 Does Not Coexist with Earlier Versions

Outlook 2003 cannot coexist with earlier versions of Outlook. This means that you can't keep a copy of Outlook 2002 (or any earlier version) on your computer when you install Outlook 2003. If you need to keep an older version of Outlook on your computer, do not install Outlook 2003.

Incompatibility with Old Versions of Word

Some features of Outlook 2003 work only when you are using Microsoft Office Word 2003 as your e-mail editor. If you are not upgrading to the full Microsoft Office System suite, or to Office Word 2003, do not configure Outlook 2003 to use Word as its e-mail editor. You will not be able to use features that depend on using Word as your e-mail editor.

Chapter 3

Set Up and Configure Outlook 2003

How to...

- Install Outlook 2003
- Start Outlook for the First Time
- Set Up E-mail Accounts
- Decide Where Outlook Stores Your Information

It's finally time to start working with Outlook itself. In this chapter, you'll install Outlook (if it isn't already installed on your system), go through product activation, and complete the basic configuration tasks. By the time you finish, Outlook should be up and running and you should be ready to send and receive e-mail.

Install Outlook 2003

Outlook 2003, and the entire Microsoft Office System as well, is available in many different forms and can be installed in various ways. Fortunately, if you're using Outlook at work, the IT department has probably already installed Outlook for you. Either that or they provided you with instructions on how to install it according to company policy.

If you have to install Outlook yourself, whether as a new installation or an upgrade, don't worry, because the process is highly automated. All you really need to do is make sure that your product key (the long sequence of letters and numbers is unique to each copy of Outlook) is handy and follow the instructions as they appear onscreen.

 If you are upgrading from a previous version of Outlook or from another e-mail program, Outlook will offer to upgrade from that program. As part of upgrading, Outlook will copy the e-mail messages, contacts, and other settings from your old e-mail program. I strongly recommend taking advantage of this option if it's offered.

During installation, an Account Configuration dialog box may appear. In it, Outlook offers to help you connect to an e-mail server. You'll learn all about the process later in the chapter, so for now, decline this option and finish the installation.

Start Outlook

Start Outlook. Assuming this is the first time Outlook 2003 has been started on your computer, you'll see the Product Activation dialog box. Product activation is an attempt by Microsoft to eliminate, or at least reduce, software piracy. The idea behind it is simple. When you install a product that requires activation, the installation program examines the hardware in your computer and generates an activation ID. Assuming your PC is connected to the Internet, the product then checks your activation ID against a central database at Microsoft to be sure that your copy of Outlook has not already been activated on another computer.

If you don't activate Outlook right away, a reminder appears each time you start the program. You can only start Outlook fifty times without activating it. After that, Outlook only lets you view items, but not create new ones until such time as you activate the product.

When you activate Outlook 2003, you can enter lots of personal information, but only your country or region is required. If your computer has an Internet connection, you can activate Outlook across the Internet. This takes a minute or two.

 *Don't be surprised if a message pops up on your screen warning you that a program is trying to connect to the Internet while you are activating Outlook. If this happens, just click OK, click Yes, or click whichever button is needed to allow the Internet connection.*

As shown in Figure 3-1, use the Activation Wizard to activate Outlook 2003 across the Internet. If the Activation Wizard is not visible, closing Outlook and opening it again should bring the Activation Wizard into view. Follow these steps to activate Outlook:

1. Read the Microsoft Office Privacy Policy in the initial Activation Wizard screen, and then click Next to go to the Customer Information screen.

2. Select your country or region in the Country/Region list. All other information is optional. Click Next to continue.

3. Follow the onscreen instructions to complete the activation process.

The main Outlook window should now be visible and should look as I described it in Chapter 1. Which folder appears when you start Outlook is determined by settings Outlook 2003 inherited from your previous version or settings that the IT department entered. You can make Outlook open in whichever folder you want,

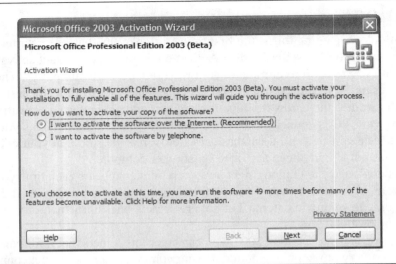

FIGURE 3-1
You can only use Outlook a limited number of times before you must
contend with the Activation Wizard.

including folders you define yourself, by following the procedures in the "How to
Specify which Outlook Folder Appears at Start Time" box.

Now that Outlook is installed and running, you might want to play around with
it a bit and check out some of the features you learned about in Chapter 1. Go right

Specify Which Outlook Folder Appears at Start Time

Microsoft makes it easy to specify which folder Outlook starts in. You can
specify any Outlook folder you wish, including ones you define yourself. The
procedure for starting in the Outlook Today view is slightly different. That
procedure follows this one. Follow these steps to choose which folder appears
when you start Outlook:

1. In the main Outlook window, click Tools | Options to open the Options
   dialog box.

2. Select the Other tab.

3. In the General section, click Advanced Options.

4. In the General Settings section of the Advanced Options dialog box, click Browse to open the list of all the available Outlook folders.

5. Select a folder from the list that appears and click OK. Your changes go into effect the next time you start Outlook.

If you want the Outlook Today page to be the default view, you need to follow these steps:

1. Open the Advanced toolbar, if it is not already visible. To do so, choose View | Toolbars | Advanced.

2. On the Advanced toolbar, click Outlook Today.

3. On the Outlook Today page, click Customize Outlook Today.

4. On the Customize Outlook Today page, set the When Starting, Go Directly to Outlook Today check box.

5. Click Save Changes.

ahead. After you're done playing, come back here to learn about setting up additional e-mail accounts.

Set Up E-Mail Accounts

If you upgraded to Outlook 2003 from an earlier version, your e-mail account should already be set up for you. Similarly, if someone from your IT department at work set up Outlook for you, your work e-mail account is probably already set up. In such cases, you may be wondering why you need to be concerned with setting up an e-mail account. The answer: Because most people have more than one e-mail account. You might have a work account that's connected to the Microsoft Exchange server at the office, as well as a personal one running on an Internet service such as Yahoo! or Hotmail. Many people have multiple work accounts and personal accounts. I have at least a half-dozen for various purposes.

Most e-mail services provide their own interfaces to their e-mail system, meaning you have to check for e-mail in two, three, or more different places. But with a little work, you can set up Outlook to handle virtually any e-mail account on virtually any system. You can arrange for all of your e-mail to come to the Outlook Inbox. You can read your e-mail and write e-mail messages for all your e-mail accounts in Outlook.

Outlook's ability to easily handle multiple e-mail accounts can save you lots of time and effort, but you need to learn a few simple rules that govern how Outlook handles multiple accounts. For now, the goal is to get Outlook connected to these accounts. You'll learn how to work with multiple accounts in Chapter 4.

> NOTE
> *Outlook 2003 works with e-mail servers using the following protocols: POP3, IMAP, and HTTP. At this writing, Outlook supports IMAP4, but not the new IMAP4rev1 standard. Your Internet Service Provider will be able to tell you which version of IMAP their servers use.*

Whenever you set up Outlook to work with an additional e-mail account, you need certain information from the e-mail administrator or Internet Service Provider (ISP) responsible for the account. The information you need is

- The type of the e-mail server you will be connecting to. Most of the time when you are working with accounts outside of work, you connect to a POP3 server.

- The name of the incoming mail server, the e-mail server that handles messages being sent to your account.

- The name of the outgoing mail server, the e-mail server that handles messages being sent from the account.

- The account's e-mail address. Outlook uses this to tell the server which e-mail account it wants to connect to.

- Your name. Whatever you enter in this field will appear in the From box of messages you send.

- The user name of the e-mail account Outlook will be connecting to. Usually, the user name is the first part of the e-mail address.

- The password for the e-mail account.

- Any special information that the ISP requires. You usually enter this information in the Internet Email Settings dialog box (the procedures that follow explain these requirements in detail).

After you have this information, you can set up the account.

 *At work, most e-mail administrators don't take kindly to the idea of employees connecting to additional e-mail accounts without permission. Assuming you get approval to go ahead, the administrator will likely set up the account for you or give you detailed instructions for setting it up.*

Set Up Exchange E-Mail Accounts

Microsoft Exchange is the corporate messaging server Outlook is designed to work with. Since it is part of the corporate messaging system, Exchange is not something you can mess around with, by, for example, setting up Exchange e-mail accounts on your own. Not only is it a bad idea to set up an Exchange e-mail account without the administrator's guidance, but you need additional information to get the job done. See Chapter 23 for more information.

Set Up Internet E-Mail Accounts

As you've learned, Outlook supports three types of Internet e-mail accounts: POP3, HTTP, and IMAP. While setting up each type of account is very similar, there are minor differences. The sections that follow walk you through setting up each type of account.

Set Up a POP3 E-Mail Account

POP3 accounts are the most common type of Internet e-mail account. POP3 stands for *post office protocol 3* (a protocol is set of rules, in this case for retrieving e-mail from a server). POP3 servers often use an SMTP server to transfer outgoing mail to the server that receives the message. SMTP, which stands for *simple mail transfer protocol*, is a set of rules for sending e-mail from one server to another. Together, SMTP and POP3 provide the ability to send and receive e-mail messages across the Internet.

Follow these steps to set up a POP3 Internet e-mail account:

1. In the main Outlook window, choose Tools | E-Mail Accounts. This activates the E-Mail Accounts Wizard.

2. In the Wizard's first screen, as shown in Figure 3-2, select Add A New E-Mail Account and click Next.

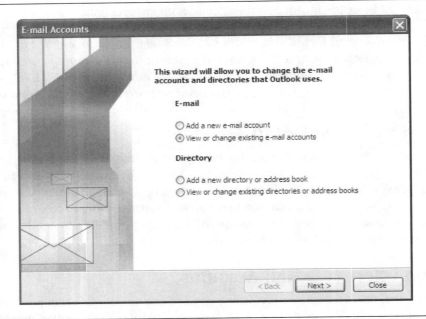

FIGURE 3-2   Tell the E-Mail Accounts Wizard what you want to do in this screen.

3. On the Server Type screen, click POP3 and then click Next. The Internet E-Mail Settings (POP3) screen appears, as shown in Figure 3-3.

4. Enter the account information you gathered earlier.

> **TIP** *If you want to prevent other people from using your e-mail account for their own purposes, you can leave the Password field blank and clear the Remember Password check box. Doing so causes Outlook to request a password the first time you connect to that e-mail account in each session. Requiring a password won't prevent someone from using your e-mail account while you're away from your desk for a few minutes, but it will prevent someone from turning on your computer, starting Outlook, and sending e-mail using this account. I prefer to enter my password when I set up the account, but this is a matter of personal discretion.*

5. If your ISP requires any special information beyond that which appears on the screen, enter the information and click More Settings. You see the Internet E-Mail Settings dialog box shown in Figure 3-4.

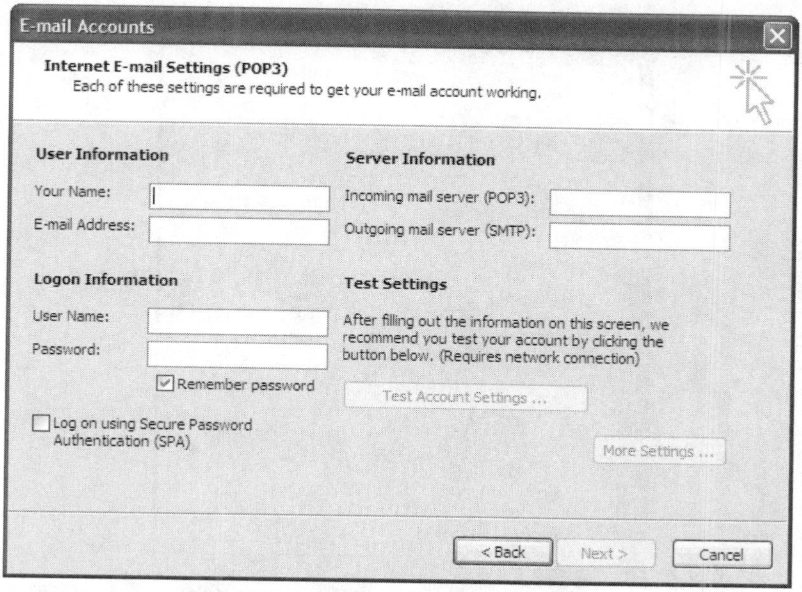

FIGURE 3-3   Use this screen to enter the settings for a POP3 Internet e-mail account.

6. Click Test Account Settings to confirm that Outlook can now communicate with the new e-mail account. If Outlook successfully connects to the new e-mail account, it will tell you so.

7. Click Next | Finish to finish the job. Outlook now has access to your POP3 e-mail account.

Set Up an HTTP E-Mail Account

While POP3 e-mail accounts are the most common, HTTP e-mail services like Hotmail and MSN also have a large number of users.

Follow these steps to set up an HTTP Internet e-mail account:

1. In the main Outlook window, choose Tools | E-Mail Accounts. This activates the E-Mail Accounts Wizard.

2. In the first screen, click Add A New E-Mail Account, and then click Next.

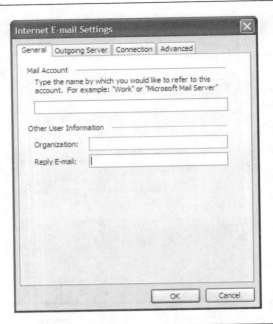

FIGURE 3-4 If your ISP has any special settings, enter them on one of the tabs in this dialog box.

3. On the Server Type screen, click HTTP, and then click Next. You see the Internet E-Mail Settings (HTTP) screen, as shown in Figure 3-5.

4. Enter the account information you gathered earlier. As you can see by comparing Figure 3-5 to Figure 3-3, the information you need for an HTTP e-mail account is slightly different from the information you need for a POP3 account.

5. Click Next | Finish to finish the job. Outlook should now have access to your HTTP e-mail account.

Set Up an IMAP E-Mail Account

IMAP e-mail accounts work somewhat differently from POP3 and HTTP accounts. With an IMAP account, messages are stored on the e-mail server, not downloaded directly to a computer. You can keep multiple folders on an IMAP server and use them to organize and store messages.

3

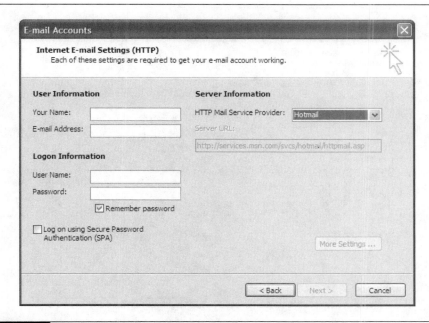

FIGURE 3-5   Use this dialog box to set up an HTTP e-mail account.

Follow these steps to set up an IMAP Internet e-mail account:

1. In the main Outlook window, choose Tools | E-Mail Accounts. This activates the E-Mail Accounts Wizard.

2. In the Wizard's first screen, choose Add A New E-Mail Account and then click Next to continue.

3. On the Server Type screen, click IMAP, and then click Next to continue. You see the Internet E-Mail Settings (IMAP) screen, as shown in Figure 3-6.

4. Enter the account information you gathered earlier. As you can see by comparing this figure to Figures 3-3 and 3-5, the information you need for an IMAP e-mail account is slightly different from the information you need for a POP3 or HTTP account.

5. Click Next | Finish to finish the job. Outlook should now have access to the IMAP e-mail account.

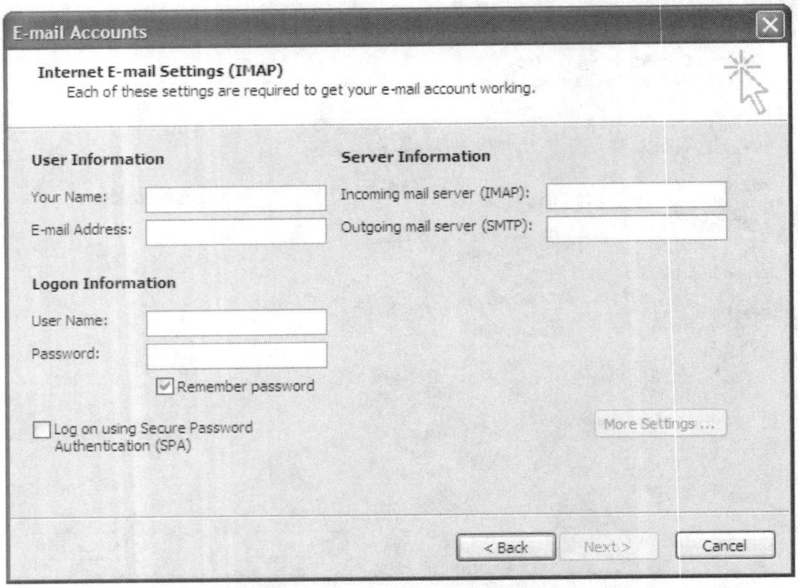

FIGURE 3-6   The information for IMAP e-mail accounts differs slightly from both POP3 and HTTP accounts.

Troubleshoot an Internet E-Mail Account

If Outlook can't connect to the new e-mail account, you can try to fix the problem by double-checking the account information you entered in the E-Mail Accounts Wizard. Next, contact the person who gave you the original account information and confirm that the information you have is correct. Also ask about any fields you did not fill in, as you might be missing a piece of required information.

Finally, confirm that the e-mail account you are using allows you to read your e-mail in Outlook. Recently, some e-mail providers have started blocking access to e-mail accounts on their servers or allowing access only if customers pay an additional fee. Yahoo!, for example, is now taking this approach. I used to be able to read my Yahoo! mail from my desktop for free, but now I have to pay an annual fee for the privilege. If you don't pay, the only way to get your Yahoo! e-mail is through the Web-based Yahoo! mail system, which hits you with multiple advertisements whenever you use it.

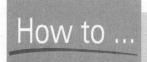

Make Outlook the Default Application for E-Mail and More

If you've been using a different program to handle your e-mail, contacts, or calendar, you'll want to make Outlook the default application for these. It only takes a moment to do so. Just follow these steps:

1. In the main Outlook window, choose Tools | Options to open the Options dialog box.

2. Select the Other tab.

3. In the General section, select the Make Outlook The Default Program For E-Mail, Contacts, And Calendar check box.

4. Click OK to put the change into effect.

Specify E-Mail Connections

Not everyone has a full-time connection to the Internet. The type of connection you have affects how Outlook works with your Internet e-mail account. Which type of connection you have for a particular account may change, depending on circumstances. If you have a laptop or Tablet PC, for example, the machine may be connected full-time when you're in the office, but require a dial-up connection otherwise. You can tell Outlook what kind of connection you have for each Internet e-mail account in the Internet E-Mail Settings dialog box. Follow these steps to specify your e-mail connection for each Internet e-mail account:

1. In the Outlook main window, choose Tools | E-mail Accounts to activate the E-Mail Accounts Wizard.

2. Click View Or Change Existing E-Mail Accounts | Next to continue.

3. Select the Internet e-mail account you want to work with, and then click Change.

4. Click More Settings to open the Internet E-Mail Settings dialog box. The Connection tab has a collection of connection options, as Figure 3-7 shows.

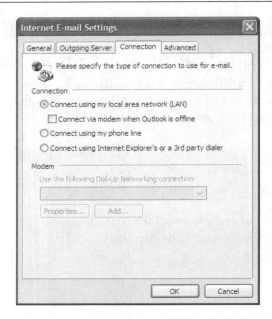

FIGURE 3-7   Select a connection type for each Internet e-mail account on this tab.

5. Select the connection type that best describes your Internet e-mail account.

6. Click OK | Next and repeat the process for any other e-mail accounts that need it.

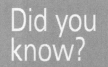

Did you know?

You Can Define Additional E-Mail Profiles?

Outlook allows you to create multiple e-mail *user profiles*. By associating e-mail accounts and connections with a user profile, you can separate your e-mail activities. For example, you can separate your personal e-mail activities from your work e-mail. This way, you can download messages from personal e-mail accounts but not work-related ones.

In the vast majority of cases, you'll do fine with a single e-mail user profile, and separate e-mail accounts for work and home. But if you do want to create separate profiles, follow these basic steps:

1. Click Start then Control Panel. If you're using Windows XP's Category view for the Control Panel, click User Accounts and then Mail. If you're not using the Windows XP Category view, double-click Mail. This opens the Mail Setup dialog box.

2. Click Show Profiles. Using the Show Profiles dialog box, you can add, remove, change, or copy e-mail user profiles.

3. If you wish to be able to choose between user profiles each time you start out, select the Prompt For A Profile To Be Used check box.

For additional information about using multiple e-mail profiles, search the Outlook Help system for the keyword "profiles."

Decide Where Outlook Stores Your Information

Outlook stores your information in various locations, depending on how you or your network administrator configured Outlook. The location where your personal information is stored is called the *primary store*. In most cases, the primary store is a *Personal Folders file* on your hard drive. Personal Folders files are often called .pst files because .pst is the file name extension.

Most of the time, you can leave Personal Folders files in the default location selected by Outlook. But you can move Personal Folders files to new locations, as well as create additional files in the Outlook Data Files dialog box.

Why create additional files? Well, if you upgraded from an earlier version of Outlook, your system probably uses the old style of Personal Folders file (see "Did You Know Outlook 2003 Uses a Personal Folders File Format?" for more information). In addition, while Personal Folders files can hold gigabytes of data, they can be difficult to manage after they reach a few hundred megabytes. Some people create new Personal Folders files every few months to simplify the task of backing up and maintaining the files.

Work with Your Personal Folders Files

To view information about your Outlook data files or create new files, follow these steps:

1. In the Outlook main window, click File | Data File Management to open the Outlook Data Files dialog box.

2. Select the Data File you want to work with and then click one of the buttons along the right side of the dialog box to make any changes.

3. Use the Settings button to view General Information about the Data File, including its location and format. Click Compact Now if you want to reduce the size of the file by compacting (or compressing) it.

Move Personal Folders Files

Moving Personal Folders files is a little more cumbersome than just working with them. To move a Personal Folders file, you start in the Data Files Management dialog box. Follow these steps to move a Personal Folders file:

1. In the Outlook main window, choose File | Data File Management to open the Outlook Data Files dialog box, shown in Figure 3-8.

2. Select the file you want to move and then click the Open Folder button.

3. With the folder containing the Personal Folders file you want to move open, close Outlook.

4. Drag the Personal Folders file to a new location and drop it there.

5. Restart Outlook. You'll see a message stating that Outlook cannot find the Personal Folders file. Click OK to continue.

Did you know?

Outlook 2003 Uses a New Personal Folders File Format?

Outlook 2003, like previous versions, stores all your information in one or more Personal Folders files (.pst files). However, Outlook 2003 uses a different file format from previous versions. This new file format provides greater storage capacity and also supports multilingual data, but older versions of Outlook cannot read the new file format.

If you need to be able to read Personal Folders files with older versions of Outlook, you need to save your data in a backward-compatible Personal Folders file format. See the Outlook Help system for more information.

6. In the Create/Open Personal Folders File dialog box, shown in Figure 3-9, navigate to the new location of the Personal Folders file, select the file, and click the Open button.

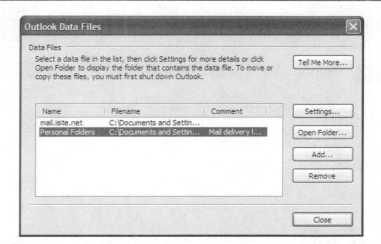

FIGURE 3-8   The Outlook Data Files dialog box allows you to manage and move your Outlook data files.

7. When Outlook displays a message saying that it is unable to display the folder, ignore the message and click one of the folders in the Navigation pane. Outlook should function normally again.

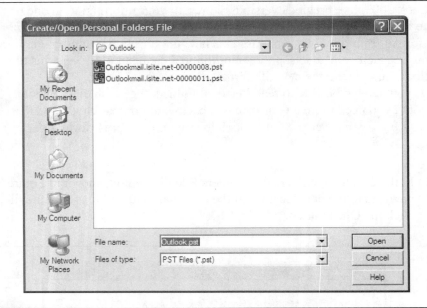

FIGURE 3-9   Use this dialog box to find Personal Folders files after you move them.

Part II

Communicate Using Outlook 2003

Chapter 4

Send and Receive E-Mail

How to...

- Navigate the New E-Mail View
- Compose and Send E-Mail Messages
- Receive and Reply to E-Mail Messages
- Choose a Format for Your Messages
- Take Advantage of Desktop Alerts
- Work with Multiple E-Mail Accounts
- Manage Send/Receive Groups
- Send and Receive Internet Faxes

While Outlook has incredibly powerful personal information management features, its primary use is for sending and receiving e-mail messages. This chapter focuses on exactly that. In it, you'll learn your way around Outlook's new Mail view, as well as how to compose, send, receive, and reply to messages.

The chapter also covers topics that are related to the basics of sending and receiving e-mail messages. Desktop Alerts, for example, let you know that new messages have arrived when Outlook is not open on your desktop. Multiple e-mail accounts and Send/Receive groups work together to let you manage all your work and personal e-mail accounts in one place: the Outlook Inbox.

You'll even learn how to send Internet faxes here. Microsoft Office System 2003 works with fax service providers to turn Outlook into a virtual fax machine, and this chapter walks you through the entire process.

Navigate the New E-Mail View

There are reportedly over 200 million users of Outlook in the world. The vast majority of them spend most of their time in Mail view. Any changes that improve the usability of this view have the potential to save vast amounts of time and effort. Microsoft has made significant changes to Mail view, and those changes will increase productivity worldwide. Figure 4-1 shows the basic Outlook 2003 Mail view.

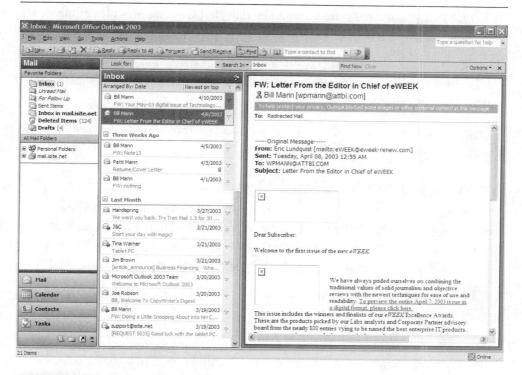

FIGURE 4-1 The new Mail view makes more efficient use of screen space than previous versions.

A Three Pane View for Better Usability

If you've upgraded from a previous version of Outlook, you've probably noticed a number of changes, the most obvious being the Outlook bar that used to run down the left side of the Outlook window. It has been replaced by the *Navigation pane*, which combines the functions of the Outlook bar and the old Folder list. The four most commonly used Outlook views—Mail, Calendar, Contacts, and Tasks— appear as clickable bars at the bottom of the Navigation pane. Other Outlook views (Notes, Folder List, and Shortcuts) appear as small icons below these.

To the right of the Navigation pane is the new Inbox pane. This pane provides a two-line presentation of messages as opposed to the one-line presentation in earlier versions of Outlook. This new layout makes it easier to see key information in messages all at once without having to open or preview messages. By default, messages in the Inbox pane are grouped by date, but Outlook provides numerous ways to group messages in this pane (you'll learn about them in Chapter 5).

The new Reading pane appears on the right side of the window. By default, this pane gives you far more room for viewing messages than previous versions of Outlook did. Besides the additional space, with its vertical orientation, the pane is just easier to read than the old Preview pane.

 *You can reposition the Reading pane and most other elements of Outlook. See Chapter 15 for details.*

Introducing the New Mail View

The organization of the new Mail view is actually quite sensible. Start in the Navigation pane on the left and select the folder containing the messages that you want to view. The Inbox pane then displays those messages. Select one of the messages in the Inbox pane to read it in the Reading pane.

 The name of the pane displaying messages changes to match the name of the folder you selected in the Navigation pane.

You can also make a message appear in its own window instead of the Reading pane. To do this, double-click the message. You might want to view messages in windows, for example, if you need to deal with several messages in the Inbox. You could go through the Inbox, open all the messages that need attention in their own windows, and handle them at your leisure. This is the approach I used with previous versions of Outlook.

 *Outlook 2003 offers Quick Flags, which are explicitly designed for marking messages that you can't deal with right now. Quick Flags are covered in detail in Chapter 5.*

You now have the basic information you need to navigate Mail view. The rest of this chapter, and Chapter 5, go into more detail about various aspects of Outlook, starting with composing and sending e-mail messages.

Compose and Send E-Mail Messages

Composing and sending e-mail messages works much the same as it did in earlier versions of Outlook. If you're familiar with doing these tasks, you know the keyboard shortcuts for creating and sending messages, and you are up to speed on the use of the spell-checker, then feel free to skip to the next section of this chapter. Otherwise, read along and you will be ready to send messages in no time.

Compose a New Message

The first step in composing a new message is to open a blank message window. If you're working in Mail view, you can do this by clicking the New button on the Outlook toolbar. You can also open a blank message window from other views by clicking the little down-arrow next to the New button and choosing Mail Message on the drop-down menu.

 *Press* CTRL-N *to open a new message window no matter where you are in Outlook.*

The new message window looks something like the one in Figure 4-2. As with most things in Outlook, the details depend on the options you selected and the ways you customized the user interface. But the default new message window should look very much like the one in the figure.

Starting from the top, you enter the e-mail address of the person to whom you are sending the message in the To field. You can look up a person's e-mail address in Outlook's Address Book by clicking the little book icon to the left of the word To. That little book icon represents the Address Book throughout Outlook. You'll learn everything you need to know about the Address Book in Chapter 6.

The CC field is for entering the address of anyone you want to receive a copy of the message. People whose addresses appear in the CC field typically are receiving a copy of the message for informational purposes only.

Enter the subject of the message in the Subject field.

You enter the body of your message in the large empty field beneath the Subject field. Because HTML is the default format for messages in Outlook, you can use different fonts for text, boldface or italicize text, include images, and enter hyperlinks to web pages.

When you're done entering text into the message body, I recommend checking your spelling using the spell-checker. Outlook shares a basic spell-checker with the other Office System products. To use it, compose your message as you normally would, and then press F7 to launch the spell-checker. If Outlook is using Word as your e-mail editor (it does so by default), you get to use the full Word 2003 spelling and grammar checker instead of a basic one. Using it goes a long way toward writing cleaner, better messages.

Address Book   To field   Subject field

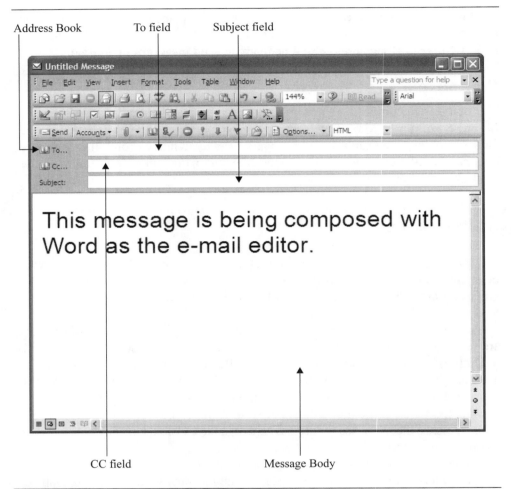

CC field   Message Body

FIGURE 4-2   A blank new message window is the starting point for composing e-mail messages.

Add a File Attachment to Your Message

E-mail messages can include *attachments* as well as the written material in the body of the message. Attachments are files that get carried along with an e-mail message to its destination. Using attachments, you can e-mail documents, pictures, music files, or any other kind of computer file. Attachments can be a great way to transfer files quickly and efficiently.

4

Unfortunately, attachments are also a great way to transmit viruses. Many people won't open messages with attachments and delete them automatically. Some companies block messages with attachments from ever even reaching their employees. And some e-mail programs, including Outlook, block certain kinds of attachments from reaching their recipients. Chapter 18 talks about this in more detail. For now, we'll concentrate on how to send attachments and leave the security ramifications for later.

The easiest way to send an attachment with a message is simply to drop a file onto the message. When you do this, Outlook automatically includes the file as an attachment to the message. Figure 4-3 shows a message with an attachment. The attachment is named "Smart Medical Home.doc". It appears in the Attach field, a field that Outlook displays in a message header whenever you attach a file to a message.

If you look closely at the file icon in Figure 4-3, you can tell that the attachment is a Word document. Outlook displays the same kind of file type icon that Windows does.

Send Your Message

When you finish composing your message and running the spell-checker on it, you're ready to send it. Click the Send button in the message window's toolbar to send the message on its way.

Outlook doesn't immediately send messages to their recipients. Messages you send go first into the Outbox. After a message arrives there, Outlook may send it on its way immediately or wait until certain conditions are met. This is controlled by the *Send/Receive groups* settings, a topic covered later in this chapter in the section titled "Manage Send/Receive Groups."

Eventually, however, Outlook does send the messages in the Outbox to their recipients. As messages are sent, Outlook's default behavior is to remove each message from the Outbox and put a copy of it in the Sent Items folder.

TIP   *If you ever want to look at the contents of a message you sent some time ago, and you didn't save a copy of it, check the Sent Items folder. You can find the Sent Items folder in the list of folders that appears in the Navigation pane in Mail view.*

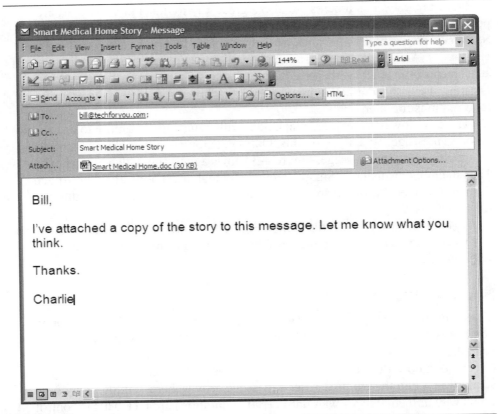

FIGURE 4-3   You can easily transfer files from person-to-person as e-mail attachments.

Choose the Editor to Use with E-Mail Messages

You can compose e-mail messages in Outlook without worrying about many of the underlying details. But once you go beyond the basics, such details begin to matter. One of those details is which editor to use for e-mail.

Outlook supports two different e-mail editors: Microsoft Word and its own built-in e-mail editor. By default, Microsoft Word is the e-mail editor. You can use either for basic e-mail editing, but there are trade-offs to each. Word is much more powerful than the built-in editor, and it offers many more options. But Word also offers many more options than you normally need to compose e-mail messages. Word also consumes many more system resources when it is running than the built-in Outlook editor does. In addition, the built-in editor is designed explicitly for editing e-mail messages. The features it does have are designed for e-mail. Chief among these features is the easy-to-use Signature feature (it is described later in this chapter).

Unless you have a real need to create fancy e-mail messages or you are a Tablet PC user (see the "How To Use Ink in E-Mail Messages" box), I recommend configuring Outlook to use its built-in editor instead of Word.

Follow these steps to choose which e-mail editor to use:

1. In the main Outlook window, click Tools | Options to open the Options dialog box.

2. On the Mail Format tab, either select or clear the Use Microsoft Word To Edit E-mail Messages check box. If you are making Microsoft Word your e-mail editor, select the Use Microsoft Word To Read Rich Text E-mail Messages check box as well.

NOTE   *Rich Text and other message formats are covered in the "Choose a Format for Your Messages" section later in this chapter.*

3. Click Apply and then OK.

How to ... Use Ink in E-Mail Messages

If you're a Tablet PC user, you may want to ignore what I said about not using Word as your e-mail editor, because with Word as the editor of an HTML-formatted e-mail message, you can use ink in the message. Ink works only within the body of e-mail messages. By accessing Word 2003's ink features, you can create ink drawings and writing, as well as insert ink annotations and comments.

To use ink in the body of an e-mail message, position the cursor where you want to write, and then tap Insert | Ink to open the Ink menu. Then select the ink option you want to use. Most recipients will have no problem dealing with messages that include ink, as long as their e-mail program works with HTML messages.

Figure 4-4 shows what the message window looks like when Outlook is configured to use the built-in editor (compare this figure to Figure 4-2). The window is clean and simple, which can only help when you're trying to be productive in dealing with your e-mail.

Enhance Your E-Mail with Signatures

When you write a letter, you surely sign it. When you write an e-mail message, you should sign that as well. If your e-mail message is business-related, you may well have to include all sorts of information in the signature—not just your contact information, but company information and legal disclaimers, too. I've seen signatures that contain more words than the body of the message does.

Manually creating a long signature every time you send an e-mail message would be crazy. It would take too much work. Outlook's Signature feature lets you

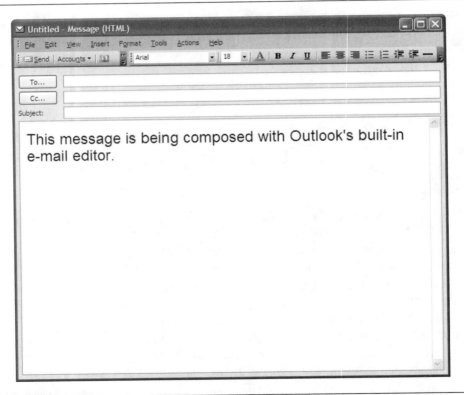

FIGURE 4-4 Outlook's built-in editor provides a streamlined approach to composing e-mail messages.

4

enter your signature once, then have it automatically appear at the end of every message you send.

Create a Signature

As I mentioned before, Outlook's built-in message editor is set up to make it easy to create and manage a set of signatures. In some ways, creating a signature is the easy part. Figuring out what information it should contain, and when to use each particular signature, can be difficult.

Follow these steps to create a signature (assuming you're using the Outlook e-mail editor):

1. In the main Outlook window, click Tools | Options to open the Options dialog box.

2. On the Mail Format tab, click the Signatures button. This opens the Create Signature dialog box.

3. Click New to create a new signature.

4. In the Create New Signature dialog box, enter a name for the signature and choose the way you'll create it. You can start from scratch by using a blank signature, or use an existing signature or file as a template. Click Next to continue to the Edit Signature dialog box shown in Figure 4-5.

5. Enter your signature in this dialog box exactly as you would like it to appear in your messages. You can paste text into this window if, for example, your company has some standard text you're required to include in all messages.

6. You can choose the fonts and paragraph formatting, and include hyperlinks in the signature as well. To do so, select the text you want to modify, and then select the font or format you want to apply. Which capabilities are available is determined by Outlook's default message format.

CAUTION *Don't click the Advanced Edit button. This starts Word as the signature editor. If you're not going to use Word to compose your messages, you certainly don't want to use it to create your signatures.*

7. When you're happy with the signature, click Finish. This returns you to the Create Signature dialog box, where you can see a preview of the signature. Repeat steps 3 through 5 if you want to create additional signatures.

8. When you're done creating signatures, click OK to get back to the Mail Format tab.

FIGURE 4-5   This dialog box is where you create signatures that Outlook automatically adds to your messages.

Tips for Creating Signatures

Now that you know how to create signatures, here are some guidelines for creating practical and useful ones:

- If you're creating a business signature, don't overdo it with fancy fonts or an outrageous quote from your favorite rapper. Instead, include your contact information and any other text required by your employer.

- If you're creating a signature for personal use, you can be a little more creative in the formatting and content. Just remember that e-mail messages tend to stick around for a while and are often forwarded to other people. Try not to include anything you will regret later.

- Consider the format of the messages that your signatures will be a part of. While you can create signatures using any of the message formats Outlook supports, signatures appear in the same format as the messages in which they appear. If you create a signature in HTML format and include it in a plain-text-formatted message, the signature will appear as plain text, not HTML.

> TIP *It can make sense to preview a signature by sending yourself a message that includes the signature to see what it looks like.*

Use Signatures

After you create signatures, you need to tell Outlook when to use them. You do this in the Signature section of the Options dialog box's Mail Format tab (click Tools | Options to get there). First, specify the account you want to select signatures for, and then specify the signatures as follows:

■ To automatically include a signature in messages you send, select the name of the signature in the Signature for New Messages list.

■ To automatically include a signature in messages you reply to or forward to others, select the name of the signature in the Signature for Replies and Forwards list.

If you want manual control over when signatures appear, make sure that no signatures are selected for this account.

To manually add a signature to a message, click Insert | Signature in the message window's menu bar. Select the signature you want to use in the list that appears.

Once you start using Outlook's Signature feature, you'll wonder how you ever got along without it.

Receive and Reply to E-Mail Messages

Whenever Outlook is online, it checks all of your e-mail accounts at regular intervals for new messages. When it finds new messages, Outlook puts a copy of them in the Inbox. They then appear in the Inbox pane.

Things to Note When Reading Messages

Earlier in the chapter, you learned how to read messages (by clicking or double-clicking them in the Inbox pane). In general, but not always, messages look the same to you as they did to the person who created them. As part of Microsoft's efforts to protect you from e-mail–borne viruses and other nastiness, Outlook doesn't display certain kinds of content. Chapter 18 covers all the details, so for now just be aware that Outlook may block certain images or e-mail attachments.

If a message you receive contains an attachment, the attachment appears as a paperclip in the Inbox, and as an icon in the message window or Preview pane. Double-click the attachment icon to open it. Right-click the attachment icon, then click Save As in the menu that appears to save the attachment as a file on your hard drive.

Reply to a Message

You'll often want to respond to an e-mail message by replying to it or forwarding it to someone else. You can reply to or forward a message that appears in the Reading pane, in its own separate window, or even one in the Inbox pane and hasn't been opened yet. But first you need to figure out which kind of response you want to make. You can reply to the sender of the message, reply to the sender and everyone else who received the message, or forward the message.

- ■ If you want to reply to the sender, click the Reply button.

- ■ To reply to the sender and everyone who originally received the message if the message was sent to more than one person, click the Reply to All button.

- ■ To forward the message to someone else, click the Forward button.

If you're responding to a message that's visible in the Reading or Inbox pane, buttons for replying appear on Outlook's toolbar. If you're responding to a message that appears in its own window, the buttons are on the toolbar.

 *You can use these keyboard shortcuts to respond to the active message (the one selected in the Inbox pane or open in the active window):* CTRL-R *for Reply,* CTRL-SHIFT-R *for Reply to All, and* CTRL-F *for Forward.*

When you respond to a message, Outlook opens a new window like the one in Figure 4-6 for your response. In the message shown in the figure, I selected Reply, so Outlook automatically entered the letters RE: (for "reply") at the start of the message subject line, and addressed the message to the person who sent it originally. In addition, Outlook included the body of the original message at the bottom of the message window and placed the cursor at the top of the window. Including the original message provides some context for my reply. Now I can easily address the relevant parts of the original message in my response.

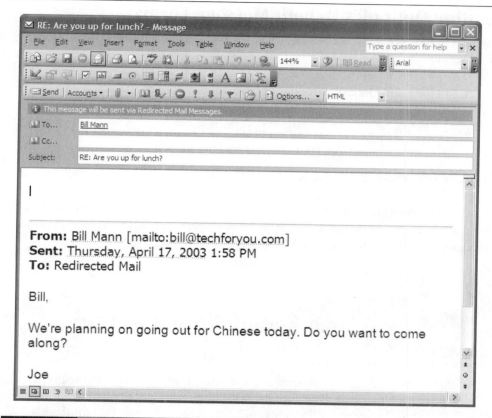

FIGURE 4-6   Outlook does what it can to make things easy for you when you respond to a message.

NOTE   *It is considerate to include only the relevant parts of the message you're responding to in a reply. This is particularly the case when you're responding to a lengthy message.*

Choose a Format for Your Messages

Earlier in this chapter, I alluded to the fact that you can create e-mail messages in more than one format. As with signatures, selecting formats is easy. Knowing which one to use is more difficult. In this section, you'll learn how to specify the default format for messages, as well as how to set the format for a specific message. Check out the "Did You Know Which E-Mail Format to Use?" box for help in choosing an e-mail format.

Setting Outlook's Default Message Format

To set Outlook's default message format, it's back to our old friend the Mail Format tab:

1. In the main Outlook window, choose Tools | Options to open the Options dialog box.

2. In the Message Format section of the Mail Format tab, select the format you want to use from the Compose in This Message Format list.

3. Click Apply and then OK.

For this point on, new message windows that you open will open in the default format you chose. Message windows that you opened in a different format before changing the default format retain their original format.

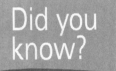

Which E-Mail Format to Use?

Another aspect of e-mail etiquette that Outlook simplifies is using the proper format for each message. By that, I mean sending messages in plain text format, HTML format, or rich text format, whichever is most appropriate for the recipient.

How do you know which format to use? I recommend following these simple rules:

- Always use the same format as the message to which you're replying because you know that it will work for the recipient. Unless you manually override it, Outlook automatically replies to messages in the format they were sent in.

- Newsgroup programs (you'll learn about these in Chapter 9) often don't understand HTML format. Before sending messages to a newsgroup, you should check the group's frequently asked questions (FAQ) file to find out which format to use. If you're still unsure what format to use, start with plain text. That's sure to work.

- When you're sending e-mail to someone and you don't know what format their e-mail program uses, send your message in plain text format. That way, the message is sure to get through, regardless of the e-mail program the recipient uses.

- If your company has set a standard format for e-mail, then, of course, use that.

Set the Format of a Single Message

To manually change the format of a single message, choose Format on the message window menu bar and select the format you want to use from the menu.

Take Advantage of Desktop Alerts

A *desktop alert* is a message that appears on your desktop to alert you to the arrival of certain Outlook items. The alerts appear when Outlook is minimized. They allow you to see what item has arrived, as well as perform certain actions on items, all without opening the Outlook Inbox.

The following list describes the types of items that can generate desktop alerts and how Outlook displays them:

- **E-mail messages**   An e-mail message alert displays the name of the sender, the subject of the message, and the first two lines of the message. If the message is encrypted or digitally signed the alert will not display the contents. In that case, you'll have to open the message to see what it says.

- **Meeting requests**   A meeting request alert displays the name of the sender, the subject of the meeting, its date and time, and its location.

- **Task requests**   A task request displays the name of the sender, the subject, and the start date of the task to be assigned.

When it receives items from the Exchange server or from Internet e-mail and the items are destined for the default Inbox, Outlook automatically generates desktop alerts. However, Outlook doesn't automatically generate alerts for items bound for a location other than the default Inbox, nor does it automatically generate alerts for messages that come in through an IMAP or HTTP account. If you want Outlook to generate desktop alerts for these types of items, you need to create rules to do so (Chapter 5 shows you how).

Work with Desktop Alerts

When a desktop alert appears, you can do several things with it. First, you can read it to see what kind of item has arrived. Alerts are designed so you can make a decision as to what to do about them at a glance. That's why they appear for a few seconds only. If you want the alert to remain visible longer, just hover the cursor over it. As long as the cursor is pointing to the alert, it will remain on the screen.

To work with the item that triggered the alert without opening the Outlook Inbox, you just click the down-arrow to open the alert's Options list. The list contains a set of options appropriate for the type of alert you are dealing with. You can choose to open the item, flag it, mark it as read, disable future alerts for this type of item, or change desktop alert settings.

Customize Your Desktop Alerts

You customize desktop alerts with the Desktop Alerts Settings dialog box shown in Figure 4-7. You can reach this dialog box from the menu of an open alert or from the Outlook window. Follow these steps to open the Desktop Alerts Settings dialog box and customize your desktop alerts:

1. On the Outlook menu bar, click Tools | Options | E-Mail Options | Advanced E-Mail Options | Desktop Alert Settings. This opens the Desktop Alerts Settings dialog box.

FIGURE 4-7   Use this dialog box to customize your desktop alerts.

2. Adjust the Duration and Transparency settings to meet your needs. The higher the transparency, the more alerts will blend into the background. If you select the Hide Desktop Alerts Behind Applications in Full Screen Mode check box, alerts will only be visible when no applications are maximized on the desktop.

3. To see the results of your changes, click the Preview button to display a dummy alert with the settings you selected.

Work with Multiple E-Mail Accounts

Chapter 3 shows you how to configure Outlook to connect to multiple types of e-mail accounts on multiple servers. After you set up these accounts, Outlook automatically receives messages directed to them. But if you're not careful, things can quickly get complicated. For example, you don't want to get your personal e-mail mixed up with your work e-mail. And it would certainly be helpful to control which e-mail account Outlook uses to send or reply to a message.

The engineers that designed Outlook had these kinds of situations in mind. Outlook can send messages using any of your e-mail accounts, and automatically keeps track of which messages are associated with which accounts. This means you can use Outlook for all your e-mail needs and still avoid embarrassing situations such as sending personal messages to business associates or forwarding confidential corporate messages to friends.

NOTE *While you can manage all your separate e-mail accounts manually, Chapter 5 shows you how to create rules that automatically process incoming messages based on which accounts they came from. For now, we'll concentrate on the things you can do manually.*

Send Messages with Multiple Accounts

One of the most important aspects of handling multiple e-mail accounts with a single program is being able to select the account that the program uses to send a message. If a message is going to a friend, you probably want to use one of your personal accounts; if you're writing to your boss, you likely want to use your company e-mail account.

Outlook applies these commonsense rules to determine which account to use when writing a message:

■ If you're replying to a message, Outlook assumes you want to reply using the same account to which the original message was sent.

■ If you're creating a message from scratch, Outlook assumes you want to use your default account. Unless you've changed it, your default account is the first e-mail account you set up with Outlook on your computer. (See the "How to Change Your Default E-Mail Account" box to find out which account is your default account and change it, if necessary.)

What if you don't want to use the default account to send a message? Changing the e-mail account Outlook uses to send a specific message is even easier than changing the default account. Before you send the message, choose Accounts on the toolbar in the message window. This opens a menu of available e-mail accounts like the one shown in Figure 4-8. The account Outlook thinks it should use appears at the top of the menu and is followed by a numbered list of all your available accounts. Click the name of the account you want to use or press the corresponding number on the keyboard. Outlook uses the account you selected when it sends the message.

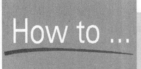 **Change Your Default E-Mail Account**

To find out which e-mail account is your default e-mail account and change it if necessary, follow these steps:

1. On the Outlook main menu, click Tools | E-Mail Accounts. This starts the E-Mail Accounts Wizard.

2. Select View Or Change Existing E-mail Accounts; then click Next. All your available e-mail accounts appear in a list on this screen. The word "Default" appears in parentheses after the default account.

3. If you want to change the default account, select the account you want to be the new default account and click the Set As Default button.

4. Click the Finish button to make the change.

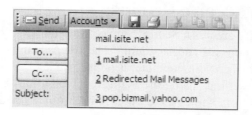

FIGURE 4-8   Setting the e-mail account for a specific message takes only a few clicks of the mouse.

Receive Messages from Multiple Accounts

Normally, Outlook checks each of your e-mail accounts one after the other. If you have a broadband (high-speed, always-on) Internet connection, you probably don't need to worry about how long it takes for Outlook to check all your e-mail accounts or how frequently it checks them. But if you have a dial-up connection, you might want to manage Outlook's schedule for checking your accounts. You can check unimportant and infrequently used accounts less often, thereby reducing the total amount of time Outlook ties up your phone line. And if you get distracted by every new message that arrives, you might want to limit how often Outlook checks for new mail, even if—particularly if—you have a high-speed, always-on connection.

Outlook uses *Send/Receive groups* to determine when accounts get checked for new mail. Send/Receive groups are collections of accounts and folders that you can apply tasks to on a schedule you define. For example, you might define a Send/Receive group that automatically sends and receives messages every three minutes when your computer is online, but doesn't try to send or receive messages at all when your computer is offline.

One thing to remember is that an account can be in more than one Send/Receive group. This actually makes a lot of sense, since it allows you much greater flexibility when you're trying to manage your accounts. If you're just working with a desktop PC that has a broadband Internet connection, you'll do just fine with a single Send/Receive group using the default options.

But if you're working with a notebook or a Tablet PC that is sometimes online and sometimes off, that sometimes uses a dial-up connection and sometimes uses broadband, you will probably be better off with a few different groups that you can use in different situations. The following sections show you how to define and manage groups, including how to tell your computer whether it is online or offline.

Manage Send/Receive Groups

Outlook automatically creates a Send/Receive group named All Accounts, which, not surprisingly, contains all your accounts. The All Accounts group holds one set of default settings for when your computer is online and another for when it is offline. You can adjust these settings using the Send/Receive Groups dialog box, as shown in Figure 4-9. (The figure shows the default All Accounts dialog box, plus two others that I use in my work.)

Follow these steps to manage the All Accounts group or any other Send/Receive groups you create.

1. On the Outlook menu bar, click Tools | Send/Receive | Send/Receive Settings | Define Send/Receive Groups. This opens the Send/Receive Groups dialog box.

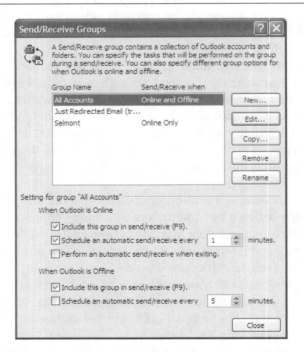

FIGURE 4-9   The Send/Receive Groups dialog box controls when Outlook checks your e-mail accounts.

 *You can also press* CTRL-ALT-S *to open the Send/Receive Groups dialog box.*

2. Select the Send/Receive group you want to work on.

3. If you want to control when Outlook sends and receives messages in this group, use the Setting For Group section at the bottom of this dialog box. As Figure 4-9 shows, you can control when sending and receiving occurs when Outlook is online and offline.

4. If you want to change the accounts that are included in a group or specify the tasks that will occur for a group, click the Edit button. This opens another dialog box, as shown in Figure 4-10. This dialog box works a little differently than the typical Windows dialog box. See the "How to Edit Send/Receive Group Settings" box for more information.

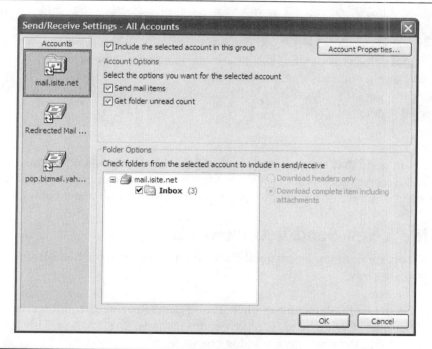

FIGURE 4-10   Use this dialog box to edit account and folder settings for a Send/Receive group.

How to ... Edit Send/Receive Group Settings

You edit the options for accounts and folders in a particular Send/Receive group by using the dialog box shown in Figure 4-10. The Accounts list on the left side of the dialog box shows all of your defined e-mail accounts. The options in the rest of the dialog box pertain specifically to an account within this Send/Receive group. To edit the account options, select the account you want to work with in the Accounts list and make any necessary changes in the rest of the dialog box.

You can remove an account from a Send/Receive group by clearing the Include the Selected Account in this Group check box.

The specific options that appear in the Account Options and Folder Options sections of the dialog box vary, depending on the type of e-mail account you've selected in the Accounts list. In most cases, you'll do best if you just leave all the default values.

If you're unsure which icons in the Accounts list represent which e-mail accounts (perhaps you didn't use descriptive names for your accounts), select the account in question and then click the Accounts Properties button. This opens an Internet E-Mail Settings dialog box with all the settings for the selected account.

Keep in mind that any settings you change in this dialog box only apply when this Send/Receive group is active. One account can appear in multiple Send/Receive groups and can have different options set in each group without any conflicts.

Define a New Send/Receive Group

The process for defining a new Send/Receive group starts in the Send/Receive Groups dialog box:

1. On the Outlook menu bar, click Tools | Send/Receive | Send/Receive Settings | Define Send/Receive Groups (or press CTRL-ALT-S). This opens the Send/Receive Groups dialog box (refer to Figure 4-9).

2. Click the New button to open the Send/Receive Group Name dialog box shown in Figure 4-11.

3. Enter the name of the new group and click OK. A Send/Receive Settings dialog box appears for the new group. The new group starts out with no accounts in it, as indicated by the little red *X* in the icons for each account in the Accounts list.

4. Select an account you want to include in the group and then select its Include the Selected Account In The Group check box.

5. Before adding the next account, look in the Folder Options section of the dialog box to ensure that the appropriate folders are selected.

6. When you're done configuring accounts, click OK. Your new Send/Receive group appears in the group list at the top of the Send/Receive Groups dialog box (refer to Figure 4-9).

7. Check the online and offline settings for the new group at the bottom of the dialog box, and click the Close button to put the changes into effect.

In addition to the settings you control using the Send/Receive Groups dialog box, Outlook automatically takes certain actions when it is online. For Exchange, IMAP, and HTTP e-mail accounts, Outlook sends and receives messages immediately. For POP3 accounts, it sends messages immediately only if you select the Send Immediately When Connected check box on the Mail Setup tab of the Outlook Options dialog box, as shown in Figure 4-12.To reach this tab, choose Tools | Options and select the Mail Setup tab. The Send Immediately When Connected check box is in the Send/Receive section of the dialog box.

FIGURE 4-11   The first step in creating a new Send/Receive group is naming it.

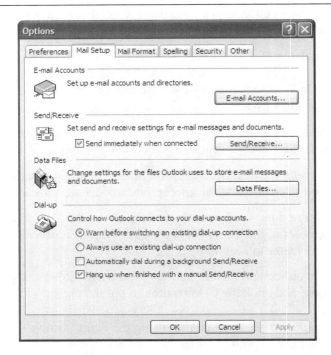

FIGURE 4-12
Select the Send Immediately When Connected check box if you want POP3 e-mail messages to be sent immediately whenever Outlook is online.

Tell Outlook Whether It Is Online or Offline

The idea that you need to tell Outlook whether it is online or not seems very strange at first. But it really makes sense. Being online is not simply a matter of whether the physical connection to the Internet or to the Exchange server is active.

Consider what happens when you use a dial-up modem to connect to the Internet. What state is your computer in when the modem is connected to the phone line but it hasn't yet dialed out to your ISP? Technically, your computer is offline, since it isn't actively connected to the Internet through your ISP. But if that's the case, then your computer is almost always offline.

And what if your computer is connected to the Internet, say, through a cable modem or other broadband connection, but you don't want to send and receive messages right now? Technically, your computer is online because it is connected to the Internet through your ISP, but you want it to behave as if it isn't online and can't send or receive messages.

4

What if you're using a laptop and you're on a trip? At home or in your office, your dial-up connection to the Internet is almost certainly through a local phone number. But in the hotel room you have to pay long-distance charges plus all sorts of surcharges for the calls you make. In this situation, do you want Outlook making calls every five or ten minutes to check for e-mail?

So "online" and "offline" turn out to be concepts that are a little more subjective than they appear at first glance. Add to this the potential technical difficulties of figuring out whether a computer is physically connected or not, and it makes sense for online or offline to be something that the user, not the computer, controls.

Now that the online-offline matter is settled, you're probably wondering how you tell Outlook whether it's online or offline. It's quite easy. In the main Outlook window choose File | Work Offline or File | Work Online. If Outlook is offline, there is a checkmark next to the Work Offline menu option. If Outlook is online, the checkmark is visible. Each time you select the Work Offline option, it switches state between online and offline.

Send and Receive Internet Faxes

Outlook 2003 (and other Microsoft Office System applications) can send faxes using Internet-based fax service providers. These service providers offer additional capabilities beyond those provided by the fax modem software that you may have on your PC. Additional capabilities may include sending faxes to multiple recipients at once, attaching multiple documents to a fax, and composing and sending faxes while your computer is offline (stored in the Outbox and sent the next time Outlook is connected).

NOTE *You must have both Outlook 2003 and Word 2003 installed to send Internet faxes. If your computer has a fax modem installed with its own faxing software, you can still use that as you would normally.*

Sign Up with a Fax Service Provider

The first time you try to send a fax, Outlook offers you the option to sign up with a fax service provider. Here's how to sign up with a fax service provider:

1. In the main Outlook window, click File | New | Internet Fax. Assuming this is the first time anyone has tried to send an Internet fax on your computer, Outlook pops up the message box shown in Figure 4-13. It prompts you to sign up with a fax service provider.

FIGURE 4-13   If Outlook displays this message, click OK to sign up with a Fax Service Provider.

2. Click OK. Outlook opens an Internet Explorer window like the one in Figure 4-14. It offers information about approved fax service providers.

3. Follow the instructions provided by the fax service provider to finish setting up the service.

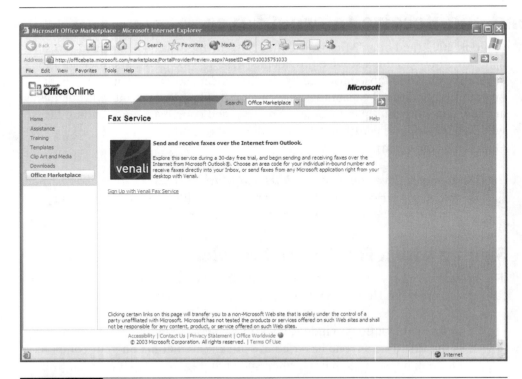

FIGURE 4-14   Select a fax service provider from among the ones on this page.

Sending an Internet Fax

After you've signed up with a fax service provider, you're ready to send Internet faxes. In Outlook, a fax is treated very much like an e-mail message, although you are required to fill in some additional fields. Here's how to send a fax:

1. In the main Outlook window, choose File | New | Internet Fax. Assuming you've successfully set up an account with a fax service provider, Outlook opens a fax message window like the one shown in Figure 4-15. This window looks very much like any e-mail message window, but it is actually a Word document.

SHORTCUT   *You can jump directly to a new fax window by pressing* CTRL-SHIFT-X.

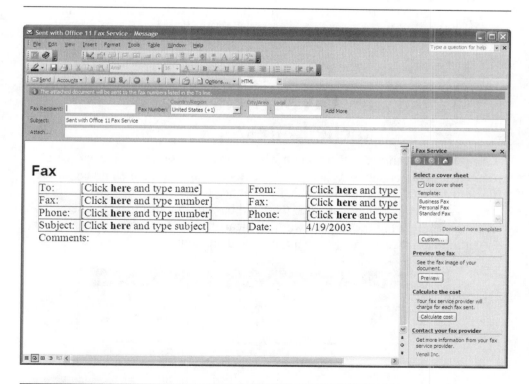

FIGURE 4-15   Fill in the fields of this message, and you're ready to send an Internet fax.

2. Fill in the Fax Recipient, Fax Number, and Subject fields. The Fax Service pane on the right side of the window provides a set of options that you can apply to your fax.

3. If you wish to have a cover sheet on your fax, make sure that the Use Cover Sheet check box in the Fax Service pane is selected, and fill in the cover sheet fields that appear in the body of the message.

4. If you're attaching documents to the fax, include them in the Attach field in the heading of the message.

5. Click the Send button to transmit the fax.

Receive an Internet Fax

Receiving a fax is incredibly easy. When someone sends a fax to your fax service provider fax number, the service accepts the fax and converts it into an e-mail message. It then sends that message to your Inbox, where it is treated just like any other e-mail message, as you can see in Figure 4-16.

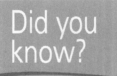

How Fax Services Treat Attached Files?

One thing that can easily trip you up when using Outlook to send faxes is the treatment of attachments. When you fax a document, you send an image of the document, not the document itself. If you attach a document to a fax, Outlook displays a warning when you click the Send button. You just need to click OK to finish sending the fax, but the warning clearly reminds you that the recipient is getting an image of the document, not the document itself.

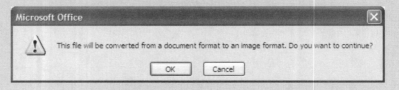

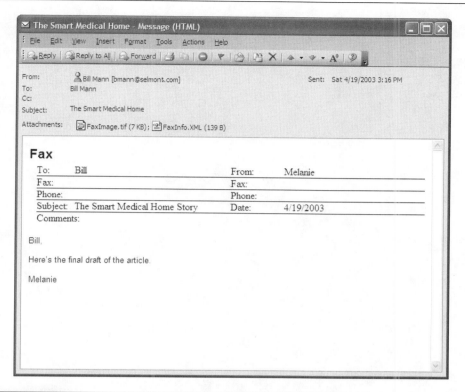

FIGURE 4-16   Faxes you receive through a fax service provider arrive as e-mail
messages.

If you look closely at Figure 4-16, you can see that the body of the message
corresponds to the cover sheet. Any attached documents arrive as attached .tif files
(a type of image file) in the Attachments line. Windows knows how to display .tif
files, so you can view the faxed information by double-clicking the attached .tif files.

NOTE   *Faxes you receive may also include attached .xml files. These files may
be useful to software developers in the future. For now, your concern is
sending and receiving faxes, so you can ignore the .xml files.*

Chapter 5

Manage Your E-Mail

How to...

- ■ Apply Intelligent Grouping to Your Messages
- ■ Take Advantage of Quick Flags, AutoComplete, and Info Tags
- ■ Automate E-Mail Handling with Rules

In the preceding chapters, you set up your e-mail accounts and learned how to send and receive messages. Outlook is a great messaging program. As time goes on, you're likely to grow ever more dependent on e-mail, and that can be a problem. The more you use e-mail, the greater the number of messages you end up with, and the harder it is to manage them all. Managing information in Outlook is a recurring theme throughout the rest of this book.

In this chapter, you'll learn to use some of the Outlook management tools that are specifically designed for handling e-mail. By intelligently grouping messages in your Inbox with the new Arrange By feature, you can find the messages you want to work with. Other new features, such as Quick Flags and AutoComplete, speed various aspects of working with e-mail messages and generally increase the usability of Mail view. The Rules feature has been with Outlook for a while now, but, as with most other major features of Outlook 2003, Microsoft has made various changes to the way rules work, making them easier to use and more effective.

Apply Intelligent Grouping to Your Messages

If you only get a few e-mail messages a day, you might not have to worry about grouping or sorting them. You can just scan the Inbox until you find the message you are interested in. For most Outlook users, however, that approach is totally inadequate. According to one study, the average e-mail user gets many thousands of messages a year. Heck, lots of people get fifty, a hundred, or even more messages a day. Anybody who gets that many messages can surely use help in sorting and grouping them.

The Outlook 2003 Mail view tries to help out by intelligently grouping messages. For example, Outlook automatically arranges messages in the Inbox pane by date. All the messages that arrive today are part of one group, and all those that arrived yesterday are part of another. The simple-minded approach would be to continue grouping messages this way, with yesterday's messages in one group and messages from the day before that in another, and so on. Outlook employs commonsense rules for grouping messages more like you or I would.

After a week has passed, Outlook places the previous week's messages in one group, messages from the week before that in another, the previous month's messages in a third, and so on. Outlook's intelligent grouping system groups messages the way human beings would do it.

Select a Grouping Method

Outlook offers a dozen predefined ways to group messages, as well as a way to create your own custom groupings. You select a grouping method by clicking the Arranged By bar at the top of the Inbox pane. This opens the Arranged By menu shown in Figure 5-1.

Group Messages by Conversation

One grouping method that has the potential to change the way you work with Outlook is called Arrange by Conversation. This arrangement is explicitly designed

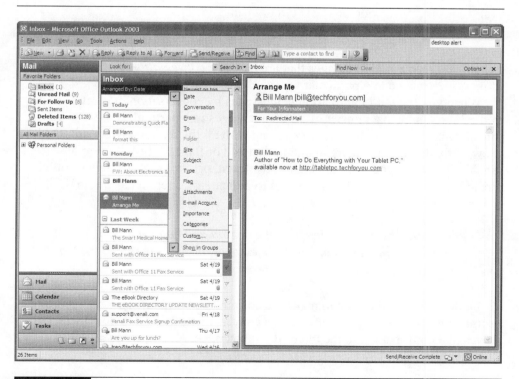

FIGURE 5-1   Use the Arranged By shortcut menu to instantly group messages in a variety of ways.

Groups Can Act Like Outlook Items?

Message groups in Mail view are more than just abstract concepts. You can treat each group is if it were an Outlook item. You can open and close groups, mark all the messages within groups as read or unread, and even delete an entire group at once.

- To open or close a group, double-click its name in the Inbox pane or folder.

- To move a group, select the group's name and drag it to the destination. The mouse pointer changes shape to let you know whether you can drop the group in any given location.

- To perform other actions on a group, right-click the group's name and select the action on the shortcut menu.

to help you read e-mail messages that are part of a *conversation*, an ongoing thread of messages related to a particular topic.

When you tell Outlook to arrange messages by conversation, it creates groups in the Inbox pane that consist of all the messages in a particular thread. Each thread consists of an initial message, along with all the replies. By default, Outlook shows only messages that are marked as unread or flagged for follow-up in each thread. This saves you from having to scroll past, or skip over, messages you've already read. Outlook indents messages to indicate who replied to whom during a conversation.

> TIP
>
> *To switch between seeing only the unread and flagged messages in a conversation and seeing all the messages, click the arrow to the left of the group name.*

Outlook does something to make the conversation arrangement even more useful. When a new message arrives in a conversation, Outlook automatically moves that conversation to the top of the Inbox pane.

> **TIP** *Moving the newest conversation to the top of the Inbox pane is the default behavior. If you prefer to work the other way around and place the newest message at the bottom, click the Newest on Top bar in the upper-right corner of the Inbox pane to switch it to Oldest on Top.*

Because all the messages in a conversation have the same subject, Outlook only displays the subject once. This way, Outlook can fit far more messages in the given space.

If you conduct discussions by e-mail, you'll find the Arrange by Conversation option incredibly useful. Please give it a try.

Take Advantage of Quick Flags, AutoComplete, and Info Tags

This section of the chapter provides a home for three e-mail–related features that don't fit anywhere else: Quick Flags, AutoComplete, and Info Tags. All three are examples of the kind of small changes that Microsoft has made to Outlook 2003 to increase your productivity. Here are the main advantages of each feature:

- Quick Flags turn the common task of flagging a message for follow-up into a one-click wonder.

- AutoComplete saves you from having to type long e-mail addresses (this is particularly useful on a Tablet PC when you're using the pen instead of the keyboard).

- Info Tags give you access to key information about a message without having to open it.

Keep Track of Your Messages with Quick Flags

According to Microsoft, research shows that people do one of three things with their messages: they respond to them immediately, discard them immediately, or plan to deal with them later when they have the time to reply or access to the information they need.

Where people get in trouble is option three, the "plan to deal with them later" bit. As I pointed out in Chapter 4, one way to deal with the problem is to open each message that needs attention in its own window and address the messages when you have the opportunity. But there are some real problems with this short-term approach. Leaving windows open on the desktop is only practical if you're never going to turn off your computer. Plus, having five, ten, fifteen, or more open message windows open on the desktop is awkward. People come up with many ways to tackle this issue, including establishing a separate "To Do" folder or leaving messages unread so that they're more visible in the Inbox, but none of these techniques works especially well.

To help you track messages, Outlook 2003 introduces Quick Flags, a much better solution to the problem. Quick Flags are flags that appear on the right side of each message in the Inbox pane. By choosing a Quick Flag for a particular message, you can, with a minimum amount of effort, signify that a message needs attention in the future or you've completed the necessary action. Outlook provides six different colors for Quick Flags, so you can come up with your own color-coded system for indicating priority, urgency, or whatever you wish.

NOTE   *Quick Flags stick with a message no matter what folder it is in. You can move messages manually or automatically without worrying about them losing their flags.*

To select a Quick Flag, click the gray flag icon next to a message. The icon immediately changes to the default Quick Flag color. When you complete the necessary action, you can click that Quick Flag icon again to indicate that you've completed whatever actions were necessary.

To select a Quick Flag in a color other than the default, right-click the gray flag icon next to a message and, on the shortcut menu, select any of the six Quick Flag colors. Figure 5-2 shows a message with a Quick Flag, a message where the flag has been replaced by a check mark to indicate that the task has been completed, and the Quick Flags shortcut menu.

In Figure 5-2, notice the gray bar under the e-mail address in the Reading pane. It contains information related to the message's Quick Flag. In Figure 5-2, the gray bar shows that the message was flagged with a follow-up flag and when the follow-up was completed.

You can also see that the shortcut menu offers additional options. The Clear Flag option does exactly that—it removes the flag from a message and leaves only the gray flag icon. The Set Default Flag option lets you specify which color flag is used when you click on a gray flag icon.

The Add Reminder option opens a dialog box where you can customize the flag for a particular message, as shown in the following illustration. You can set the meaning of the flag on this message to any of a half-dozen different possibilities,

A flagged message   A completed flag   The Quick Flag information bar

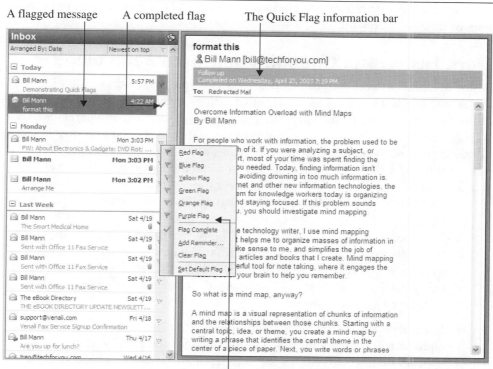

The Quick Flags shortcut menu

FIGURE 5-2 Quick Flags, a new feature in Outlook 2003, make it easier to organize your messages.

change the color of the flag, change the due date and time for dealing with the message, mark the message as complete, or clear the flag altogether.

This dialog box exists to give you the maximum amount of control over a message's flag, but you should use it sparingly. The point of Quick Flags is to mark a message with one or two clicks of the mouse and then move on, not spend a lot of time fiddling with flags.

Work Faster with Outlook's Improved AutoComplete

AutoComplete has been part of Outlook for some time, but Outlook 2003's AutoComplete has some enhancements that make it even more useful than before. AutoComplete helps you work faster by suggesting e-mail addresses as you type them in the To and CC fields of a message. If the list of e-mail addresses that AutoComplete suggests contains only one address or the address you want to enter is highlighted in the list, you can immediately press ENTER to enter that address in the field without typing the rest of it.

The new version of AutoComplete has two distinct advantages:

- In earlier versions of Outlook, AutoComplete offered addresses after you typed the first three letters of an address. The new version offers addresses as soon as you type the first letter. The addresses appear sooner and, in many cases, you need to type only one or two characters and press ENTER to enter an e-mail address.

- In earlier versions of Outlook, AutoComplete displayed addresses in alphabetical order. In the new version, the most frequently used address appears first, which reduces the number of characters you must enter.

Figure 5-3 shows AutoComplete in action. For the figure, I typed the letter *b* into the To field, and AutoComplete opened a menu containing all the e-mail addresses I've used before that start with that letter. The addresses in the list are arranged by frequency of use, with the one I use most frequently highlighted at the top of the list.

If the highlighted address is the one you want to enter, all you need to do is press ENTER and AutoComplete enters it in the To field. If the highlighted address isn't the address you want to enter, manually select a different address from the list or keep typing. Eventually, the address you want to use will either be highlighted in the AutoComplete list or you will have typed the entire address manually. Every time you type an address manually, AutoComplete adds it to its own list of addresses to offer next time around.

What if AutoComplete offers a bunch of addresses that you don't want? You can delete addresses from the AutoComplete menu easily. When you see an AutoComplete menu with an address that you don't want, press the UP or DOWN arrows to select the address and press DELETE. Doing so removes the address from the set that AutoComplete offers.

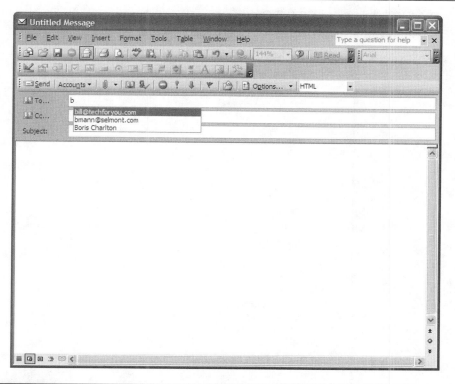

FIGURE 5-3   AutoComplete helps you enter e-mail addresses faster and more accurately.

How to ...   **Turn Off AutoComplete**

Not everyone likes AutoComplete or finds it helpful. If that describes you, you can turn off the feature altogether by following these steps:

1. In the main Outlook menu, click Tools | Options to open the Options dialog box.

2. On the Preferences tab, click E-Mail Options to open the E-Mail Options dialog box.

3. Click Advanced E-Mail Options to open the Advanced E-Mail Options dialog box shown here.

Advanced E-mail Options

Save messages

Save unsent items in: Drafts

☑ AutoSave unsent every: 3 minutes
☐ In folders other than the Inbox, save replies with original message
☑ Save forwarded messages

When new items arrive

☑ Play a sound
☑ Briefly change the mouse cursor
☑ Show an envelope icon in the system tray
☑ Display a Desktop Alert

Desktop Alert Settings...

When sending a message

Set importance: Normal
Set sensitivity: Normal

☐ Messages expire after: days
☑ Allow comma as address separator
☑ Automatic name checking
☑ Delete meeting request from Inbox when responding
☑ Suggest names while completing To, Cc, and Bcc fields
☐ Add properties to attachments to enable Reply with Changes

OK   Cancel

4. Clear the Suggest Names While Completing To, CC, and BCC Fields check box in the When Sending a Message section of the dialog box.

Scan Your Inbox with Message Info Tags

While Outlook's new user interface makes much more information about each message visible, the information you can see isn't always enough. For that reason, Info Tags provide additional information when you hover the mouse-pointer over a message.

The information that appears in an Info Tag depends on what information is visible in the Inbox pane. For example, if the sender and subject of a particular message are completely visible but the date and message size are not, the Info Tag shows only the date and size of the message. Info Tags aren't an earth-shaking enhancement, but they are a definite usability improvement.

Automate E-Mail Handling with Rules

Being able to send and receive messages using multiple e-mail accounts is one of Outlook's strengths, but bringing all your e-mail into the Inbox exacerbates the problem of handling it all. You don't want to worry about mixing up personal and business e-mail, and you certainly don't want to spend even more time sorting and arranging messages. To help you handle all that e-mail, Outlook lets you automate much of your message handling through the use of rules and the Rules Wizard.

TIP *Another important way to use rules is in the seemingly endless battle against junk e-mail, commonly known as spam. Chapter 18 covers security issues when using Outlook, including techniques to protect yourself against spam.*

5

If e-mail is a regular part of your personal and work life, you probably get dozens, even hundreds of messages each day. Even if you have a great organizational system set up, manually sorting so many messages into the right places can take up much of your day. Instead of wasting time manually sorting messages, you can set up rules that deal with the most common messages you receive, and let Outlook do most of the sorting and filing for you.

NOTE *Rules have become even more useful now that Outlook employs search folders to give you access to messages no matter where they are stored. Chapter 14 is dedicated to the powerful search folders feature.*

Here are some examples of what rules can do.

- Move or copy messages to an Outlook folder
- Flag messages for follow-up
- Delete messages or entire conversations
- Display a message or play a sound when a message arrives
- Send an alert to a mobile device

One common use of rules is to automatically sort incoming messages. You can create rules that sort all messages from friends into a Personal folder or organize work-related messages by project. Suppose you sometimes get urgent messages from your boss, complete with all sorts of dire consequences if you don't respond quickly. You could create a rule that causes Outlook to alert you whenever a message from your boss arrives. A set of well-thought-out rules can definitely make your life easier.

Ways to Create a Rule

Outlook gives you two ways to create a rule. For simple rules that require the most common actions, the Create Rule dialog box is the way to go. For anything beyond the simplest rules, you'll want to enlist the help of the Rules Wizard.

Use the Create Rule Dialog Box

The simplest way to create a rule is to right-click the name of a message in the Inbox pane and select Create Rule on the shortcut menu. This opens the Create Rule dialog box, shown in the illustration. The Create Rule dialog box is the best place to create simple message-handling rules.

To start with, Outlook uses information from the message you selected to fill in the dialog box. The From, Subject, and Sent To check boxes all contain information taken from the message you selected when you opened the Create Rule dialog box.

Those first three check boxes are conditions that you can use to trigger the new rule you are creating. In Figure 5-6, I could, simply by selecting the appropriate check boxes, create a rule that is triggered whenever a message arrives from the eBook Directory that is addressed to me only. If you select more than one condition in the Create Rule dialog box, all of them must be satisfied before the rule is triggered.

The Do the Following section of the dialog box is where you specify what happens when the rule is triggered. By choosing the appropriate check boxes, you can have Outlook:

- Display the message in the New Item Alert window

- Play a sound

- Move the message to a folder

As with the Conditions section of the dialog box, you can select more than one action and all of them will occur when the rule is triggered.

After you create the rule, click OK to exit the Create Rule dialog box. If you successfully created a new rule, a Success message box like the one in the illustration appears. This message box lets you apply your new rule to all the messages in the Inbox right now. Select the check box if you want Outlook to apply the new rule to all the messages in the Inbox as well as future messages.

Use the Rules Wizard

The Create Rule dialog box is great for simple rules. But if you need to create more complex rules, rules triggered by conditions other than those in the Create Rule dialog box, or rules that perform other than the most common actions, the Rules Wizard is the way to go. It gives you access to the full power of Outlook's rules.

To activate the Rules Wizard, click Tools | Rules and Alerts in the Outlook main menu. This opens the Rules and Alerts dialog box. Select the E-Mail Rules tab if it isn't already visible. Using this tab, you have complete control over the rules that Outlook uses. Return here if you want to change, copy, delete, or disable a rule.

To activate the Rules Wizard, click New Rule. As shown in Figure 5-4, the Rules Wizard appears.

The Rules Wizard helps you get started by providing a collection of rule templates. These templates are organized into two broad categories: Stay Organized and Stay Up to Date. When you have more experience with rules, you can dispense with the templates altogether, but when you're starting out, the templates are definitely the way to go.

FIGURE 5-4 The Rules Wizard provides several rule templates to help you create useful rules quickly.

NOTE *If you want the most flexibility in creating Outlook rules, start the Rules Wizard, and then select Start from a Blank Rule on the first screen. This gives you access to all of Outlook's options and conditions for creating rules.*

You have access to the templates when Start Creating A Rule From A Template is selected in the Rules Wizard. Using a template is a multi-step process. In Step 1, you select a template from the list of available templates. The rule description for the template you selected appears in the Wizard's Step 2 box.

If you look at the Step 2 box shown in Figure 5-5, you can see underlined values in the rule description. You customize the rule by selecting specific values for these placeholders. When you click an underlying value, the Rules Wizard displays a dialog box that helps you fill in that value. Once you replace the placeholders with specific values in the rule, click Next to continue.

Work your way through the Wizard's screens to complete and customize the rule, as well as indicate any necessary exceptions to the rule. In its last screen, as shown in Figure 5-5, the Wizard lets you name the rule, turn it on, and review it before putting it into effect. Finally, you have the option to apply the rule to all

FIGURE 5-5   The last Rules Wizard screen lets you select rule options and put the rule into effect.

the messages currently in the Inbox. When you're done selecting these options, click Finish and you're done.

Some Rules Tips

Outlook's rules are very powerful and flexible. While you can use them in the most straightforward manner—create a specific rule for each message, for example, and let the rules run all the time—you can get more out of Outlook rules if you know some simple tips. Here are two good ones:

- Combine rules if you can
- Carefully consider the order of your rules

Combine Rules if You Can

Whenever possible, combine rules. It's easy to end up with redundant or nearly identical rules, particularly when you use the Create Rule dialog box to create rules. The more rules Outlook has to process, the longer it takes to process them. A large collection of rules can have a noticeable impact on Outlook's performance. Also, rules that are similar to one another can make it hard to update your rules list, because you have to update all the related rules instead of a single rule.

The answer to the problem of too many rules is to combine rules whenever possible. Suppose you have a rule that moves all messages from Joe and Sandra to the Project X folder, and Michael joins the project. You could easily use the Create Rule dialog box to create a rule that moves messages from Michael to the Project X folder. However, if you need to update the rules related to Project X, you need to remember to do it in two places.

A better approach would be to add Michael to the existing rule that moves messages from Joe and Sandra to the Project X folder. As shown in Figure 5-6, you can do that by opening the Rules and Alerts dialog box and directly editing the rule description in the Rule Description window. You can also double-click the name of a rule to open the Rules Wizard and directly edit the rule there. And you can also make certain changes by clicking Change Rule and choosing a change from the menu that appears.

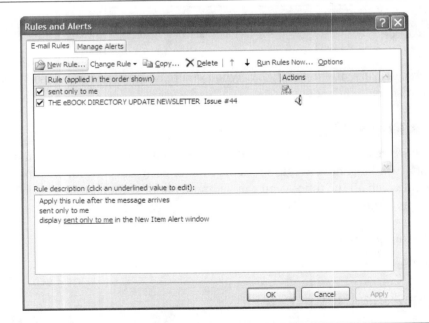

FIGURE 5-6   Use the Rules and Alerts dialog box when you want to modify an existing rule.

Carefully Consider the Order of Your Rules

Outlook executes rules in the order in which they appear in the Rules and Alerts dialog box. You can take advantage of this fact along with the Stop Processing More Rules action to speed the processing of rules and deal with special situations.

Moving messages that meet certain conditions into folders is a common use for rules. If you create a rule that moves messages from Joe into the Buddies folder, and that's the only (or last) thing you want to happen when a message from Joe arrives, you can add the Stop Processing More Rules action to the rule that moves Joe's messages. This way, Outlook doesn't need to check any of the following rules for messages from Joe, and Outlook can start processing the next message sooner.

5

Chapter 6

Work with Contacts

How to...

- Navigate the New Contacts View
- Add New Contacts
- Use Your Contacts
- Manage Your Contacts

Outlook's Contacts folder is its storage center for information about people and organizations. The information you can store for each contact is quite extensive, including e-mail addresses, an IM address, multiple phone numbers, a postal address, employer and title information, as well as personal information such as a spouse's name and birthday. New to Outlook 2003 is the ability to attach a picture to each contact, allowing you to put a face to each name.

In this chapter, you'll learn what you need to know to use Outlook 2003 contacts effectively. From navigating the new Contacts view, to adding, using, and managing your contacts, this chapter shows you all the key information.

Navigate the New Contacts View

Like Outlook's new Mail view, the new Contacts view has been redesigned to use screen space more efficiently. It, too, dispenses with the Outlook bar and the Folder List. In their place is the Contacts pane. The result, as Figure 6-1 shows, is a less cluttered view with more working space compared to previous versions of Outlook.

Did you know?

About Microsoft Office Outlook with Business Contact Manager?

For Office System 2003, Microsoft created two versions of Outlook. This book primarily covers the standard version, Microsoft Office Outlook 2003. The other version is one especially enhanced for small businesses. It is called Microsoft Office Outlook with Business Contact Manager.

That version includes a number of features intended to add basic Customer Relationship Management (CRM) features to Outlook. If that sounds interesting to you, check out Chapter 22, which is dedicated to that version of Outlook.

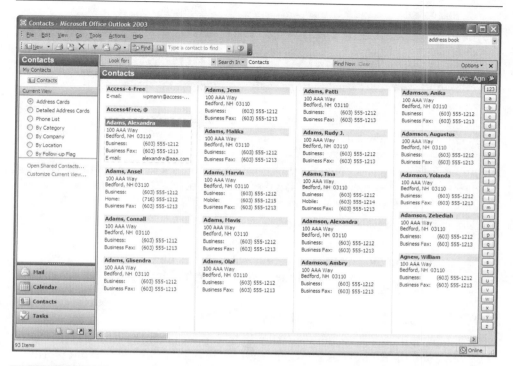

The new Contacts view provides a clean, efficient way to work with your contacts.

A Two Pane View for Better Usability

Like the new Mail view, the new Contacts view is a two-pane view. The Contacts pane, visible on the left side of Figure 6-1, replaces the old Outlook bar and Folder list. The Contacts pane has four main sections, starting from the top:

- **My Contacts** gives you access to all your contacts, whether local to your PC, on a SharePoint server, or shared by another Outlook user.

- **Current View** lets you switch between different Contact views easily.

- **Links** contains links to Contacts view features such as opening shared contacts, sharing your own contacts, and customizing the current view.

NOTE   *The exact links that appear in this section vary, depending on whether Outlook is connected to Exchange, connected to SharePoint, or is being used standalone.*

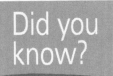

You Can Change the Contacts Pane Button Size?

By default, commonly used buttons in the Contacts pane are large, but less frequently used ones appear as small icons at the bottom of the column of buttons. You can change this behavior by moving the *splitter*.

The splitter is the thick bar that appears right above the Mail button. By dragging the splitter up or down, you can change the size of the buttons. Large buttons are ideal when you are using a Tablet PC or you are otherwise having trouble clicking the tiny buttons. On the other hand, smaller buttons mean more room in the Contacts pane for other information. It's your choice.

■ **Buttons** on the bottom of the pane work just as they do in Mail view. For example, click that Mail button to go to the Mail folder.

How to Use the New Contacts View

After using Mail view, Contact view should look pretty familiar to you. There are, however, enough differences between Mail and Contact view to make it worth spending a minute or two going over them.

Contacts appear in the large View pane. How they appear is controlled by which option you select in the Current View section of the Contacts pane. Try selecting a few options to see how they affect the appearance of the contacts in the View pane.

The View pane has features designed to make it easier to handle large numbers of contacts. In Address Card view, the upper-right corner of the View pane contains an entry that—similar to a paper dictionary or encyclopedia—shows you the range of entries visible right now. Also in Address Card views, Outlook displays a list of buttons down the right side of the View pane. Use these buttons to jump to a specific section of your contact list. Click the letter K, for example, to immediately jump to the first address card beginning with that letter.

In the Phone List, By Category, By Company, By Location, and By Follow-Up Flag views, your contacts appear in a table very similar to a spreadsheet. And they behave like a spreadsheet, too. For example, you can scroll through your contacts or sort them by field. At the same time, they work a lot like Mail view's Grouped by Conversation feature. They are grouped according to the View you selected. You can collapse or expand the groups and treat them as if they were single objects.

> TIP
> *The By Company view can be particularly useful at work because it groups all people from the same company together. If you frequently deal with multiple contacts from the same company, this view can really help you stay organized.*

Each icon on the My Contact section of the Contacts pane represents a different source of contacts. Click an icon to view contacts from that source.

The Contact view normally runs with the Reading pane turned off to leave the maximum amount of room possible for contacts in the View pane. To see information for a Contact, double-click it so it opens in its own window.

Now you should be ready to start working with your contacts. The first step is to add some if you don't already have them.

Add New Contacts

There are a few ways to add new contacts. You can create a contact from scratch or create a contact from information in an e-mail message. Let's first take a look at creating a new contact from scratch.

> NOTE
> *You can also create Contacts in public folders, but doing so requires you to be using Microsoft Exchange. See Chapter 23 for information about creating Contacts in public folders.*

Create a New Contact from Scratch

To create a new contact from scratch, you open a New Contact dialog box and manually enter the information. Follow these steps:

1. From anywhere in Outlook, click File | New | Contact to open a blank Contact dialog box like the one shown in Figure 6-2.

> SHORTCUT
> *You can open a new Contact dialog box from anywhere in Outlook by pressing* CTRL-SHIFT-C.

2. On the General tab, enter the name of the contact in the field next to the Full Name button. Outlook automatically breaks the name into its constituent parts and stores each part in its own field. You can confirm that Outlook parsed the name correctly with the Check Full Name dialog box. See the "How to Check a Full Name" box for details.

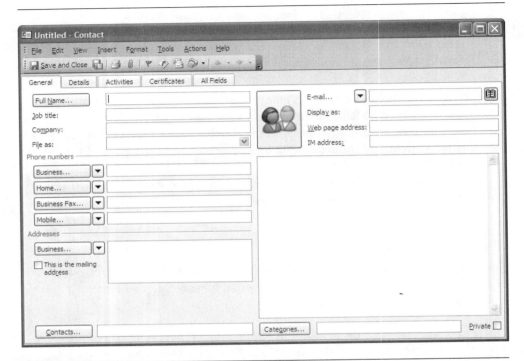

FIGURE 6-2   Open an empty Contact dialog box when you want to enter contact information manually.

3. Enter the rest of the information you want to include for the contact. The most basic information goes on the General tab. Information such as the contact's boss's name or birthday goes on the Details tab.

When you're entering information for a contact, here are some things to keep in mind:

■ To tell Outlook how to file a contact, choose an option from the File As list on the General tab. When you open this list, Outlook displays a number of options for filing the contact. Which options appear depends on what information you entered into the Contact dialog box fields.

■ You can customize many of the fields on the General tab. For example, if you look in the Phone Numbers section of the page, the first option is Business, but if you click the down-arrow next to the Business button, you'll see an entire list of possible names for that field on the card. Here's what's going on: Outlook supports many more phone number fields than are visible on the General tab. By clicking the down-arrow, you can change which field appears in that location. This not only allows you to control which fields appear on the General tab, it also allows you to enter information into fields that are not otherwise visible.

■ When a field name appears as a button (Full Name or Business, for example), you can click that button to see more detailed information that Outlook may have about the information in that field. The "How to Check a Full Name" box shows one example of the type of Check dialog box that appears.

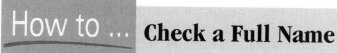

How to ... **Check a Full Name**

Checking a name is one specific example of checking the detailed information Outlook has stored in a particular field. To check a full name, click the Full Name button to the left of the name field after you've entered the name. This opens a small dialog box that displays all the detailed information that Outlook stored for the name you entered, including the title (Dr., Miss); the first, middle, and last names; and any suffix (Jr., III).

If any of this information is incorrect or incomplete, you can correct it or add it here. Note that this dialog box will automatically appear when Outlook believes the name information is incomplete or unclear.

■ If you entered more than one address for a contact in the Addresses section (by using the down-arrow button described previously), you can designate one address as the primary address by selecting the This Is the Mailing Address check box when the appropriate address is visible.

> **TIP** *If you're entering multiple contacts with the same company information, you can save yourself some time with this trick: In the current contact, click Actions | New Contact From Same Company. This opens a new Contact dialog box with all the company-related information fields already filled with information copied from the current contact.*

Create a New Contact from an E-Mail Message

If you've been exchanging e-mail with someone and you want to create a contact for your correspondent, you can save some time by automatically entering his or her name and e-mail address into a new Contact dialog box. Here's how to do it:

1. In the Mail view, select a message that contains the person's name or e-mail address in the Two, From, or CC fields.

2. Right-click the person's name or e-mail address.

3. In the shortcut menu, click Add To Outlook Contacts. This opens a new Contact dialog box containing whatever information Outlook gleaned about that person from the e-mail message.

Include Pictures in Contacts

Microsoft says that one of the most commonly requested improvements to contacts has been the ability to include a picture in a contact. Including a picture is really a great idea when you think about it. The ability to match a face to the contact information you have can only help your relationship with that contact. Figure 6-3 shows a Contact dialog box containing a photo of yours truly.

Assuming you already have a picture of the person in question, adding that picture to the person's Contact dialog box is a simple, three-step process:

1. Open the person's Contact.

2. Click Actions | Add Picture. This opens a Find dialog box that you can use to locate the picture on your system or anywhere on a network.

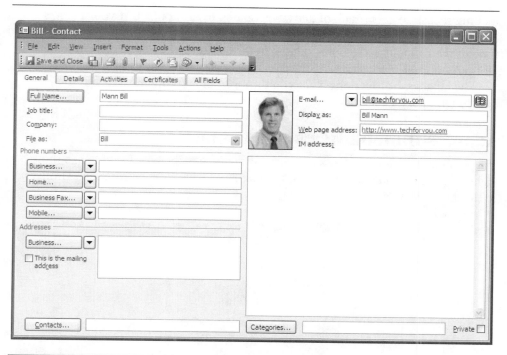

FIGURE 6-3   Outlook 2003 makes it simple to add pictures to contacts.

3. Locate the picture you want to use and double-click it. Outlook copies the picture, resizes it to fit the contact picture space, and adds it to the Contact dialog box.

Changing or removing a picture involves virtually the same process. The only difference is that when you go into the Actions menu, the Add Picture option is gone and the Change Picture and Remove Picture options are available instead. Select the appropriate option to accomplish your objective.

Use Your Contacts

While you can use contacts simply as storage areas for information about users and organizations, they can be more than that. With a contact selected, it only takes a few clicks of the mouse to address a meeting request, an e-mail message, or a task to that contact. You can link Outlook items or Office documents to a contact, making it easy to keep track of activities related to the contact. If your PC has a dial-up modem, you can also have it dial the contact for you, and even track the time of the call and make notes related to the call under the contact's name in Outlook Journal.

The next several sections walk you through some of the most useful things you can do with contacts.

Address Outlook Items to a Contact

You can have Outlook address a variety of items to a contact. To do this, simply right-click the contact in any one of the Contact views. A shortcut menu similar to this appears.

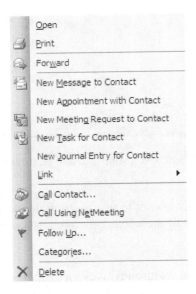

Select any of the "New" options (New Message To Contact, for example) and Outlook opens a new window for that type of item with the contact's address information already filled in. Another way to get the same result is to select the contact, click Actions, and select the option from the Actions menu that appears.

Link Outlook Items and Office Documents to a Contact

Linking Outlook items and Office documents to a contact creates an association between the item or document and the contact. If you open a Contact window and select the Activities tab, Outlook displays a list of the items that are linked to that contact.

Linking items to a contact is similar to addressing an Outlook item to a contact. Start by right-clicking the contact. On the shortcut menu, click Link, and then either Items (for an Outlook item) or File (for an Office document). If you select Items, the Link Items to Contact dialog box shown in Figure 6-4 appears.

Find the folder containing the item you want to link to the contact in the Look In list, and then select the item in the Items list. Click Apply if you want to continue linking items to the contact, and OK when you're done.

Linking Office documents to a contact works similarly, except, instead of a Link Items To Contact dialog box, you work with a Choose A File dialog box.

Set a Contact Reminder

Calendar allows you to set appointments with reminders attached to them. Tasks allows you to create reminders that are not associated with a particular time of day. Both features are great, but sometimes what you really need is a reminder associated with a particular contact. For that, you can set a contact reminder. With a contact reminder, the reminder is associated with a person or company instead of a particular time or date.

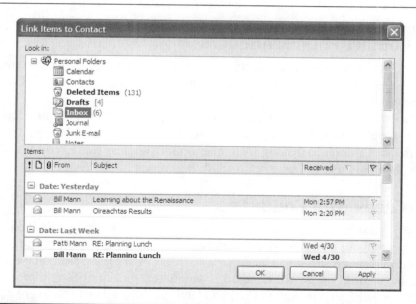

FIGURE 6-4   Linking items to a contact helps you keep track of activities related to that contact.

To create a contact reminder, follow these steps:

1. Open the contact for which you wish to set a reminder, and click Actions |
    Follow Up. This opens the Flag For Follow Up dialog box shown here. You
    use this dialog box when directly attaching a reminder to a contact.

 *You can also open the Flag For Follow Up dialog box by pressing*
CTRL-SHIFT-G.

2. Set the type of flag you want to use in the Flag To list, or remove the flag
    from the contact with the Clear Flag button.

3. Set the date and time of the reminder by using the Due By list boxes.

Dial Contact Phone Numbers

If your PC has a dial-up modem installed and connected to the phone system, you
don't even have to dial a contact's phone number yourself. You can have Outlook
do it for you.

To have Outlook dial a contact's phone number, open the contact and then click
Actions | Call Contact. This opens a new menu containing all of the Contact phone
numbers that Outlook has, along with other options such as Redial and Speed Dial.
Click a phone number or menu option and let Outlook do the rest.

Use vCards with Contacts

When you want to exchange contact information in the physical world, you
give someone your business card. When you want to exchange contact information
with someone online, you give him or her a vCard. A *vCard* is the electronic equivalent
of a business card. The vCard standard is widely recognized by e-mail programs
and contact managers, including Outlook. Outlook 2003 allows you to create and

read vCards from contacts, as well as e-mail vCards to others or make a vCard part of your e-mail signature.

CAUTION   *Some corporate firewalls remove vCards from messages as a security measure.*

Follow these steps to create a vCard from an existing contact:

1.   Open the contact you want to use as the source for the vCard.

2.   Click File | Export To vCard File. When the vCard File dialog box appears, select a name and location for your new vCard.

3.   Click Save.

From time to time, you might receive vCards attached to e-mail messages. You can easily convert a vCard into an Outlook contact by double-clicking the vCard attachment. Outlook opens the attachment as a new contact. Click Save to save the information.

Sending information to someone as a vCard is quite easy. Just open the contact containing information you want to send as a Card, then click Actions | Forward As vCard. This opens up an Outlook e-mail message that you can use to send the information.

Including a vCard as part of your e-mail signature is a little more complicated. You can add a vCard to an existing signature or attach one to a new signature at the time you create it. In either case, you need to open the Edit Signature dialog box. You'll get there automatically if you're creating a new signature.

If you're adding a vCard to an existing signature, here's how to open the Edit Signature dialog box:

1.   In the Outlook main window, click Tools | Options to open the Options dialog box.

2.   On the Mail Format tab, click Signatures to open the Create Signature dialog box.

3.   In the Signature list, select the signature you want to attach to the vCard, and then click Edit to open the Edit Signature dialog box.

Working in the Edit Signature Dialog Box

After you open the Edit Signature dialog box, look at the vCard Options section at the bottom. Either select an existing card from the Attach This Business Card (vCard) To This Signature list, or click New vCard From Contact.

If you go for the new vCard, you see the Select Contacts To Export As vCards dialog box shown in Figure 6-5. In this dialog box, you can select one or more of your existing contacts; Outlook will create vCards from them.

After Outlook creates the vCards for you, return to the previous dialog box and select the vCard you want to use from the Attach This Business Card (vCard) to This Signature list. Once you return to the main Outlook window, whenever you create a new e-mail message using this signature, Outlook will automatically attach the vCard to the message.

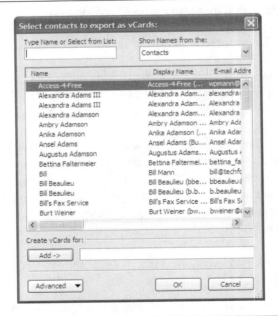

FIGURE 6-5   You can convert multiple contacts into vCards simultaneously by using this dialog box.

Manage Your Contacts

There is one troublesome thing about contacts: they accumulate. Unlike e-mail messages, tasks, or appointments, you naturally tend to hang onto contacts. Some people accumulate hundreds, even thousands. Long before you get into the thousands, contacts can become cumbersome to deal with. That's why you need to learn some techniques for managing them. Aside from a general suggestion that you delete old contacts that you are sure you don't need anymore, I have two techniques to help you manage your contacts.

Find a Contact

When you have lots of contacts, the most difficult management task may just be finding the right one. Fortunately, the Contact view menu makes it easy to search contacts without having to scan through all 5000 of them.

To search for a particular contact, type any information you can remember about the contact into the Type A Contact To Find box. You can find this box directly above the Contacts View pane. When you press Enter, Outlook opens the contact if only one contact matches your search, or displays the Choose Contact dialog box shown in Figure 6-6 if more than one contact is found. If the Choose Contact dialog box appears, select the contact you want and click OK.

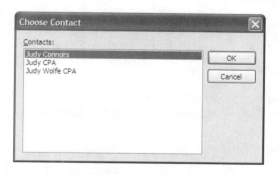

FIGURE 6-6   Given a little information, Outlook can help you find the contact you're looking for.

When searching for contacts, you can enter a full name, a partial name, an e-mail alias, a display name, or a company name. Searches with only a limited amount of information may return a large number of possibilities, but you're sure to find the contact you're looking for.

Deal with Duplicate Contacts

One final headache when managing contacts is dealing with duplicates. Sooner or later, virtually everyone ends up with one or more duplicate contacts. Finding that you have duplicates is easy, however, because Outlook tells you when you have them. The more difficult task is figuring out what to do about it.

When you try to save a duplicate contact, Outlook displays the Duplicate Contact Detected dialog box shown in Figure 6-7. Now you have to make a decision. You can either add the new contact anyway, or update the existing contact with any new information from the new contact.

If there is a valid reason to have two contacts with the same name, you can select the Add This As A New Contact Anyway option and click OK. But before you do, consider coming up with a way to distinguish between the two contacts (perhaps include the middle initial for one). Doing so will make it easier for you to tell them apart when you look in the contact list later, and prevent any further confusion about duplicate entries.

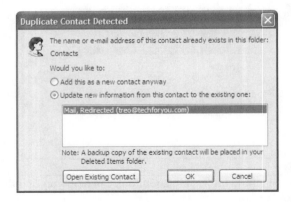

FIGURE 6-7   When Outlook detects duplicate contacts, use this dialog box to resolve the problem.

If you would like to update the existing contact with information from the new contact, select Update New Information From This Contact To The Existing One option and click OK. While Outlook can automatically transfer basic information from the new contact to the existing one, certain links from the Activities tab and other information will not get copied. This is the reason why it's best for you to deal with duplicate contacts as soon as possible. Doing so reduces the chance of losing information that you've entered into the duplicate contact.

TIP *If you're not sure how to handle duplicate contacts, you can click the Open Existing Contact button at the bottom of the Duplicate Contact Detected dialog box (refer to Figure 6-7) to see what's in the existing contact already.*

6

Chapter 7

Use the Address Book and Distribution Lists

How to...

■ Understand and Use the Address Book

■ Create and Use Distribution Lists

Understand and Use the Address Book

The Address Book is actually a collection of address books and address lists on your PC, your corporate network, or even sites on the Internet. Using the Address Book window shown in Figure 7-1, you can look up any people or organizations stored in any of the address books or lists you have access to. When searching for the appropriate address in the Address Book, you can search on names, e-mail addresses, or distribution lists.

NOTE   *You will learn all about distribution lists in the second part of this chapter.*

The Address Book can contain the following types of address books or lists:

■ **Global Address List**   The Global Address List (GAL) is the corporate address book that's available when your computer is connected to Microsoft Exchange. You can learn more about the GAL in Chapter 23.

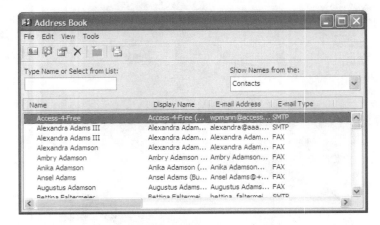

FIGURE 7-1   The Address Book window is a single point for access to all of your address books and lists.

■ **Outlook Address Book**   Outlook creates the Outlook Address Book automatically. It contains every contact that has either an e-mail address or a fax number. If you have more than one Contacts folder, you can configure the additional folders to also appear in the Outlook Address Book.

■ **Personal Address Book**   Personal Address Books (PABs) are the predecessors of the Contacts folder. Unlike previous versions, Outlook 2003 cannot create PABs.

■ **Internet Directory Services**   Internet Directory Services give you access to e-mail addresses that are not stored either on your PC or on the corporate network. Internet Directory Services use LDAP (Lightweight Directory Access Protocol) to communicate with e-mail clients like Outlook. For you to use an Internet Directory Service (often called an LDAP server), you'll need to get the appropriate information from either your network administrator or your Internet service provider.

■ **Third-party address books**   Outlook supports third-party address books. The way they're installed or the way they work is determined by the third-party vendor and not by Outlook. I won't go into further detail on third-party address books in this chapter. If you are required to use one, your IT department or the vendor will provide you with the information you need.

The addresses that you see in the Address Book depend on which address book or address list is selected. To choose an address book or list to view, select it from the Show Names From The list box in the Address Book dialog box.

Outlook's Contacts folder is generally faster and easier to work with than the Address Book. I recommend that whenever possible you work with the Contacts folder, and use the Address Book only when you need access to addresses that are not stored in your Contacts folder.

Use the Address Book

The primary use of the Address Book is, of course, to address e-mail messages. To open the Address Book, click the Address Book button (it looks like an open book) on the main Outlook toolbar. When you do, you'll see something very much like Figure 7-1. The simplest way to find an address is simply to scroll through the address list and look for it. Assuming the address you're after is in the default address book, that's all it should take to find it. If the address you want is in another address book, you can search that address book by selecting it in the Show Names From The list.

7

 *You can also open the Address Book with the* CTRL-SHIFT-B *keyboard shortcut.*

While this approach works, it isn't the most efficient way to do things. If you know the name of the address you want, start typing it in the Type Name Or Select From List box. As you type, Outlook searches through the selected address book and finds the first address containing the letters that you enter. If, for example, you type the letter *b* into this box, Outlook would automatically find and select the first address in the list that begins with that letter. If you then typed an *i,* so that the box contained the letters *bi,* Outlook would find and select the first address that begins with those letters.

This process continues until you press ENTER to open the address that Outlook has selected, or until there's only one address that matches the letters you've typed. At that point, Outlook opens the address for you.

There is yet a third way to find the address you're looking for. If you know at least part of the name that you're looking for, you can have Outlook track down all the addresses in the current address book that contain the bit you know. This is the most general way to find an address from within the Address Book dialog box. Follow these steps to conduct a search this way:

1. In the Address Book dialog box, click Tools | Find. This opens the Find dialog box.

 *You can also open the Find dialog box with the* CTRL-SHIFT-F *keyboard shortcut.*

2. In the Find dialog box, enter all or part of the name in the Find Names Containing box and click OK. The Address Book dialog box reappears, but this time, only addresses containing the name (or piece of the name) that you enter appear. The result will look very similar to Figure 7-2. Note that the Show Names From The list box now says Search Results. This lets you know that you're looking only at the results of your last search and not a full address book.

3. Select the address you want to use from among the ones that appear in the list, or display a different address book by selecting it in the Show Names From The list box.

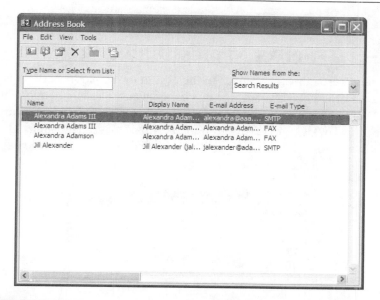

FIGURE 7-2   When you see the words "Search Results" in the Show Names From
The list box, you know you're looking at a subset of an address book.

Address an E-Mail Message from the Address Book Dialog Box

Once you have an address selected in the Address Book dialog box, it's easy to
create a new e-mail message using that address. With the address selected, click
the New Message button in the Address Book dialog box toolbar. Outlook immediately

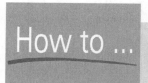 **Get Details about an Address**

You can get more detailed information about an address that you have selected.
In some cases, you may even be able to change that information. It all depends
on the type of address book you're working in.

   To get more details about an address, right-click the address in the Address
Book dialog box. Click Properties in the shortcut menu that appears. Outlook
displays whatever information is available on that address.

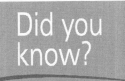

Microsoft Redesigned the Select Names Dialog Box?

While there were in many changes to the design of the Address Book and its associated dialog boxes, one welcome change was the redesign of the Select Names Dialog box. The Select Names dialog box is the one that appears when you click the To, CC, or BCC button in an e-mail message header. The old dialog box was relatively small and cluttered, and you couldn't resize it. That sometimes made it hard to select the right name.

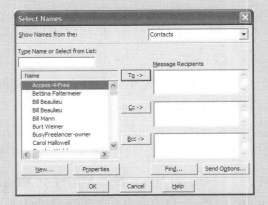

The new dialog box is much less cluttered and can be resized to show more information when necessary. It's a significant usability improvement.

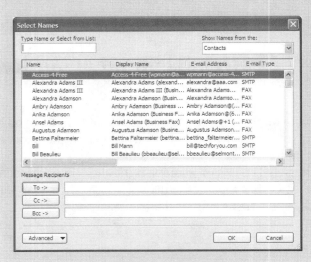

opens a new Message window with the address you selected in the To field. It couldn't be easier.

The Address Book allows you to send a message to more than one address at a time. When you click New Message, Outlook puts every address you have selected in the To field of the message. You can select multiple addresses in the Address Book dialog box by holding down the CTRL key as you click each name. This works best if you are manually selecting addresses from a single address book.

Add an Internet Directory Service (LDAP) Address Book

Adding an Internet Directory Service (LDAP) address book takes a few steps but isn't hard. Before you start, ask the network administrator or your ISP to provide the LDAP server name and any other information you need to connect to the server. Once you have that information, follow these steps:

7

1. In the main Outlook window, click Tools | E-Mail Accounts. This activates the E-mail Accounts Wizard. Figure 7-3 shows the first screen of the wizard.

2. Under the Directory heading, select Add A New Directory Or Address Book, then click Next.

3. On the Directory Or Address Book Type screen, select Internet Directory Service (LDAP), then click Next.

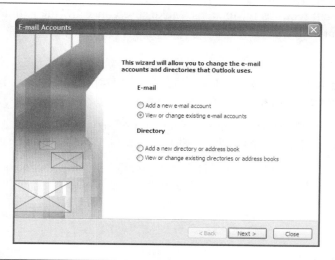

FIGURE 7-3   You use the E-mail Accounts Wizard to add or remove directories and address books as well as e-mail accounts.

4. On the Directory Service (LDAP) Settings screen, enter the information the network administrator or your ISP provided to you.

NOTE *On the next step, Outlook may display a message warning you that you cannot use the service until after you choose Exit from the File menu, then restart Outlook. If that warning does appear, click OK and continue with the step.*

5. Click More Settings to open the Microsoft LDAP Directory dialog box. Enter a user-friendly name in the Display Name section of the Connection tab page, and fill in any information in the Connection Details section if it was provided to you.

6. On the Search tabbed page of this dialog box, enter any Server Settings or Search Options that were provided to you. Click OK, then complete the wizard.

7. After you finish running through the wizard, click File | Exit to exit Outlook, then restart Outlook. The new address book should now be visible in your Address Book.

Add a Non–Internet Directory Service (LDAP) Address Book

Adding a non–Internet Directory Service (LDAP) address book (an existing PAB or a third-party address book, for example) is similar to adding an LDAP address book but requires fewer steps. Make sure you know the path to the address book you want to add before starting, then follow these steps to add a non-LDAP address book:

1. In the main Outlook window, click Tools | E-Mail Accounts. This activates the Email Accounts Wizard as shown previously in Figure 7-3.

2. Under the Directory heading, select Add A New Directory Or Address Book, then click Next. This opens the Directory Or Address Book Type screen.

3. Select Additional Address Books, then click Next. This opens the Other Address Book Types screen shown in Figure 7-4.

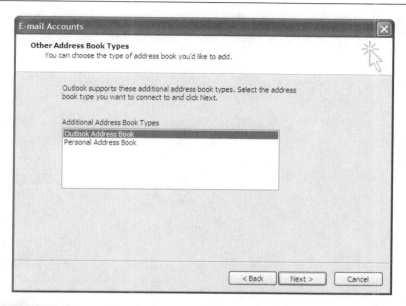

FIGURE 7-4   Use this screen to tell Outlook which type of non-LDAP address book you want to connect to.

4. Select the type of address book you would like to connect to, then click Next.

5. In the dialog box that appears, enter the path to the address book and set any options, then click OK.

6. In the Outlook main window, click File | Exit to close Outlook.

7. Restart Outlook. The new address book should be visible in the Address Book.

Change or Remove an Address Book

You use the E-Mail Accounts Wizard to remove address books. Start the wizard (click Tools | E-Mail Accounts) and in the first screen select View Or Change Existing Directories Or Address Books. Then click Next.

The wizard opens the Directories And Address Books screen shown in Figure 7-5. Select the directory or address book you want to change or remove,

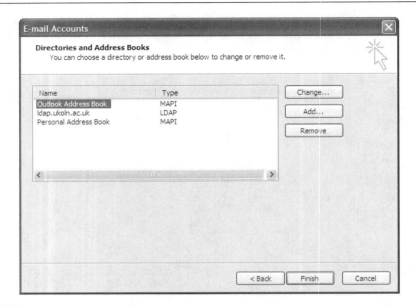

FIGURE 7-5   This screen in the E-mail Accounts Wizard lets you change or remove
address books and directories from a single location.

click the appropriate button, and let the wizard walk you through the rest of
the process.

Create and Use Distribution Lists

Outlook *distribution lists* are nothing more than lists of contacts. They exist to
make it easy to send a message, meeting request, or other Outlook item to a group
of people without having to enter each person's e-mail address whenever you want
to send a message. Here's an example of one way to use a distribution list:

I maintain the web site for the Irish dance school my daughter attends. Since
the site doesn't change often, we offer people the opportunity to sign up for a
notification list that sends them a message when the site changes. While there are
lots of sophisticated ways to handle something like this, I use a simple Outlook
distribution list. Whenever someone wants to join the notification list, I add them
to an Outlook distribution list that I maintain for the school. When I make a change
to the site, I simply address the notification message to the e-mail list and send it.
Outlook handles the details of sending the message to each individual contact on
the list. It's simple and effective.

Outlook stores distribution lists in the Contacts folder. When working in the Contacts folder, you can distinguish a distribution list from a regular contact by the two-headed icon that appears after the name of the distribution list in card views, or by the fact that the name of the distribution list is bold in other views.

Dance Notification List   🐾
Full Name: Dance ...

Working with distribution lists hasn't changed much in this new version of Outlook. The one big change is that distribution lists are now expandable. In previous versions of Outlook, you could only treat the distribution list as a single entity. In Outlook 2003, you can expand a distribution list to remove recipients for a particular situation without having to modify the list itself. The benefits of this change will become clearer as you learn more about creating and using distribution lists.

7

Create and Update Distribution Lists

The process for creating a distribution list is simple, with only minor variations depending on whether you are creating the list from scratch or creating it using addresses from an e-mail message. You might create a list from scratch when a new project team is formed and you know you'll be sending more than a few messages to the group. You might create a distribution list from an e-mail message if, for example, you've just joined an existing team and the team leader hasn't provided you with a list.

Create a Distribution List from an Existing E-mail Message

If you want to create the distribution list from an existing e-mail message, then follow these steps:

1. In the e-mail message, select the addresses in the To, CC, and BCC boxes that you want to add to the distribution list.

2. In the Outlook main menu, click File | Copy to grab a copy of the addresses.

SHORTCUT   *You can also use the CTRL-C keyboard shortcut to grab a copy of the addresses.*

3. Click File | New. In the menu that appears, click Distribution List to open the new distribution list dialog box shown in Figure 7-6.

 *You can also open a new distribution list dialog box with the* CTRL-SHIFT-L *keyboard shortcut.*

4. Enter a name for the new distribution list in the Name box.

 *If you want to include more information about the distribution list than just the descriptive name, click the Notes tab and enter as much information as you want on the Notes tabbed page. Then return to the Members tabbed page and continue with this procedure.*

5. Click Select Members to open the Select Members dialog box.

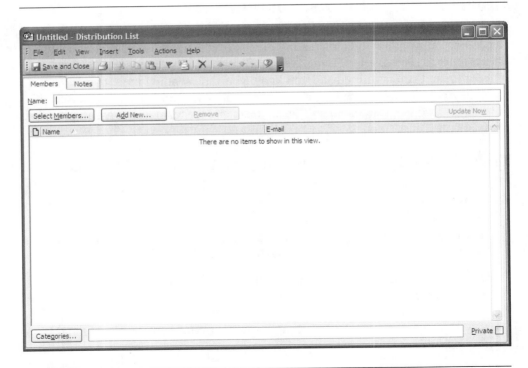

FIGURE 7-6 You use this dialog box to create and update distribution lists.

6. In the Select Members dialog box, right-click the Add To Distribution List box, then click Paste in the shortcut menu that opens to add the addresses you selected in the e-mail message.

7. Click OK to return to the distribution list dialog box. The names that you added should now appear in the list.

8. Click Save And Close to save you new distribution list.

Create a Distribution List from Scratch

If you want to create the distribution list from scratch, then follow these steps:

1. In the Outlook window, click File | New. In the menu that appears, click Distribution List to open the new distribution list dialog box.

SHORTCUT *You can also open a new distribution list dialog box with the* CTRL-SHIFT-L *keyboard shortcut.*

2. Enter a name for the new distribution list in the Name box.

3. Click Select Members to open the Select Members dialog box.

4. In the Show Names From The list, select the address book containing the addresses you want to add to your new list.

5. In the Type Name Or Select From List box, enter the name of a contact you want to add to the distribution list. Select the name from the contacts list, then click Members to add this contact to the list.

6. Repeat the process for each contact you want to add to the distribution list.

7. Click OK to return to the distribution list dialog box. The names that you added should now appear in the list.

8. Click Save And Close to save you new distribution list.

Move a Distribution List Someone Sent You into Contacts

If someone e-mails you a distribution list, you can easily add it to your Contacts folder. Just open the message containing the distribution list, and drag the list into the Contacts folder.

7

Update the Addresses in a Distribution List

If you have changed the e-mail addresses of any of the contacts included in a distribution list, you'll need to update the list before using it again. To do this, find the distribution list in your Contacts folder. Double-click the list to open it, then click Update Now. Click Save And Close to save the changes.

Modify a Distribution List

Once you've created the distribution list, you can also modify it. To do so, find the distribution list in your Contacts folder. Double-click the list to open it, then use the Select Members, Add New, and Remove buttons to make any changes necessary.

Use a Distribution List

In general, you use a distribution list the same way you use any regular contact. The only time there's a noticeable difference is when you only want to work with part of the distribution list. And in those cases, you can just expand the list, then work with the individual contacts as normal. The rest of this section talks about the most common situations you'll encounter when using distribution lists.

Send a Message to a Distribution List

Once you have a distribution list saved in the Contacts folder, you can use it in an e-mail message just like a regular contact. Enter the distribution list in the To field of an e-mail message and Outlook sends the message to everyone in the distribution list. It works the same way with the CC and BCC fields.

TIP

If you are in a situation where you don't want to automatically give the people on your distribution list access to everyone else on the list, you can send the message to yourself and BCC the distribution list. That way, everyone on the list will get the message, but only your e-mail address will appear in the message.

Because distribution lists are expandable in Outlook 2003, you also have the flexibility to send a message to only part of the distribution list. The next section shows how.

Send a Message to Part of a Distribution List

If you need to send a message to only some of the people on a distribution list, you don't need to type everything in by hand. Instead, you can expand the distribution list and remove the contacts you don't want to receive the message. Because Outlook expands the distribution list in the To, CC, or BCC box of the message, adding or removing names affects only the current message and doesn't change the actual distribution list.

When you add a distribution list to the To, CC, or BCC box of a message, you'll notice a plus sign (+) to the left of the name of the list, as shown in Figure 7-7. This, by the way, is easy way to tell if you're looking at a distribution list as opposed to a regular contact.

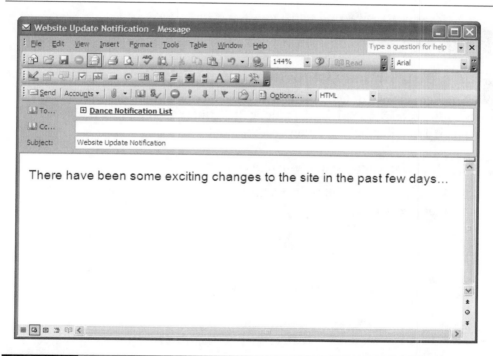

FIGURE 7-7   The plus sign to the left of a distribution list in a Message tells you that you can expand that list.

If you click the plus sign, Outlook expands the distribution list, replacing the single entry for the list with each of the contacts the list contains. Once the list is expanded, you can easily remove the contacts you do not want to receive the message. Be aware that unless you disabled it, Outlook will display an Expand List message box, giving you a chance to cancel the expansion of the distribution list.

 *You cannot collapse a distribution list once you expand it in a message.*

Send a Distribution List to Someone by E-Mail

With earlier versions of Outlook, people often reported problems sending distribution lists by e-mail. With Outlook 2003, there should be no problems. To e-mail a distribution list, follow these steps:

1. Open and address a new e-mail message.

2. Drag the distribution list from the Contacts folder into the body of the message and send it.

Chapter 8

Communicate with Instant Messaging

How to…

- Learn about Instant Messaging
- Use Windows Messenger with Outlook

The Internet is primarily a means of communication. And humans love to communicate. That's why e-mail became so popular so fast. But humans prefer to communicate face to face, in real-time. Conversations by e-mail are good, but conversations with instant feedback are even better. That's where *instant messaging* (IM) comes in. With instant messaging, you can communicate with other people in real-time, using the Internet to connect you whether you're in the next office or thousands of miles apart. Figure 8-1 shows part of an IM conversation.

Note the informal tone of the messages and the occasional typo. Exchanging instant messages is more like chatting with a friend than publishing a formal document.

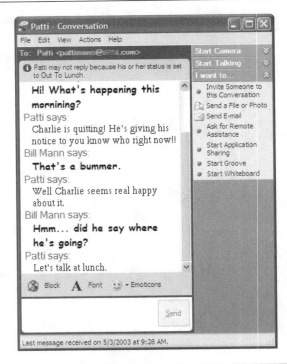

FIGURE 8-1   Instant messaging makes for quick and casual online conversations.

Not long ago, instant messaging was primarily a tool for socializing, as anyone with a teenage child can attest. But adults have quickly caught on, and now instant messaging is an important business tool. Project teams often use instant messaging in place of the telephone as a quicker, less intrusive way to ask questions and exchange information. I once managed a team of writers scattered across five locations in four states. Instant messaging was our primary means of regular day-to-day communication, and it worked out great.

Instant messaging is truly a powerful tool, and an important part of modern electronic communication. Recognizing this, Microsoft has integrated an instant messaging client, Windows Messenger, with Outlook. This chapter explains how to set up and use Windows Messenger, and how it works with Outlook.

NOTE   *This chapter assumes that you are using Windows XP, which comes with the Windows Messenger instant messaging client pre-installed. If you're not using Windows XP and Windows Messenger, don't worry about it. Most of the material in this chapter applies just as well to MSN Messenger, Microsoft's non-XP instant messaging client.*

8

Learn about Instant Messaging

Instant messaging systems work differently than e-mail systems or newsgroups (see Chapter 9 for more on newsgroups). Instant messaging systems are *client/ server* systems. In an instant messaging system, the client program runs on your PC. The client program communicates with a server program running on one or more central computers.

When you log on with the client program on your PC, it begins exchanging information with the server. This information includes, among other things, a list of all your instant messenger contacts. The server program checks to see which of your contacts are online, and passes information back to the client program so you can see who is available right now.

Knowledge of who is online right now, known as *presence*, is one of the key distinguishing features of instant messaging programs. When you send e-mail to someone, you have no idea whether the other person is online and likely to receive your message soon. With instant messaging programs, you know that the person you want to talk to is available right now (or at least that the person's instant messaging client is online). Outlook takes advantage of presence to help you communicate with your contacts in the most efficient way.

Use Windows Messenger with Outlook

As shown in Figure 8-2, Windows Messenger is the instant messaging program included with Windows XP. It allows instant text chatting between any two Windows Messenger users who are online at the same time. In addition, Windows Messenger permits you to exchange files, engage in group chats, and make voice calls to other computers or even telephone calls from your PC. The rest of this chapter is dedicated to helping you use this powerful communication tool.

Set Up Windows Messenger

Setting up Windows Messenger is easy, and may well be unnecessary. Most Windows PCs come with Windows Messenger or MSN Messenger pre-installed and set up to start automatically when you start Windows. If you see an icon

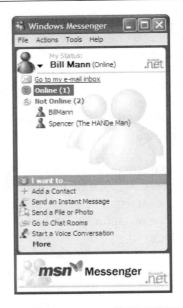

FIGURE 8-2   Windows Messenger provides Outlook's instant messaging capabilities, and a lot more!

showing two people in silhouette in the notification area of the taskbar, Windows Messenger is installed and running on your computer. To use Windows Messenger you need only sign in. But before you can sign in, you need to have a .NET Passport.

If you have a HotMail account or you signed up for any of the incarnations of Microsoft's Passport service, you should already have a .NET Passport. If you don't, skip ahead to the section "Get a .NET Passport" and get a password before continuing.

After you've successfully created your .NET Passport account, you'll see a dialog box like the one in Figure 8-3, where you can sign in to the *.NET Messenger Service*. .NET Messenger Service is the instant messaging service that Windows Messenger uses. Consider selecting the Sign Me in Automatically check box so you don't have to log in to the Windows Messenger Service every time you start Windows Messenger.

8

FIGURE 8-3   You'll have to face this dialog box every time you start Windows Messenger unless you select the Sign Me In Automatically checkbox.

Did you know?

Many Companies Manage or Ban IM?

Instant messaging originally found its way into the workplace through individual users, but corporations have increasingly seized control of IM use in the office. Just as they have telephone and Internet policies, many companies now have IM policies.

While IM programs use up relatively few computer and network resources, consumer-grade services are not secure and pose real security risks. One way that companies address the security issue is with IM policies. Don't install Windows Messenger or any other IM program on a business PC before consulting your company's IM policy, if it exists.

Software vendors are also attacking the security problem by developing secure enterprise instant messaging systems. Microsoft, for example, has developed something called Microsoft Real Time Communications Server 2003, a secure version of Windows Messenger that's designed for enterprise use. It provides secure instant messaging across corporate networks, as well as a bridge to existing consumer-grade systems.

Get a .NET Passport

Before you can sign in with Windows Messenger, you must have an account with *.NET Passport*, Microsoft's online user identification service. The easiest way to sign up is to start Windows Messenger. Until you set up an account, the .NET Passport Wizard dialog box appears whenever you start Windows Messenger.

If you use Microsoft's HotMail e-mail service, you already have a .NET Passport account that you can use with the wizard. If you don't use HotMail, you can create a .NET Passport by giving the wizard the name of one of your current e-mail accounts. The best choice is to give the wizard one of your primary e-mail addresses. This way, Windows Messenger users can send e-mail to that address if they want to get a message to you but you aren't online.

 *Be sure to give the wizard a valid e-mail address. The address you enter will receive a confirmation message that you must reply to before you can use your .NET Passport account.*

After you finish answering the wizard's questions, you'll be ready to start using Windows Messenger.

Enable Instant Messaging in Outlook

To use the integrated instant messaging capabilities of Outlook, you must first enable them. Enabling instant messaging in Outlook means activating the Person Names *Smart Tags*. Smart Tag icons look like the silhouette of a person's head and shoulders. Clicking them causes Outlook to display context-sensitive menus and options.

 You can find more information on Smart Tags in general in Chapter 25.

Follow these steps to enable instant messaging in Outlook:

1. In the main Outlook window, click Tools | Options. You see the Options dialog box.

2. In the Person Names section of the Other tab, select the Enable the Person Names Smart Tag check box (see Figure 8-4).

8

FIGURE 8-4   Enable instant messaging in Outlook by choosing options in the Person Names section of this tab.

3. Select the Display Messenger Status in the From Field check box.

4. Click OK.

Add Instant Messaging Contacts

Contacts are the key to using Windows Messenger. The program tracks your contacts so you know who is online. It uses contacts to know which instant messages to accept, which to block, and when to ask you what to do with incoming messages. And it lets you communicate with your contacts with only a few clicks of the mouse. So how do you add contacts to Windows Messenger?

To add contacts manually, click Add a Contact in the I Want To list at the bottom of the main Windows Messenger window. This starts the Add a Contact Wizard shown in Figure 8-5, which walks you through the process of adding a contact. You can manually enter the person's Windows Messenger sign-in name or their e-mail address, or you can search for that person in the central Windows Messenger Service user database.

TIP *You can also use Outlook Express contacts with Windows Messenger, as the two programs share the Outlook Express Address Book. Any Outlook Express contacts who are also Windows Messenger users automatically appear as contacts in Windows Messenger.*

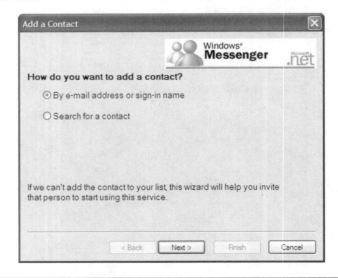

FIGURE 8-5   The Add a Contact Wizard gives you two ways to add a contact to Windows Messenger.

Send and Receive Instant Messages

After Windows Messenger is set up and running properly, all you need to do is
sign on, and Windows Messenger will be ready to receive messages. It will receive
messages automatically if the person sending the message is on your Windows
Messenger contacts list.

> **TIP** *Standards for etiquette in corporate phone conversations and e-mail
> messages have been around for some time. Instant Messaging etiquette is
> still evolving (heck, telephone etiquette is still evolving, and those things
> have been in the office forever), but there are some basic guidelines you can
> follow. Instant Messaging Planet has a helpful article about IM etiquette at
> this web address: http://www.instantmessagingplanet.com/enterprise/
> article.php/10816_1379121.*

When someone sends you an instant message, Windows Messenger pops up a
small box in the corner of your screen. That box stays there for a few seconds and
then disappears. If you click the box, a Conversation window connecting you to
the sender appears. If you don't click the little box in time, you don't lose the
conversation—it's still available on the taskbar.

If the sender is not on your list, Windows Messenger opens a dialog box
similar to the one shown here. From there, you can do one of the following:

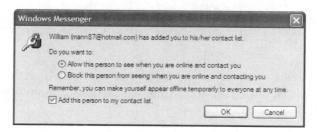

- Accept messages from this person.

- Block this person from seeing when you're online and from contacting you.

- Add this person to your Windows Messenger Contacts list.

8

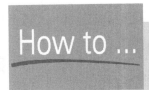 **Block and Unblock Instant Messages**

You may find that you want to prevent someone from sending instant messages to you, and keep him or her from seeing when you're online. Windows Messenger gives you the ability to do exactly that. There are two ways to go about it:

- If you're in the midst of an instant message conversation with the person, click Block on the Conversation window toolbar. When the Block menu appears, click the name of the person you want to block.

- In the main Windows Messenger window, right-click the name of the person you want to block and click Block on the shortcut menu.

You can follow analogous procedures to unblock someone who is already blocked:

- If you're in the middle of a conversation with someone you have blocked, click Unblock in the Conversation window.

- In the main Windows Messenger window, right-click the name of the person you want to unblock and click Unblock on the shortcut menu.

Sending messages is slightly different, as you can do so directly from Windows Messenger or from Outlook. The following two sections explain how you do it in each case.

Sending Messages from Windows Messenger

To send an instant message to someone when you're working directly with Windows Messenger, find that person's name or e-mail address in the Windows Messenger main window. If the person is online, double-click his or her name or e-mail address to open a new instant messenger window. If the person is off-line, you can send an e-mail instead. See "How to Send E-Mail to a Windows Messenger Contact" for more information.

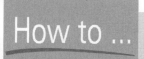

You Can Save Conversations?

As a matter of protecting your privacy, Windows Messenger (and the servers it works with) is explicitly designed *not* to save your conversations. Particularly in a business environment, however, you might find it important to save a conversation. To save a conversation, click File | Save As in the Conversation window. This opens a Save As dialog box, where you can specify the location to save the conversation. The conversation is stored as a plain-text file so you can read it with Word, Widows Notepad, or any other editor capable of handling plain text.

Send Messages from within Outlook

When you're working in Outlook, you can send an instant message to anyone whose Smart Tag is visible and shows any status other than offline. Assuming you've enabled Smart Tags, the tags are visible when you hover the mouse-pointer over a person's e-mail address in the To, From, or CC field of an e-mail message, or the e-mail address field in a Contact.

8

How to ... Send E-Mail to a Windows Messenger Contact

If a Windows Messenger contact is offline, or if you're more interested in preserving a record of a message than you are in instant communication, you can e-mail a message to a Windows Messenger contact. Windows Messenger offers two ways to send e-mail:

- Click the person's Smart Tag in an existing e-mail message or in the e-mail field of their contact. Then click Send Mail in the menu that appears to open a new message window in Outlook.

- Go to the Windows Messenger main window and double-click the person's name or e-mail address. A menu appears where you can click Send Mail to open a new message window in Outlook.

NOTE
Curiously enough, you can't initiate an instant message by hovering the cursor over the Instant Messenger Address field in a Contact.

To send an instant message from within Outlook, follow these steps:

1. Point to the person's e-mail address in a message or contact to cause the person's Smart Tag to appear. After a moment, the person's online status also appears.

2. If the person is not offline, click the Smart Tag, and then click Send Instant Message in the menu that appears.

3. Complete and send your instant message as you normally would.

Did you know?

Windows Messenger Can Do More than Chat?

When a Conversation window is open, Windows Messenger lets you do more than just type messages and send them back and forth. It displays a list of options to the right of the message window that, depending on the equipment connected to your PC, lets you do any or all of the following:

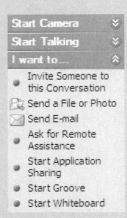

- **Add video to your conversation.** If your computer has a video camera connected to it, you can send live video as part of your conversation. The video images appear in the upper-right corner of the recipient's Conversation window.

- **Speak to the other person.**   If your computer has a microphone and speakers connected to it, you can add voice to your conversation. Of course, the computer on the other end must also have speakers and a microphone to conduct a voice conversation.

- **Invite more people into the conversation.**   While all Windows Messenger conversations begin with two participants, you can add others simply by inviting them.

- **Send a file or photo.**   This option lets you send a file or photo to someone in your conversation. The recipient must accept the file or photo before Windows Messenger will transmit it. By default, Windows Messenger stores files and photos you receive in the My Received Files folder, a subfolder of the My Documents folder.

- **Send e-mail.**   This option opens Outlook 2003 so you can e-mail the person quickly and easily.

- **Request help.**   You can invite someone to initiate a Remote Assistance session to help you fix a problem with your PC.

- **Make a phone call.**   If you sign up with a Voice Service Provider (Windows Messenger helps you do this), you can use Windows Messenger to make voice calls from your computer to a regular telephone. You'll have to pay an additional fee to use any of these providers.

- **Share applications.**   Everyone in the conversation can work on one application at the same time. You run the application on your computer and then share it with everyone else.

- **Share a whiteboard.**   Whiteboards are the online equivalent of the white, dry-erase marker boards you may have in your office at work. Everyone in the conversation shares the whiteboard.

- **Start Groove.**   Groove is a collaboration program that I use for various projects. Like a number of other programs, it can hook into Windows Messenger to take advantage of its IM capabilities. Since Groove is hooked into Windows Messenger on my computer, this option allows me to activate Groove. It's possible that you'll see Groove or other programs in this list on your computer.

8

Set Your Windows Messenger Status

Remember that the Windows Messenger Service knows when you're online and when you're not, and passes this information along to other users. When people see that you're online, they assume that you're available and willing to accept instant messages. Suppose you don't want others to know you're online? It would be a pain to shut down your instant messaging service every time you want to concentrate on your work and not exchange messages with other people. A better approach is to let people know your situation by setting your instant messaging status.

To set your status, click the words My Status at the top of the main Windows Messenger window. This opens the menu shown in Figure 8-6. The menu contains more than a half-dozen status settings that you can use to keep others informed of your situation.

FIGURE 8-6   Choose from among the status settings on this menu when you want to let others know your instant messaging situation.

As of this writing, Windows Messenger offers seven options for describing your online status: Online, Busy, Be Right Back, Away, On the Phone, Out to Lunch, and Appear Offline. By setting the right status at all times, you can better control the way people interact with you through Windows Messenger.

You now have all the information you need to use Windows Messenger as Outlook's instant messaging tool. But don't stop there. As you've seen, Windows Messenger can do far more than just exchange instant messages. I strongly suggest you experiment with some of its other features. They can really enhance your online communications.

8

Chapter 9

Enter the World of Newsgroups

How to...

- Learn about Newsgroups
- Use Outlook Express as Outlook's Newsreader

While e-mail is the most popular way to communicate on the Internet today, some older, more public means of communicating also exist. Many millions of people around the world use newsgroups to share information and discuss literally tens of thousands of topics in open conversations that virtually anyone can join. Newsgroups are an exciting and useful means of communication.

 *With the rise of the World Wide Web, the value of newsgroups as information sources has declined somewhat. Even so, there is still plenty of value in the world of newsgroups.*

Outlook 2003 doesn't directly work with newsgroups. Instead, it relies on another program, one that is shipped with every version of Windows. That program is Outlook Express, a combined e-mail client and newsreader. As an Outlook user, you really have no need for the e-mail client side of Outlook Express. But Outlook Express works great as a newsreader in conjunction with Outlook.

This chapter explains newsgroups and teaches you how to use Outlook Express as Outlook's newsreader.

Learn about Newsgroups

A *newsgroup* is the Internet equivalent of a bulletin board. Subscribers to a newsgroup can post messages to the group, and these messages can be viewed by other subscribers. People can respond to messages they see posted, and others can respond to their responses, and so on, creating what are known as *discussion threads*.

Newsgroups have been around a long time. Usenet, a network of *news servers* (computers that host newsgroups), which hosts most of the newsgroups in the world, is more than twenty years old. Google, the Internet search site at www.google.com, maintains an archive containing the last twenty years' worth of Usenet newsgroup messages. This archive contains over 700 million messages.

In addition to the vast array of public newsgroups, an unknown number of private newsgroups are available on corporate news servers. These newsgroups usually have restricted memberships and deal, not surprisingly, with issues of importance to the company or organization that hosts them.

Most newsgroups are unmoderated. That means no one is responsible for controlling the messages that appear in the newsgroup. While not having a moderator saves someone a lot of work, particularly on busy newsgroups, it does have some serious drawbacks. Unmoderated newsgroups often contain many messages unrelated to the subject of the newsgroup, junk e-mail, sales come-ons, and even obscenity and pornography. Despite these drawbacks, unmoderated newsgroups are by far the most common type of newsgroup.

Moderated newsgroups, on the other hand, are owned or managed by someone. A moderator determines whether incoming messages are allowed to appear on the newsgroup, and tries to keep the focus on the topics at hand. Moderated newsgroups are better at staying on track but depend heavily upon the efforts of the moderator or moderators.

Some newsgroups are open to anyone at all, but others limit membership to employees of a certain company, members of a particular group or organization, or another qualification established by the moderator.

9

TIP

One of the nicest things about newsgroups is that you don't have to pay to join them. Membership in the vast majority of newsgroups is completely free of charge (not counting whatever it costs to connect to the Internet in the first place) and open to anyone with a newsreader and access to a news server.

You use a *newsreader* to view the messages in newsgroups. Newsreaders display a list of the newsgroups available on a particular news server, and allow you to download and read messages from newsgroups, as well as compose your own messages that the newsreader posts to newsgroups. Some newsreaders, such as Microsoft's Outlook Express, provide significantly more than just basic news-reading capabilities. They allow you to organize and filter newsgroup messages as well as read and write them.

Now that you know a bit about newsgroups and newsreaders in general, it's time to get specific and learn about Outlook Express and how you can use it as Outlook's newsreader.

CAUTION

The people who send junk e-mail (spam) also haunt newsgroups. Chapter 18 contains information you can use to protect yourself from newsgroup and e-mail spammers.

Use Outlook Express as Outlook's Newsreader

Outlook Express is a free e-mail client and newsreader that Microsoft includes with Windows. It can manage multiple e-mail and newsgroup accounts for you under a single user identity, as well as manage multiple identities. Outlook 2003 is a much more capable e-mail program than Outlook Express, so we won't spend any time on the e-mailing aspect of Outlook Express. Instead, we'll concentrate on using Outlook Express as a newsreader. Unless you install and configure your own newsreader, Outlook assumes that you want to use Outlook Express as your newsreader.

Outlook Express is an NNTP (Network News Transport Protocol) newsreader, which means it will work with any public or private newsgroup. Because Outlook Express supports accounts with multiple news servers, it can access all the new servers you have accounts on. But before you go any further with Outlook Express, you need to configure Outlook to use Outlook Express as its newsreader.

Configure Outlook to Use Outlook Express

Before you can use Outlook Express as your newsgroup newsreader, you need to add Outlook Express to the Outlook Go menu. You only have to do this procedure once to be able to open Outlook Express as your newsreader directly from the Go menu. Follow these steps:

1. In the main Outlook window, find the Standard toolbar. While the exact contents of this bar vary, it normally contains the Print, Send/Receive, and Find commands, among others.

2. Click the Toolbar Options arrow on the right side of the Standard toolbar, as shown here. The Toolbar Options arrow on the end of the Standard toolbar lets you add a newsreader to the Go menu.

3. In the menu that appears, click Add or Remove Buttons, and then click Customize.

4. In the Customize dialog box, select the Commands tab.

5. In the Categories list, select Go. This allows you to alter the commands that are visible on the Go menu.

6. In the Commands list, select News.

7. Without releasing the mouse button, drag News to the Go menu on the Standard toolbar. After a moment, the Go menu appears.

8. Drag News to the position in the Go menu where you want it, and then release the mouse button. This assigns News to that position in the Go menu, as the illustration shows. You can place the News option anywhere on the Go menu that makes sense to you.

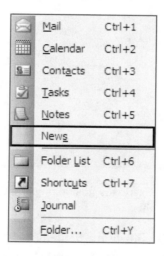

Now that you've configured Outlook to start Outlook Express as its newsreader, all you need to do is open the Go menu and choose News to start Outlook Express.

Meet Outlook Express

When you choose Go | News to activate Outlook Express as Outlook's newsreader, Outlook Express opens in newsreader mode, as shown in Figure 9-1. The pane on the left side of the screen is the Folders list, which shows all of Outlook Express's folders. The e-mail–related folders in the Local Folders section of the list are of little interest when using Outlook Express as a newsreader. What's important is the list of newsgroups that appears under your news server in this list.

You probably don't have any news servers or newsgroups listed when you first start Outlook Express. In Figure 9-1, you can see the news server I use: netnews.attbi.com.

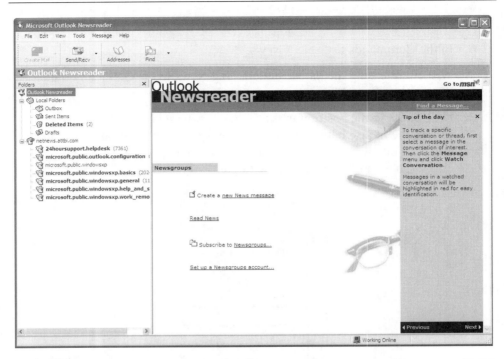

FIGURE 9-1   When Outlook Express is functioning as Outlook's newsreader, it looks very much like this.

The large pane on the right side of the figure is the View pane. This pane is where basic information about the message appears (the subject, who sent it and when, and similar information), as well as the complete text of messages you are reading. The exact information you see in the View pane depends on what you're doing at the moment.

Set Up a Newsgroup Account

Configuring Outlook Express to work with a news server is very similar to configuring Outlook to work with a mail server. You need to know the name of the news server before you start. Your ISP (for public news servers) or network administrator (for corporate news servers) can give the name of the news server to you.

Once you know the name of your news server, follow these steps to set up the account:

1. Start Outlook Express by clicking Go | News from the Outlook main window.

2. In the Outlook Express main window, click Tools | Accounts to open the Internet Accounts dialog box.

3. On the News tab shown in Figure 9-2, click Add and choose News to start the Internet Connection Wizard. It will guide you through the process of entering the name of your news server and setting up the account.

View a List of the Available Newsgroups

After you finish setting up a new server account, Outlook Express gives you the option to download a list of the newsgroups available on your news server. Downloading the list can take a while, as most new servers carry quite a few newsgroups. For example, the news server I use supports in excess of 36,000 newsgroups.

After Outlook Express finishes downloading the list of available newsgroups, you can start looking for some to join. To do this, click Newsgroups in the Outlook Express View pane. Doing so opens the Newsgroup Subscriptions dialog box shown in Figure 9-3.

9

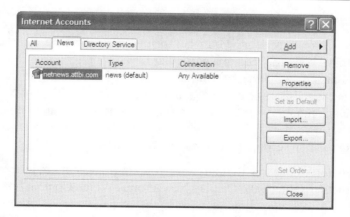

FIGURE 9-2   Use the News tab of the Internet Accounts dialog box to tell Outlook Express about your news server.

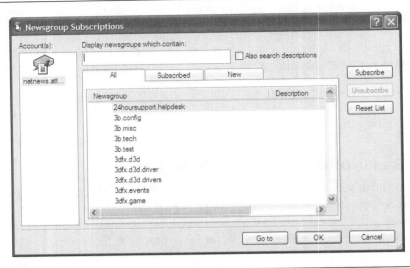

FIGURE 9-3   Use the Newsgroup Subscriptions dialog box to search for, and subscribe to, interesting and useful newsgroups.

As you learned earlier, your news server probably has thousands or even tens of thousands of available newsgroups. With so many newsgroups to choose from, how can you figure out which ones to subscribe to? Here are three ways to tackle the problem:

■ Know which newsgroup you want to subscribe to before you start. You may have been referred to a particular newsgroup by a friend or co-worker, or perhaps by a directive from the IT department at work. In this case, your task is easy. Enter the name of the newsgroup in the Display Newsgroups Which Contain box of the Newsgroup Subscriptions dialog box. Assuming your news server carries the newsgroup, its name will appear in the list. Select the newsgroup, and then click Subscribe.

■ If you don't have a particular newsgroup in mind, but are interested in a particular subject, the Display Newsgroups Which Contain box can be very helpful. Enter a word describing the subject you're interested in to see a list of each newsgroups on the news server whose name contains the word you entered. Enter "fishing" for example, and Outlook Express will list every available newsgroup on the news server that has the word "fishing" in its name.

> **TIP**
> *You can increase your chances of finding a newsgroup that covers your subject by selecting the Also Search Descriptions check box. Some newsgroups publish a description that explains the purpose of the newsgroup. This description may include the name of the subject you're interested in, even if the newsgroup's name doesn't.*

■ As an Outlook user, you might find Microsoft's Outlook, Office, and Windows newsgroups to be of use. Try entering the words "Microsoft" and "Outlook." Doing so returns dozens of newsgroups that cover Microsoft Outlook (and Outlook Express). Other searches containing the word "Microsoft" and the name of the application or operating system you're interested in will return similar results.

> **TIP**
> *If your news server doesn't carry the newsgroup you're looking for, try using a different news server. One place to find publicly available news servers is newszbot.com (http://www.newzbot.com/serverlist.php).*

Subscribe to a Newsgroup

You can read newsgroup messages without subscribing to a newsgroup. You can even post messages to a newsgroup without subscribing. So why subscribe?

When you subscribe to a newsgroup, your newsreader includes that newsgroup in a list that appears each time you start the newsreader. This gives you access to the newsgroup with as little as one click of the mouse, instead of requiring you to search for the newsgroup each time you want to view it.

To subscribe to a newsgroup, follow these steps:

1. Click Tools | Newsgroups to open the Newsgroup Subscriptions dialog box if it isn't already open.

> **SHORTCUT**
> *You can also open the Newsgroup Subscriptions dialog box by pressing* CTRL-W.

2. Find and select the newsgroup you want to subscribe to in the Newsgroup Subscriptions dialog box.

3. Click Subscribe or double-click the newsgroup's name.

When you subscribe to a newsgroup, an icon—it looks like a manila folder with a piece of paper tacked to it—appears to the left of the newsgroup's name in the Newsgroup list. When you finish selecting newsgroups to subscribe to, click OK to exit the Newsgroup Subscriptions dialog box. The newsgroup you subscribed to appears in the Outlook Newsreader Folders list, as shown in Figure 9-4.

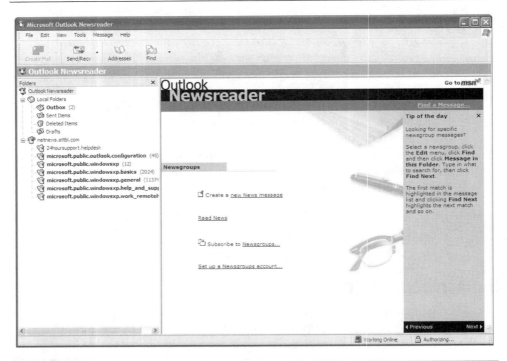

FIGURE 9-4   Newsgroups you subscribe to appear in the Outlook Newsreader
Folders list.

Read Newsgroup Messages

After you subscribe to some newsgroups, you're almost ready to start reading
messages. First you need to download the message headers from the newsgroup
that you want to read. If you're only interested in working with a single newsgroup
right now, just click that newsgroup's name in the Folders list. Outlook Express
automatically downloads the headers for that newsgroup. Downloading message
headers this way is called "synchronizing with the newsgroup."

TIP   *Newsgroup message headers contain information such as the subject of
the message, who sent it, when it was sent, and its size.*

Another approach is to download all the headers for all the newsgroups you subscribe to on this news server. To do this, click Tools | Synchronize All.

Similar to downloading the list of available newsgroups, downloading the headers of all the messages in one or more newsgroups can take a while. Between them, the six newsgroups shown in Figure 9-5 contain something like 20,000 messages, including about 19,000 messages that I haven't read yet. I know that I haven't read about 19,000 messages because the number of unread messages appears to the right of each newsgroup name in the Folders list.

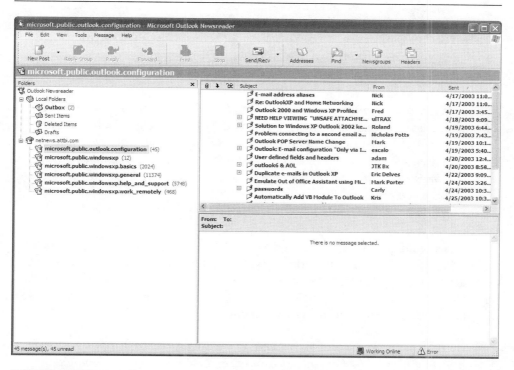

FIGURE 9-5   Few people can keep up with all the messages flowing in busy newsgroups.

Newsgroups Can Be Dangerous?

While newsgroups can be great places to share information or just chat, not all newsgroups are benign. The vast majority of newsgroups are unmoderated. That is, no one is on duty to make sure that the messages that are posted are clean, wholesome, or even legal. Some newsgroups are full of tasteless commentary or profanity. Others cater to virtually any vice you can think of.

In some ways the world of newsgroups is very much like a big city. Parts of it are very businesslike; parts are great fun; and parts are places where decent people don't want to go. Your best bet is to stick with newsgroups to which you have been referred or web sites that you trust.

TIP

If you're not careful, newsgroups can become a major time sink. If you subscribe to busy newsgroups, you're likely to see tens, hundreds, and maybe even thousands of unread messages every time you open your newsreader. You could spend vast amounts of time reading and replying to messages, and not get any of your real work done. To avoid wasting too much time, try just skimming the subject names of the messages you haven't read yet, and only select messages that really interest you.

To start reading messages in a particular newsgroup, click the name of the newsgroup in the Folders list. Outlook Express displays the headers of messages from that newsgroup in the View pane. Click a message in the View pane to make its contents appear in the Preview pane. Double-click a message in the View pane to make the message appear in its own window.

TIP

If the newsgroup contains no unread messages, the name of that newsgroup in the Folders list is in normal type. If the newsgroup does contain unread messages, its name appears in boldface in the Folders list.

 **Block Unwanted Newsgroup Messages**

You may someday find it necessary to block newsgroup messages. Perhaps a certain newsgroup participant uses language you don't approve of or is harassing you. Perhaps a long-running conversation doesn't interest you anymore. Perhaps you're getting lots of junk mail from addresses on a particular domain. Whatever your reason, Outlook Express gives you the option to block messages.

There are two ways to block a sender's messages. If you've already received a message from a sender, the easiest approach is to select the message and choose Message | Block Sender.

To block messages from a particular sender or domain when you haven't received messages from these senders, follow these steps:

1. In the Outlook Express main window, choose Tools | Message Rules | Block Senders List. This opens the Message Rules dialog box. On the Blocked Senders tab is a list that contains the e-mail addresses or domain names of all blocked senders.

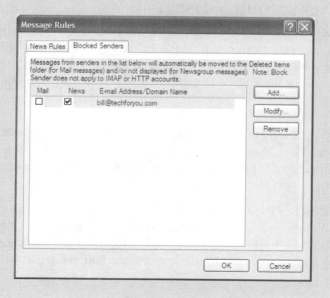

2. Click Add to open the Add Sender dialog box.

3. Add the e-mail address or domain name of the sender you want to block.

4. Choose the kind of messages sent by this sender that you want to block by selecting Mail Messages, News Messages, or Mail and News Messages in the Block the Following section of the dialog box.

 *You can modify or remove senders from the list by selecting them in the list and then clicking the Modify or Remove button.*

5. Repeat the process for each e-mail address or domain name you wish to block.

 *You can only block messages coming from standard POP3 mail servers. You cannot block messages from senders who use HTTP or IMAP e-mail or services.*

Reply to Newsgroup Messages

You'll eventually want to reply to a message you read in a newsgroup. Doing so is very much like replying to an e-mail message, except for the fact that you're using Outlook Express instead of Outlook and you're replying to a newsgroup instead of an individual. Follow these steps to compose and post a reply to a newsgroup message:

1. Decide what kind of reply you want to make. No, I don't mean deciding whether to be sarcastic or funny, I mean deciding whether you want to reply directly to the person who sent the message or to the newsgroup as a whole.

2. Click Reply or Reply Group. If you're replying to a message that you're reading in the Preview pane, click the Reply or Reply Group button on the main Outlook Express toolbar. If you're replying to a message that you're reading in its own separate window, use the buttons in that window.

Whichever method you choose, Outlook Express opens a message window similar to the one in the following illustration. The message is addressed either to the newsgroup or to an individual.

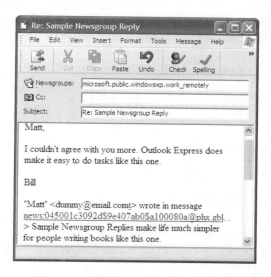

3. Type your reply in the message window. Note that Outlook Express automatically includes the contents of the message you're replying to. Outlook Express provides rudimentary formatting and editing tools that you can use while composing your message, including the Check Address and Check Spelling buttons.

4. Click Send to post a message to the newsgroup or send it to the individual recipient.

Compose and Post New Newsgroup Messages

Composing and posting new newsgroup messages is almost the same as replying to a newsgroup message. Select the newsgroup you want to post to in the Folders list, and then click New Post in the toolbar.

Outlook Express opens a New Message window that you can use to compose your message. Outlook Express fills in the address of the destination newsgroup for you, but, of course, you must type in the subject and body of the message yourself. Click Send when you're ready to post your message to the newsgroup.

Organize Your Newsgroup Messages

If you become a regular newsgroup participant, you quickly find that the thousands of message headers and bodies that Outlook Express downloads can become difficult to work with. To help you deal this information, Outlook Express offers several ways to manage newsgroup messages. You can

- Find a message in a newsgroup

- View only certain types of messages

- Group messages and replies

- Delete messages (but only on your PC)

- Create rules for managing messages

- Create custom message views

This chapter covers the first four techniques in the list. I'll leave learning how to create newsgroup rules and custom views as an exercise for those of you who are big fans of newsgroups.

Find a Message in a Newsgroup

You can search for messages in a newsgroup by entering keywords you specify. To do this, select the newsgroup you want to search in the Folders list, and then click Edit | Find | Message. You see the Find dialog box shown here.

 *You can also open the Find dialog box by pressing* SHIFT-F3.

Enter the word or words you want to search for in the Look For box. By default, Outlook Express searches only in message headers. To make it search in the message bodies as well, select the Search All the Text in Download Messages check box. Click Find Next to start the search. Outlook Express highlights the next message it comes to that contains the words you're searching for. Click Find to find the next message containing the search words.

TIP *If your search doesn't find what you want, or you're finding too many messages, try clicking Advanced Find. This opens a new dialog box for entering more information and refining your search.*

View Only Certain Types of Messages

Outlook Express supports several views that you can use to look at certain categories of messages. For example, one view hides messages that you have already read. Applying these predefined views takes only a few clicks of the mouse.

Select the newsgroup you want to work with in that Folders list, choose View | Current View, and select one of the predefined views on the submenu.

Group Messages and Replies

Just as Outlook can group e-mail messages by conversation (grouping messages and their replies together), Outlook Express can group newsgroup messages. When messages are grouped in this manner, you can choose to view only the original message or the message and all its replies.

To group messages by conversation, select the newsgroup you want to work with in the Folders list and choose View | Current View | Group Messages by Conversation. Message grouping is turned on when there is a checkmark next to the Group Messages by Conversation menu option.

When grouping messages by conversation, the original message in each conversation has a plus sign (+) or minus sign (−) to its left. Double-click the symbol to switch between showing just the original message and the message with all its replies.

Delete Messages

You probably won't want to keep all the newsgroup messages you download. You can't remove messages from the newsgroup itself, but you can delete copies of messages on your PC. The messages are still part of the newsgroup. They just won't appear in Outlook Express on your PC. Here are instructions for deleting messages and otherwise handling messages:

- To delete a newsgroup message, select the message in the View pane and press DELETE.

- To unsubscribe from a newsgroup, select it in the Folders list and press DELETE.

9

■ To completely delete a newsgroup and all its messages from your PC (not just unsubscribe from a newsgroup), click Tools | Options. In the Options dialog box, open the Maintenance tab and click Clean Up Now. In the Local File Clean Up dialog box, click Browse. Select the newsgroup folder you want to delete and click OK. In the Local File Clean Up dialog box, click Delete to remove the message header and bodies.

Part III

Manage your Personal Information

Chapter 10

Stay on Schedule with Calendar

How to...

- Navigate the New Calendar View
- Use the Calendar
- Make Your Free/Busy Information Available Online

The Calendar view lets you track and schedule your daily activities. Like a paper calendar, it gives you a place to record appointments, track upcoming events, and figure out how much longer until the weekend or your big vacation.

But the Outlook Calendar can do far more. It can remind you when it's time for various activities. And it can also help you schedule meetings by showing everyone's free and busy times, transmitting meeting invitations, and tracking the responses for you. Calendar also helps you reschedule meetings and compare schedules.

This chapter shows you how to use Calendar to keep your life on schedule. In particular, it covers the efficiency-enhancing changes that Microsoft has made for this version of Calendar, things like faster handling of meeting requests and the side-by-side Calendar view.

Navigate the New Calendar View

To open the Calendar view, click the Calendar button in the navigation pane. The Calendar view is similar to the Contacts view: it has two panes, with the Calendar pane on the left and varying views of your calendar information in the View pane on the right.

However, as Figure 10-1 shows, the Calendar view has some additional elements. In date-oriented views, the standard toolbar contains a set of buttons that controls the number of days that are displayed. There's also a small calendar that appears at the top of that Calendar pane. This is the Date Navigator, a tool for quickly moving from day to day within the current month, or any month at all.

 *You can switch to the Calendar view from anywhere in Outlook with the* CTRL-2 *keyboard shortcut.*

Leaving aside the Date Navigator for a moment, the Calendar pane has four main sections, starting from the top:

- **My Calendars** gives you access to all your calendars, whether local to your PC, on a SharePoint server, in an Exchange public folder, or shared by another Outlook user. One of the slick new features of Outlook 2003 (and one that was heavily requested) is the ability to view multiple Calendars at the same time.

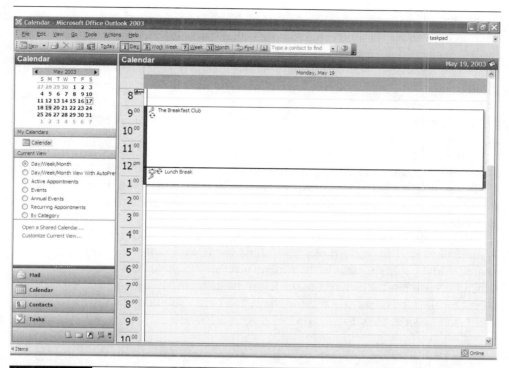

FIGURE 10-1 The Calendar view is the standard Outlook two-pane view, with special features for handling dates.

- **Current View** lets you switch easily between different Calendar views.

- **Links** contains links that allow you to open shared Calendars, share your Calendar, or customize the current view.

NOTE *The exact links that appear in this section vary, depending on whether Outlook is connected to Exchange, is connected to SharePoint, or is being used stand-alone.*

- **Buttons** at the bottom of the pane work just as they do in Mail view. Click the Mail button to go to the Mail folder and so on.

Now about that Date Navigator: When you have Calendar in a standard two-pane view, the Date Navigator appears at the top of that Calendar pane. But the Calendar view can also include an additional pane, called the TaskPad. When the TaskPad is visible, the Date Navigator moves from the top of the Calendar pane to the top of the TaskPad pane. The TaskPad is off by default, but you may well want to turn it on. You'll learn more about the TaskPad later in this chapter.

Now that you know how to find the Date Navigator, you're probably wondering what to do with it. The first thing to note is that it doesn't just show the days of the month. Dates that appear in bold text in the Date Navigator are days with some sort of activity scheduled. Not surprisingly, you can use the Date Navigator to navigate through time. Click a date in the Date Navigator and the View pane switches to show that date.

The Date Navigator becomes particularly handy when you are scheduling activities more than a few days in advance. Click a date in the Date Navigator, and Calendar displays that date in the View pane. Click the right and left arrows in the header of the Date Navigator to see the next or preceding month. With only a few clicks on the Date Navigator, you can quickly get to the date you want to work on, without having to fool around with your view or the buttons on the standard toolbar.

The ability to view Calendars side by side is a big addition to Outlook. And it is incredibly easy to use. All of your Calendars, as well as the ones that are being shared with you, are visible in the Calendar pane. When you have more than one Calendar, each has a check box to the left of its name in My Calendar. Set the check boxes for the Calendars you want to view, and Outlook automatically displays them side by side, as in Figure 10-2.

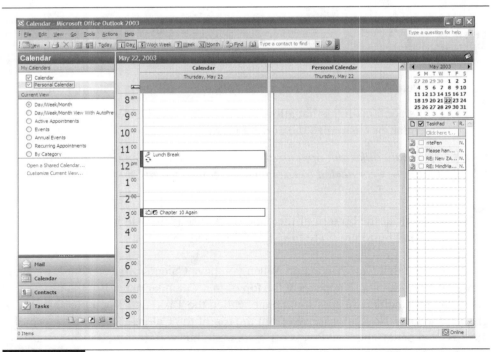

FIGURE 10-2   The ability to display Calendars side by side can simplify many tasks.

Use the Calendar

Once you understand the different things it can do, Calendar isn't hard to use. Calendar supports three types of activities: appointments, meetings, and events.

- **Appointments**   An appointment is an activity that doesn't require you to invite other people. Use an appointment to set aside some time to work on a special project. Or use an appointment to set aside time for an upcoming doctor's or dentist's appointment. While other people are involved in such an appointment, as far as Calendar is concerned, there's only you. You can set a reminder for each appointment, and you can schedule recurring appointments.

- **Meetings**   Meetings are appointments that involve other people or resources. When you create a meeting item, you specify the people who are invited to the meeting, and select a meeting time. Outlook automatically sends invitations to everyone on the list. In addition to scheduling a meeting and inviting people, you can reschedule meetings, add people to the list of invitees, even set up recurring meetings.

- **Events**   Events are activities that last for at least 24 hours. They differ from normal appointments and meetings in that they don't occupy a particular time slot in the Calendar. Instead, events appear as a banner across the top of your schedule. You can set events to recur. Holidays are good examples of annually recurring events.

10

How to ... Display Holidays in Calendar

Do you observe the national holidays of the United States or other countries? Would you like those holidays to appear in Calendar? If so, you've come to the right spot.

CAUTION   *If you upgraded from an earlier version of Outlook, and Calendar already displays holidays for a country or region, you must first remove them before adding the current holiday calendar in Outlook 2003. Instructions on how to do so are at the end of this box.*

To make holidays appear in the Outlook Calendar, follow these steps:

1. In the Outlook main window, click Tools | Options, to open the Options dialog box.

2. On the Preferences tabbed page, click Calendar Options to open the Calendar Options dialog box.

3. In the Calendar Options section of the dialog box, click Add Holidays. This opens the Add Holidays To Calendar dialog box.

4. In the list of countries, select the names of the countries or regions whose national holidays you want to display.

 *Calendar automatically selects your own country or region for you.*

5. Click OK. The Import Holidays dialog box appears and shows progress as Outlook imports the national holiday information.

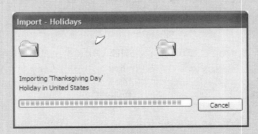

6. When the download is complete, a message box appears to tell you so. Click OK to finish.

You can also remove holidays from Calendar, but you use a totally different process. To remove holidays from Calendar, open the Calendar view if it isn't already open, then follow these steps:

1. Click View | Arrange By to open the Arrange By menu.

2. In the Arrange By menu, click Current View to open the Current View menu.

3. In the Current View menu, click Events to see a list of all the events (including holidays) in Calendar.

4. Select the holidays you want to delete, then click Delete on the standard toolbar to remove them from Calendar.

When you look at a day in Calendar, any scheduled appointments or meetings block out the section of the day allocated for them. If there are activities that aren't visible at the moment (you usually can't display a full day's activities at once), Outlook lets you know. If there are activities early in the day that aren't visible, Outlook displays a tiny up arrow and an ellipsis (...) near the top of the schedule. If there are activities late in the day that aren't visible, Outlook displays a tiny down arrow and an ellipsis (...) near the bottom of the schedule. Use the scroll bar on the right side of the view pane to scroll up or down so that you can see the invisible activities.

Add Activities to the Calendar

Activities get into Calendar in any of three ways. If you're using Outlook with Microsoft Exchange server, Exchange can add activities to your Calendar. You can accept meeting invitations or otherwise receive copies of Calendar items from other people. Third, you can add the information and activities yourself.

Microsoft Exchange adds activities to your Calendar automatically, so there really isn't much more to say about it.

Receiving meeting invitations from others is common when you use Outlook for work. If you accept a meeting request, Outlook creates a meeting item and adds it to Calendar. Similarly, someone can drag an event or appointment item into an e-mail message and send it to you.

SHORTCUT *You can accept a Meeting request with the* CTRL-C *keyboard shortcut and can decline a Meeting request with the* CTRL-D *keyboard shortcut.*

10

The most common way for activities to make it onto your Calendar is for you to put them there yourself. Scheduling an appointment or event is easiest.

Schedule an Appointment

To create a new appointment, follow these steps:

1. In the Outlook main window, click File | New, then Appointment. This opens a blank Appointment window like the one in Figure 10-3.

 *You can also open a new Appointment window with the* CTRL-SHIFT-A *keyboard shortcut.*

2. Enter at least the Subject of the meeting, the Start Time, and the End Time. Set a Reminder if you wish.

3. If this is an appointment that will recur at regular intervals, click Recurrence on the Appointment window toolbar to open the Appointment Recurrence dialog box shown in Figure 10-4 and set the Recurrence Pattern (when the appointment will recur) and the Range Of Recurrence (how long the recurrence pattern will continue).

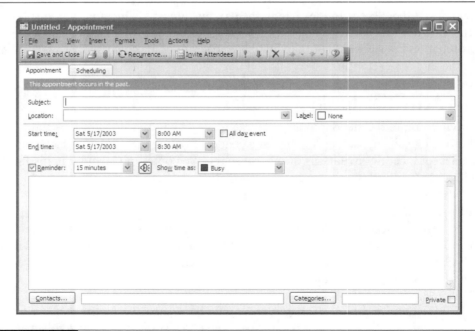

FIGURE 10-3 Fill in a few fields in this blank Appointment window to schedule an appointment on your Calendar.

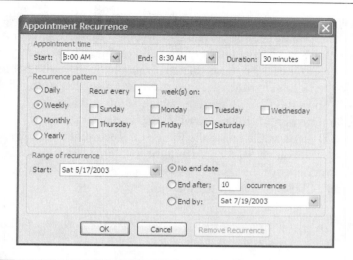

FIGURE 10-4   You set the repetition pattern for all types of recurring activities using this Appointment Recurrence dialog box.

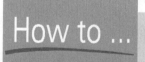   *For instructions on creating recurring activities, see the "How to Create a Recurring Activity" box.*

4. Click Save And Close to add the new appointment to your Calendar.

How to ... **Create a Recurring Activity**

Recurring activities are activities that repeat on some sort of schedule. That schedule can have the activity repeat at regular intervals, or it can repeat a certain number of days after the date when it was last completed. You can make an activity a recurring activity when you first create it, or you can make a nonrecurring activity that's already in your Calendar into a recurring activity. In all of these cases, you turn the activity into a repeating activity using the Appointment Recurrence dialog box shown in Figure 10-4.

To set the Start and End times of an activity, you work in the Appointment Time section of the dialog box. Set the Start time and either the End time or the Duration. Outlook automatically calculates that Duration if you give it Start and End times, or the End time if you give it a Start and a Duration. Furthermore, if you change the Start time, the End time will automatically move as well.

To set when an activity will repeat, you work in the Recurrence Pattern portion of the Appointment Recurrence dialog box. Start by selecting a Daily, Weekly, Monthly, or Yearly pattern in the left column. The pattern you select in this column determines the options that are available on the right. Set the pattern you want in the right side of the Recurrence Pattern section of the dialog box. Figure 10-4 shows the Weekly pattern, which is the default.

To set the time period (the range of dates, not the time of day) during which the activity will recur, you work in the Range Of Recurrence section of the dialog box. Begin by selecting a Start date from the available list. Then set an End date, using whichever of the three possibilities makes the most sense for this particular task. Click OK to exit the dialog box.

 *Don't forget to Save And Close the activity after you set the recurrence pattern.*

Schedule a Meeting

Scheduling meetings is a little more complicated than scheduling appointments, since meetings involve inviting other people and matching everyone's schedule to find an appropriate date and time.

 Scheduling meetings assumes that the people involved in the meeting are either on a company network using Microsoft Exchange or have registered with the Microsoft Office Free/Busy Service. The Free/Busy Service is covered later in this chapter.

To create a new meeting request, follow these steps:

1. In the Outlook main window, click File | New, then Meeting Request. This opens a blank Meeting window like the one in Figure 10-5.

 *You can open a new Meeting request window with the* CTRL-SHIFT-Q *keyboard shortcut.*

2. On the Appointment tabbed page, enter a list of the people you want to invite to the meeting in the To field. You can enter the names or e-mail addresses directly into the To field, or click the To button to select people from the Address Book.

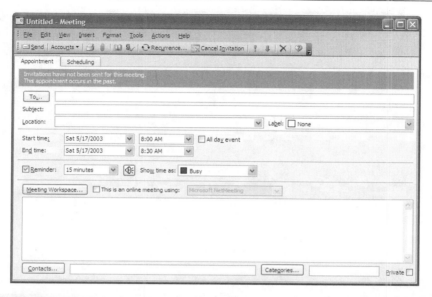

FIGURE 10-5   Filling in this blank Meeting window is the first step in scheduling a meeting.

3. Fill in at least the Subject of the meeting, the Location, the Start time, and the End time. You can also set a Reminder.

4. If this is a meeting that will recur at regular intervals, click Recurrence on the Meeting window toolbar to open the Recurrence dialog box shown in Figure 10-4 and set the Recurrence Pattern (when the appointment will recur) and the Range Of Recurrence (how long the recurrence pattern will continue).

> **TIP**   *For instructions on creating recurring activities, see the "How to Create a Recurring Activity" box.*

5. Now this is where things begin to deviate from setting up an appointment. Click the Scheduling tab to view the Scheduling tabbed page shown in Figure 10-6.

6. The name (or e-mail address) of each person you are inviting appears in a list, followed by a timeline showing the free and busy periods in that person's schedule. Find an open slot in everyone's schedule to hold your meeting, and enter a Meeting Start Time and Meeting End Time at the

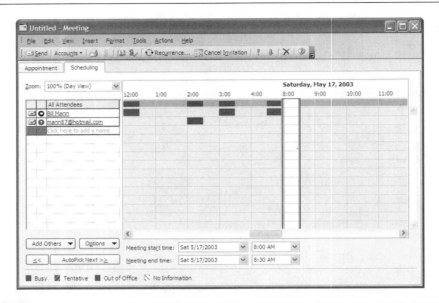

FIGURE 10-6   Outlook gives you this dialog box to help with the most difficult part of setting up a meeting: finding an open spot in everyone's schedule.

bottom of the dialog box. Switch back to the Appointment tabbed page and you'll see that the meeting times you selected are now visible here.

7. Click Save And Close to add the new meeting to your Calendar and send the request to the people you specified. When the people respond to the meeting invitation, their responses appear in your Inbox as e-mail messages stating whether they accepted or declined (or tentatively accepted) the meeting.

Schedule an Event

Scheduling events is a lot like scheduling appointments and meetings. The thing that makes events different than appointments and meetings is that events don't have start or end times. Instead, they run all day for any day or days on which they occur. For example, a two-day meeting might run from, say, 8 A.M. to 5 P.M. Thursday and Friday. Change that two-day meeting into a two-day event, and Outlook will show it as running all day Thursday and all day Friday.

The fact that events have no specific times of day associated with them makes them great for scheduling things like your birthday or a vacation, which normally don't have particular times associated with them. On your birthday, your Calendar might include a 5:00 P.M. dinner appointment with your spouse to celebrate your birthday, while your birthday itself would appear as an all-day event having no particular times associated with it.

To create an event, you first need to decide what kind of event you want to create. There are two kinds: standard events, and invited events. A standard event just marks an all-day occurrence of some sort. An invited event not only marks the occurrence, it lets you invite people to it. I can see invited events being particularly useful for things like conferences or general get-togethers along the lines of "Why don't you come on over on Saturday?"

To create a standard event, you start by creating a new appointment (use the CTRL-SHIFT-A keyboard shortcut). Now complete the appointment as you would normally, but don't click Save And Close yet.

On the Appointment tabbed page in the Appointment window, set the All Day Event check box and watch what happens to your appointment. The title bar of the window now says this is an Event, rather than an Appointment. The fields where you enter the Start time and End time disappear, leaving only Start and End date fields. Even the Reminder field changes so that the reminder occurs 18 hours before the event. Setting the All Day Event check box converts an Appointment into an Event. Similarly, clearing the All Day Event check box converts the Event back into an Appointment.

10

CAUTION   *When you convert an appointment into an event, the value in the Reminder field changes to a default value (18 hours) regardless of what you had it set for. If you had set the Reminder field to more than the default value (two days or more), Calendar changes it to the default value anyway. This isn't a good thing at all. Likewise, when you convert an event to an appointment, Calendar sets the Reminder field to another default value (usually one hour). The way to deal with this is to set the reminder time after you're done switching between Appointment and Event. That way, you can be sure that you get the reminder when you want it.*

To create an invited event, first open a new Meeting request (use the CTRL-SHIFT-Q keyboard shortcut). Now fill in the fields of the Meeting Request as you would normally. On the Appointment tabbed page, set the All Day Event check box, which triggers a transformation similar to the one that occurred when you did this in the Appointment window. Setting or clearing the All Day Event check box switches the activity between a Meeting and an invited Event.

TIP   *Outlook also has the ability to do group scheduling. Since group scheduling is most commonly used in Microsoft Exchange environments, this topic is covered in Chapter 23.*

Quickly Respond to Invitations

If you get invited to a lot of meetings, you'll like this feature. In Outlook 2003, you don't even need to open a meeting invitation to reply to it. When a meeting invitation is visible in the Preview pane, you can not only see the message, but Outlook displays your options for responding to the invitation at the top of the pane, too. As Figure 10-7 shows, you have these options:

- Accept
- Tentative (tentatively accept the invitation)
- Decline
- Propose New Time (or date for the meeting)
- Calendar (open Calendar so that you can check your schedule)

If you click Accept, Tentative, or Decline, Outlook immediately sends the appropriate reply. If you click Propose New Time, Outlook opens the Propose New Time dialog box shown in Figure 10-8. Use it to propose another time and date that works for everyone invited to the meeting.

FIGURE 10-7   Use the new buttons in the Preview pane to reply to invitations without even opening them.

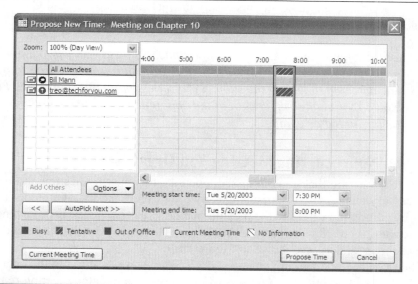

FIGURE 10-8   Use this dialog box to suggest a new time (and possibly date) when the proposed time for a meeting doesn't work for you.

Use the tools in the Propose New Time dialog box to come up with a new time for the meeting, then click Propose Time. This causes Outlook to create a New Time Proposed message you can send to the meeting organizer.

Change Your Schedule

While it is best to stick with a schedule once you make it, we all know that's not always possible. Sometimes you just have to make a change. The difficulty of making that change varies depending on the type of event you want to change. There are five cases to consider, in rough order of difficulty:

1. Changing a scheduled activity that isn't part of a recurring task

2. Changing a nonrecurring meeting you organized

3. Changing a nonrecurring meeting you didn't organize

4. Changing someone else's meeting request

5. Changing recurring activities

Change a Scheduled Activity That Isn't Part of a Recurring Task

Scheduled activities that aren't part of a recurring series are the easiest to change. To change an appointment or event that isn't part of a recurring series, open it by

double-clicking it, then make any necessary changes. Click Save And Close to put
the changes into effect.

*You can make some changes to appointments and events without opening
them. If an appointment appears in your schedule, you can drag it to a
new date and time, edit the subject (click the appointment and type the new
subject), or change the length of the appointment by clicking and dragging
the beginning or ending.*

Change a Nonrecurring Meeting You Organized

To change a meeting that you organized, open the meeting in question and make
any necessary changes. You can change anything except the list of attendees
simply by editing the values in the meeting window. To change the list of attendees,
click Actions, then Add Or Remove Attendees. This opens the Select Attendees
And Resources dialog box shown in Figure 10-9.

When you're done making changes, click Save And Close to put the changes
into effect. When you do this, Outlook offers to send an updated meeting request
to the attendees. You should normally do this, since if you don't, the attendees
won't know about the changes you made.

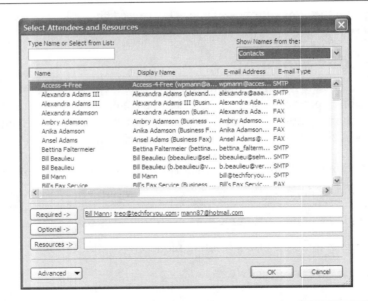

FIGURE 10-9   Use this dialog box to add attendees to a meeting or remove them.

Change a Nonrecurring Meeting You Didn't Organize

If you want to change a meeting you didn't organize, the way you can change it is limited by the fact that it is someone else's meeting. You can make changes to the copy of the meeting that's in your Calendar, but those changes don't get sent to anyone else. If you know a meeting is going to change, but the change hasn't been sent out yet (say the person responsible is in another meeting and unable to make the change until later), you can make the change to your copy of the meeting request so that at least your Calendar reflects the latest information.

Change Someone Else's Meeting Request

If you want to make changes to someone else's meeting request, and you want those changes to be published to others involved in the meeting, your options are more limited. All you can do is revoke your acceptance of the meeting request, make your acceptance tentative, or propose a new time for the meeting.

To change a meeting request you didn't organize, open it and look at the top part of the request. You'll see some special toolbar buttons, Accept, Tentative, Decline, and Propose New Time. Click any of the first three to indicate whether you will attend the meeting.

Change Recurring Activities

There's only one more thing to consider when you want to change an existing scheduled activity. That's when the activity you want to change is part of a recurring series. If it is, you need to choose between changing the entire series of recurring activities or changing this particular activity in the series, without changing the rest of the series.

To change an activity that is part of a series of recurring activities, double-click the activity you wish to change. Calendar opens a dialog box that asks you if you want to open this particular occurrence of the series or open the entire series. Choose one, then click OK to begin editing the activity as you would normally.

View and Color-Code Your Activities

To get more detailed information on an activity or to edit it, you can double-click it. Outlook displays a window containing all the information about the activity. You can modify the information in this window simply by changing it. When you're finished, you just click Save And Close on the window's toolbar to make the changes go into effect.

10

Color-Code Your Activities

The ability to apply color coding to your Calendar came in with Outlook 2002. You can manually color-code appointments, meetings, and events as well as create rules for automatically color-coding activities. Outlook provides ten color-coded labels you can apply to your activities. Figure 10-10 shows the default labels and their colors.

You can manually color-code an activity whether it is open or not. If the activity window is open, select the label you want to use from the Label list in the window. If the activity window isn't open, right-click it to open the window's shortcut menu. Click Label and select the label you want to use from the list that appears.

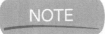 *You can also change the text of the color-coded labels, if you wish. To do this, start with a closed activity. Right-click the activity and click Label in the shortcut menu. Click Edit Labels at the bottom of the shortcut menu. This opens another dialog box, where you can edit the text of each label.*

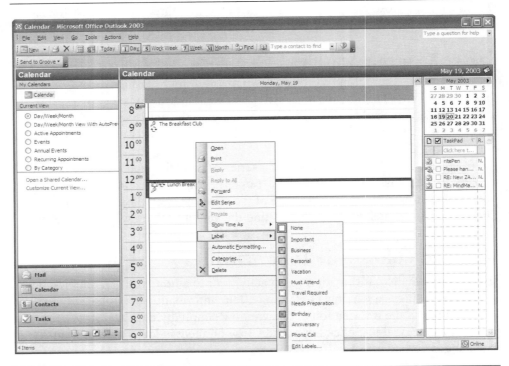

FIGURE 10-10 Use color-coded labels to easily scan your schedule for important activities.

You can also automatically color-code your calendar. Being able to do this automatically takes the drudgery out of color-coding activities by hand. By setting up the proper rules, you can have all messages from your boss appear in red, all your personal activities appear in green, and so on. If you put some thought into setting up these rules, you can really improve your effectiveness by reducing the chance of missing something important in your busy schedule.

To automatically color-code your activities, follow these steps:

1. Right-click any activity in the schedule to open a shortcut menu. In the shortcut menu, click Automatic Formatting to open the Automatic Formatting dialog box shown in Figure 10-11.

2. Click Add to create a new rule. The rule will appear in the Rules For This View list box with the name of Untitled and a marked check box next to it to show that the rule will be active when you exit the dialog box.

3. In the Properties Of Selected Rule section of the dialog box, fill in the Name box and select a Label from the available options.

4. Click Condition to open the Filter dialog box shown in Figure 10-12.

The three tabbed pages of options in the Filter dialog box give you incredible flexibility for setting up almost any kind of conditions you can think of. It may take a little experimentation, but you should be able to come up with filter conditions that meet your needs.

FIGURE 10-11   The Automatic Formatting dialog box allows you to color-code activities in your Calendar.

10

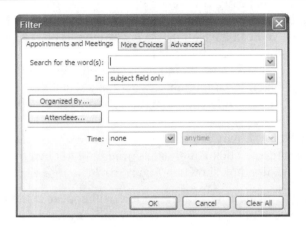

FIGURE 10-12   Use this Filter dialog box to set the conditions under which a label will be applied to an activity.

> **TIP**   *If you assign a manual label to an activity, that manual label overrides any automatic label that might be assigned to the same activity.*

Send Internet Meeting Requests

Whether or not your free/busy information is online, you can send people meeting requests over the Internet using the Internet Calendaring (iCal) format. Using iCal, other Outlook users (and anyone else using an iCal-compliant e-mail program) can accept or decline meeting requests, as well as add them to their e-mail program's calendar.

To configure Outlook to send meeting requests over the Internet using the iCal format, follow this procedure:

1. Click Tools | Options to open the Options dialog box.

2. On the Preferences tabbed page, click Calendar Options to open the Calendar Options dialog box.

3. In the Advanced options section of the dialog box, set the When Sending Meeting Requests Over The Internet, Use iCalendar Format check box.

4. Click OK and Outlook will begin sending Internet meeting requests in the iCal format.

Take Advantage of the TaskPad

The TaskPad is a minimalist view of the Tasks folder that you can use while in any of the Day/Week/Month Calendar views. By default, Outlook has the TaskPad turned off, but if you find yourself doing a lot of jumping back and forth between the Task and Calendar views, you may want to activate it.

Activate the TaskPad

To activate the TaskPad, click View | TaskPad. Normally, the TaskPad will show up on the right side of the Calendar view pane, with the Date Navigator positioned directly above it as shown in Figure 10-13.

As Figure 10-13 shows, the TaskPad is nothing more than a list of the tasks assigned to you. However, the TaskPad doesn't necessarily show all of your tasks. Which tasks appear is determined by the TaskPad view you choose.

To choose a TaskPad view, click View | Taskpad View, then on the TaskPad View menu that appears, choose the view you need.

10

FIGURE 10-13   The TaskPad gives you a quick view into your Tasks folder while you remain in Calendar view.

Use the TaskPad

Using the TaskPad is simple. For any task that's visible, you can mark it complete (by setting the check box next to the name of the task), view the task (by double-clicking it), or turn the task into an appointment (by dragging it into the Calendar View pane and filling out the new Appointment window that appears).

You can also customize the appearance of the TaskPad and modify the ways that the tasks are displayed. To change the way the TaskPad displays tasks, right-click the TaskPad header and choose from among the many options that appear on the shortcut menu.

 *You can customize the appearance of the TaskPad in numerous ways. The basics are covered in Chapter 15.*

Set Calendar Options

Most people can work just fine with the default Calendar settings. Even so, there are a few options you could well need to adjust to adapt Outlook for your company's work week or your personal schedule and habits. For example, I often start work at 4:30 or 5:00 A.M. Other people prefer to start their work day at 10:00 A.M. or later. Calendar can be adjusted to match these starting times, as well as many other individual schedule variations.

To set Calendar Options, follow these steps:

1. In the main Outlook window, click Tools | Options to open the Options dialog box.

2. In the Calendar section of the dialog box, click Calendar Options. This opens the Calendar Options dialog box.

3. In the Calendar Work Week section of the dialog box, tell Outlook which days are part of your work week by setting the appropriate day check boxes. Set the First Day Of Week, First Week Of Year, Start Time, and End Time appropriately as well.

Make Your Free/Busy Information Available Online

If you work with people who don't have access to your Outlook Calendar, you can publish your free and busy time information (free/busy information) to a shared location on the Microsoft Office Internet Free/Busy Service web site, or to an

Internet or intranet page. Once you do this, people with Outlook 2002 (Outlook XP) or later can connect to these locations and use your free/busy time information to plan meetings with you.

The best way to publish your free/busy information online depends on your situation. If the people you want to meet with are on the same intranet as you, then publishing your information on the intranet makes the most sense. Anybody with access to that intranet can see your free/busy information, but no outsiders can.

You can also publish your information to any web page, but that has some problems. Specifically, you have no control over who sees the page.

If the people you're working with are not on the same intranet as you, then using the Microsoft Office Internet Free/Busy Service is your best choice. This service provides you with security, and control over who sees your free/busy information. Since the Microsoft Office Internet Free/Busy Service is easy to use and free of charge, we'll start with that.

Use the Microsoft Office Internet Free/Busy Service

The Microsoft Office Internet Free/Busy Service is a web-based service provided by Microsoft to give users of Outlook 2002 and later a common location to publish and share their free/busy information. There are several important things to know about this service:

- It is free of charge.

- You control who has access to your free/busy times.

- The only information about your schedule that the service has is when you are free and when you are busy. It doesn't have information about what you have scheduled during your busy times.

- It is completely independent of Microsoft Exchange and your corporate network. You can use the service from any computer that runs Outlook and has Internet access.

 To use the Microsoft Office Internet Free/Busy Service, you'll need to have a .NET Passport account.

In other words, this service is as safe, affordable, and as under your control as anything you'll find on the Internet. Only people who join the service can see your free/busy information on the service.

10

Configure Outlook to Publish Your Free/Busy Information

To publish your free/busy times to the Microsoft Office Internet Free/Busy Service, you need to set up an account with the service and configure Outlook to use it. When you're ready to set up the Microsoft Office Internet Free/Busy Service, follow these instructions:

1. In the Outlook main window, click Tools | Options. On the Preferences tabbed page of the Options dialog box, click Calendar Options to open the Calendar Options dialog box.

2. In the Advanced options section of the dialog box, click Free/Busy Options to open the Free/Busy Options dialog box shown in Figure 10-14.

3. In the Options section of the dialog box, adjust the amount of information that Outlook publishes, and how frequently it does so. I recommend leaving the two months of published information as is, but consider increasing the amount of time Outlook takes between updates, unless you have a full-time, high-speed Internet connection and people make frequent use of your information.

4. In the Internet Free/Busy section of the dialog box, set the Publish And Search Using Microsoft Office Internet Free/Busy Service check box. When you do this, two additional options become available.

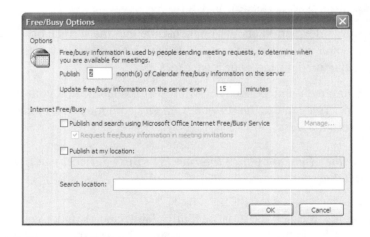

FIGURE 10-14   Use the Free/Busy Options dialog box to publish your free/busy information online.

5. If you set the Request Free/Busy Information In Meeting Invitations check box, Outlook adds a message to meeting requests it sends to people whose calendar it cannot see. This message asks the person to join the Microsoft Office Internet Free/Busy Service, and to give you access to their free/busy information.

6. Click Manage to open your web browser and go to the Microsoft Office Internet Free/Busy Service web site. The site walks you through the process of registering with the service and enabling Outlook to publish information to the service.

7. Follow the instructions that appear on the site to finish signing up for the service and configuring Outlook to use it. When you're done, close the browser window and click OK until you get back to the main Outlook window.

TIP   *To ensure that your free/busy information gets posted right away, I suggest you manually send the information to the Microsoft Office Internet Free/Busy Service as soon as you complete the setup. To do this, click Tools | Send/Receive; then in the Send/Receive menu which appears, click Free/Busy Information.*

10

View Other People's Free/Busy Information

The best way to view other people's free/busy information on the Microsoft Office Internet Free/Busy Service is to create a meeting request. You don't actually have to send the request to use it to see the free/busy information, and it beats logging onto the Microsoft Office Internet Free/Busy web site to get the information. Here's what you need to do:

1. Use the CTRL-SHIFT-Q keyboard shortcut to open a new meeting request.

2. In the To field, enter the names of the people whose free/busy information you want to check.

3. Click the Scheduling tab to see the Meeting Request Scheduling tabbed page shown in Figure 10-15. The free/busy information for all the people you entered appears (as well as your own).

4. If you really want to send a meeting request to these people, fill out the rest of the request and click Send. If you just wanted to see their free/busy times, simply close the window when you're done.

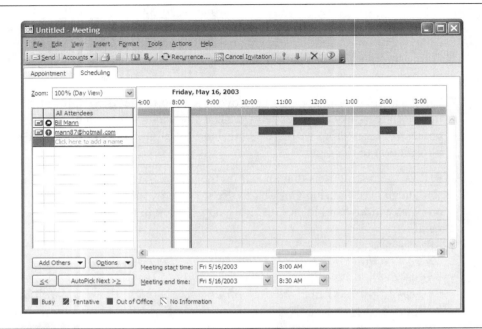

FIGURE 10-15   A dummy meeting request is often the best way to check someone's free/busy times.

Use an Internet or Intranet Site

If you don't mind leaving your free/busy information out in the open where anyone who can find it can look at it, you can publish it to a web server or an FTP server, or even post it as a file on a network somewhere. Conceptually, posting your free/busy info to the Internet or an intranet site is easy; the trick is getting all the paths set correctly. That's what we'll concentrate on here.

Set Up the Site

There really isn't anything much to setting up the site that will hold the free/busy files. Any folder on an HTTP or FTP server will do, as will a regular folder on a server somewhere. There are a few things to keep in mind, though:

- Everyone who needs to see your free/busy information must be able to reach the folder. That means you can't put it in a password-protected area, unless you're willing to give everyone the password.

- Anyone who can reach the folder can read your free/busy information. That means you should probably use the most secure location you can, consistent with its being accessible to the people who need to reach it.

- Since people are going to have to enter the path into Outlook, you want it to be a relatively permanent location.

- For housekeeping purposes, I recommend you create a subfolder (in the destination folder) named "FreeBusy" or something similar, and use that as the place to store the free/busy information.

Free/busy information is stored in any of these locations as a file with the extension ".vfb." The first part of the filename is typically your name as it appears in the first part of your e-mail address. That being the case, my free/busy file would be called bill.vfb.

To store the free/busy information on the Internet or an intranet, you (and the people who will view your free/busy information) will need to know the fully qualified path to the location that will hold your free/busy information as well as the name of your free/busy information file. The path could look like any of these:

- **Stored on the Web**   The path should look like: http://ServerName/ FreeBusy/YourName.vfb, where ServerName is the name of the server or domain (www.techforyou.com, or something similar), and YourName.vfb is the name of your free/busy information file.

- **Stored on a server**   The path should look like: file://ServerName/ FreeBusy/YourName.vfb, where ServerName is the name of the server or domain, FreeBusy is the name of the folder that stores the free/busy information, and YourName.vfb is the name of your free/busy information file.

- **Stored on an FTP site**   The path should look like: ftp://ServerName/ FreeBusy/YourName.vfb, where ServerName is the name of the server or domain (ftp.techforyou.com, or something similar), FreeBusy is the name of the folder that stores the free/busy information, and YourName.vfb is the name of your free/busy information file.

- **Stored on an FTP site with Anonymous Login disabled**   If Anonymous Login is turned off on the server, the path should look like this: ftp:// UserName:Password@ServerName/FreeBusy/YourName.vfb, where UserName and Password are the username and password that give access to the folder, ServerName is the name of the server or domain (ftp.techforyou.com, or something similar), FreeBusy is the name of the folder that stores the free/busy information, and YourName.vfb is the name of your free/busy information file.

Once you have this information, you're ready to publish your free/busy information and view other people's information.

10

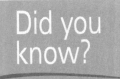

Using FTP for Free/Busy Information Carries Some Risk?

While FTP sites offer the benefit of password protection for your free/busy information folder, there is a drawback. As you've learned in this chapter, you need to include the username and password of any password-protected FTP site in the fully qualified path. This information is clearly visible, in plain English (not encrypted or hidden in any way), in the Free/Busy Options dialog box. Anyone with physical access to a computer that uses the free/busy location can get the username and password in seconds.

If the security of your free/busy information is important to you, you should really consider using the Microsoft Office Internet Free/Busy Service.

Publish Your Free/Busy Information

To publish your free/busy information to the Internet or an intranet, follow these instructions:

1. In the Outlook main window, click Tools | Options. On the Preferences tabbed page of the Options dialog box, click Calendar Options to open the Calendar Options dialog box.

2. In the Advanced Options section of the dialog box, click Free/Busy Options to open the Free/Busy Options dialog box shown in Figure 10-14.

3. In the Options section of the dialog box, adjust the amount of information that Outlook publishes, and how frequently it does so. I recommend leaving the two months of published information as is, but consider increasing the amount of time Outlook takes between updates, unless you have a full-time, high-speed Internet connection and people make frequent use of your information.

4. In the Internet Free/Busy section of the dialog box, set the Publish At My Location check box. When you do this, the box for entering the path to your location becomes active.

5. Enter the fully qualified path into the Publish At My Location text box.

Set the Free/Busy Search Path

When you want to view other people's free/busy information that is posted on the Internet or an intranet, you need to give Outlook a search path it can use to look for the information. You can set individual search paths for each contact, or you can use the global free/busy search path. Here I'm assuming that you'll have all of the free/busy information in a single location so that you can use the global search path. To set the global free/busy search path:

1. If the Free/Busy Options dialog box is not already visible, click Tools | Options in the Outlook main window. On the Preferences tabbed page of the Options dialog box, click Calendar Options to open the Calendar Options dialog box shown in Figure 10-16.

2. In the Advanced options section of the dialog box, click Free/Busy Options to open the Free/Busy Options dialog box.

3. In the Internet Free/Busy section of the dialog box, enter the fully qualified path to the location of the free/busy information files in the Search Location text box. Getting this right is tricky. Read the How To Enter Global Search Paths box for instructions.

10

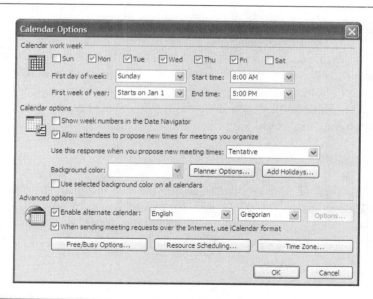

FIGURE 10-16   Most Calendar configuration activities occur in, or pass through, this dialog box.

How to ... Enter Global Search Paths

When you enter the global free/busy search path, Outlook needs you to enter a fully qualified path. That means you need to enter the name of the file containing the free/busy information for each person. You can't do that directly, but Outlook can make some substitutions based on the e-mail address of the person whose free/busy information it needs.

Specifically, Outlook can use the %NAME% and %SERVER% substitutions. When the %NAME% substitution appears in the path, Outlook extracts the person's name from his e-mail address and substitutes it for %NAME% in the path. %NAME% is the part of the e-mail address before the @ sign.

For example, if Outlook was looking for the free/busy information associated with my e-mail address, bill@techforyou.com, it would replace %NAME% with the word "bill" in the global free/busy search path.

When the %SERVER% substitution appears in the path, Outlook extracts the server name from their e-mail address and substitutes it for %SERVER% in the path. %SERVER% is the part of the e-mail address after the @ sign.

For example, if Outlook was looking for the free/busy information associated with my e-mail address, bill@techforyou.com, it would replace %SERVER% with techforyou.com in the global free/busy search path.

With the %NAME% and %SERVER% substitutions available, you can construct a flexible search path without too much effort. Here's an example:

I want to store free/busy information on the Internet, in a web folder. The folder that will hold the free/busy information files is named FreeBusy, and it sits in the root folder of my web site, techforyou.com. The fully qualified path to the search location would look like this:

    http://%SERVER%/FreeBusy/%NAME%.vfb

With this path, if Outlook wanted to find the free/busy information for me (bill@techforyou.com), it would substitute techforyou.com for %SERVER% and bill for %NAME%, resulting in this path: http://techforyou.com/FreeBusy/bill.vfb.

Chapter 11

Get Everything Done with Tasks

How to…

- Create Tasks, Assign Tasks, and Receive Assignments
- Work with Recurring Tasks
- Track Tasks

Outlook's Tasks view helps you keep on top of all those personal work-related areas that you must negotiate in your day-to-day life. Tasks can have reminders associated with them. You can keep track of the details and status of each task. By generating tasks for all those errands that you have to do, and by keeping those tasks up to date, you can really cut down on those "Oops, I forgot!" moments in life.

This chapter shows you how to create tasks. It also tells you how to assign tasks to others, deal with tasks assigned to you, keep track of the changing status of tasks you assigned to others, and work with the sometimes confusing recurring tasks.

Navigate the New Tasks View

Like the rest of the new views in Outlook 2003, the new Tasks view uses screen space more efficiently than the previous version of Outlook did. The result, as Figure 11-1 shows, is a clean, almost sparse view.

A Two-Pane View for Better Usability

As you can see in Figure 11-1, the new Tasks view is divided into two panes. The Tasks pane on the left is for navigation and has four main sections. Starting from the top, they are

- **My Tasks**   Gives you access to all your tasks—those that are local to your PC, in public folders, or shared by another Outlook user.
- **Current View**   Lets you switch between different Task views easily.
- **Links**   Contains links to features such as opening shared tasks, sharing your own tasks, and customizing the current view.

NOTE   *The exact links that appear in this section vary, depending on whether Outlook is connected to Exchange, connected to Windows SharePoint Services, or is being used as a standalone program.*

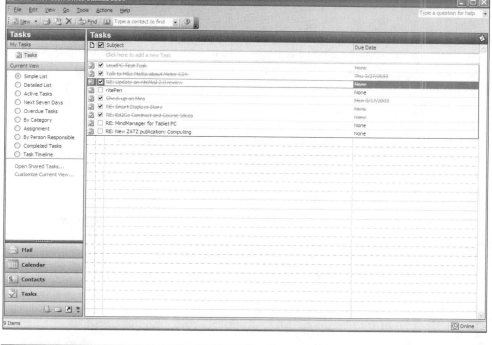

FIGURE 11-1   The new Tasks view is spacious and uncluttered.

■ **Buttons**   Buttons at the bottom of the pane work just as they in other navigation panes. Click the Mail button, for example, to go to the Mail folder.

If you've been working in Mail, Contacts, or Calendar view, you already know how to use the Tasks view, so it's time to get to it.

Create Tasks, Assign Tasks, and Receive Task Assignments

You can get tasks either by creating them yourself or having someone else assign them to you. Similarly, you can assign tasks to others or to yourself. This section shows you how to create, assign, and receive tasks.

Create a Task

You can create a task in three ways: starting from scratch, starting from an existing task, and starting from some other Outlook item. This section explains the first two techniques for creating a task. To learn how to create a task from another type of item, see "Did You Know You Can Turn an E-Mail Message into a Task?" later in this chapter.

Create a Task from Scratch

Creating a task from scratch is the most common way it's done. The most convenient way to create a task is to do it from Tasks view. If you're not in Tasks view, click the Tasks button on the navigation pane. Follow these steps to create a task from scratch:

 *You can go directly to Tasks view from anywhere in Outlook by pressing* CTRL-4.

1. Click File | New | Task to open a new blank Task window, as shown in Figure 11-2.

 *You can also open a new Task window by pressing* CTRL-SHIFT-K.

2. On the Task tab, enter the subject of the task and all other relevant information such as the due date and status. Aside from the subject, all the fields on the Task tab are optional.

3. Click Save and Close to save the task.

Create a Task from an Existing Task

Creating a task from an existing task is a great way to go if the task you are creating is similar to an existing task. This can be particularly useful if you're creating multiple similar tasks, making the work go faster and reducing the chances of making typographic mistakes. To create a new task from an existing one:

1. In Tasks view, select the task you want to duplicate. When doing this, make sure that you click the checkmark icon and not the name of the task.

2. Click Edit | Copy.

3. Click Edit | Paste. A duplicate task appears in the Tasks list directly below the original task.

4. Customize the new task as necessary.

TIP   *If you want to create a task that recurs, I suggest reading "Work with Recurring Tasks" later in this chapter.*

Assign a Task

While it's likely that most of the tasks you'll create will be for your own use, you can also assign tasks to others. Assigning tasks is very useful when you're managing a team and you want to assign tasks to team members without anyone getting confused about which task belongs to whom. By creating the task yourself

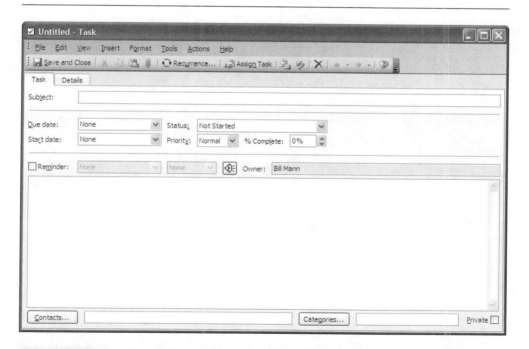

FIGURE 11-2   You will likely see this blank new Task window a lot if you create your own tasks.

11

and assigning it to someone, you can be sure that the assignment gets relayed properly.

CAUTION *All team members must be using Outlook for assigning tasks to work properly.*

To assign a task to someone, create a task as you would normally, but instead of saving it, follow these instructions:

TIP *You can also assign an existing task to someone by opening the task and then following these same instructions.*

1. Click Assign Task. Outlook adds a To field to the Task window, as shown in Figure 11-3.

2. Enter the address of the person you are assigning the task to as if you were sending the person an e-mail message.

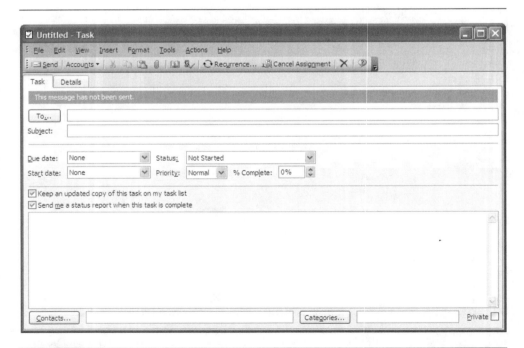

FIGURE 11-3 When you're ready to assign a task to someone, Outlook adds a few additional fields to the standard Task window.

3. Select or clear the Keep an Updated Copy of This Task on My Task List and the Send Me a Status Report When This Task Is Complete check boxes. You'll learn more about these check boxes in "Track Tasks" later in this chapter.

4. Use the body of the task to provide detailed information about the task to the recipient.

If you want to create a task that recurs, read "Work with Recurring Tasks" later in this chapter.

5. Click Send to send the task request to the recipient, or click Cancel Assignment to keep the task for yourself.

Receive Task Assignments

Task assignments arrive in your Inbox in the same manner as e-mail messages. However, a task-assignment message icon looks different. It consists of a hand holding a clipboard in front of an envelope. And a task assignment looks significantly different when you double-click the message to open it.

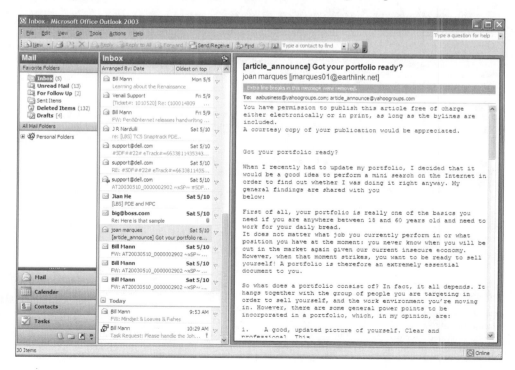

Figure 11-4 shows what a typical task assignment looks like. The Task tab has basic information about the task, while the Details tab contains the kind of information you need to track a task. But the most interesting thing about a task assignment is the Accept and Decline buttons on the task's Standard toolbar.

If you click Accept, Outlook creates an Acceptance message and adds the task to your Tasks list. You can add comments to the Acceptance message before sending it or send it as is. Clicking the Decline button produces a message as well, except the task does not get into your Tasks list.

You can also press ALT-C *to accept a task or* ALT-D *to decline it.*

Work with Recurring Tasks

Recurring tasks are tasks that repeat on some sort of schedule. A task can recur at regular intervals, such as once a week or once a month, or recur at regular intervals

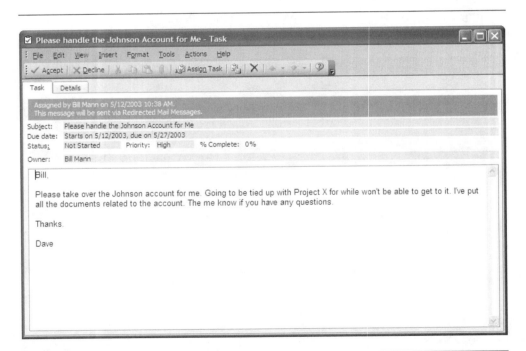

FIGURE 11-4   Task assignment messages contain Accept and Decline buttons that you can click to tell the sender whether you accept the assignment.

beginning on the date when it was last completed. You can make a task a recurring task when you first create it, or you can make a nonrecurring task that's already in your Tasks list into a recurring task. In any case, you turn the task into a repeating task by using the Task Recurrence dialog box shown in Figure 11-5. To open the Task Recurrence dialog box, click the Recurrence button on the Standard toolbar.

To determine when a task will repeat, you work in the Recurrence Pattern portion of the Task Recurrence dialog box. Start by selecting a Daily, Weekly, Monthly, or Yearly pattern in the left column. The pattern you select in this column determines the options that are available on the right side of the dialog box. Set the pattern you want in the right side of the Recurrence Pattern section of the dialog box. Figure 11-5 shows the Weekly pattern, which is the default.

To set the time period during which the task will recur, work in the Range of Recurrence section of the Task Recurrence dialog box. Begin by selecting a Start date from the available list. Then choose an end date, using whichever of the three possibilities makes the most sense for the particular task. Click OK to exit the dialog box. Don't forget to click Save and Close after you set the recurrence pattern.

NOTE   *You can assign recurring tasks to other people as well as create them for yourself.*

11

Did you know?

Certain Types of Recurring Tasks Can Be Tricky?

Creating tasks that recur at set intervals works the way you would expect it to, but you need to be a little careful when defining tasks that recur a certain amount of time after they are completed. To make a task recur a certain amount of time after it last occurred, select the Regenerate New Task option button and enter the time interval in the text box. What you need to remember is that the next task will only be regenerated after the current instance is marked as complete. If you finish the task and forget to change its status to Completed, Outlook will not generate the next occurrence of the task.

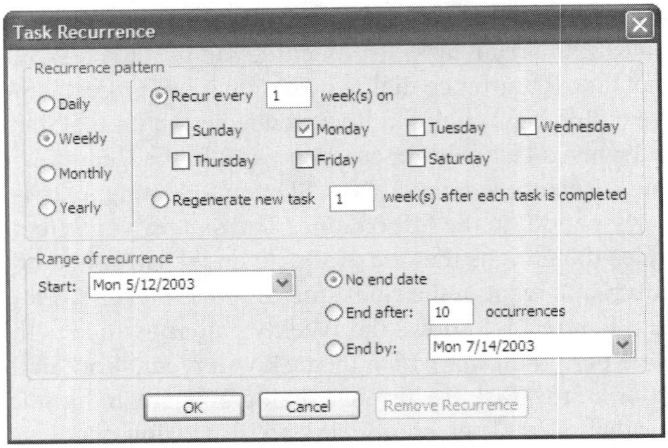

FIGURE 11-5   Use this dialog box to control when a task repeats.

Did you know?

You Can Turn an E-Mail Message into a Task?

I don't know about you, but a lot of my tasks come to me in the form of e-mail messages. Instead of task items created by someone else and assigned to me, they come as e-mail messages along the lines of, "Bill, can you deal with the Johnson account? Here's the information they need…" I could turn an e-mail message like this into a task by opening a new Task window and retyping (or cutting and pasting) the relevant parts of the e-mail message into the task, but there's a better way.

You can turn virtually any Outlook item into another kind of Outlook item by dropping it on the appropriate navigation button. In this case, all I need to do is drag the e-mail message to the Notes button in the Task pane and drop it there.

When I drop the e-mail message on the Tasks button, Outlook opens a new Task window and copies the content of the e-mail message into the body of the Task. Then all I need to do is fill in details like the start and end dates, and I'm done.

Track Tasks

You can use tasks as simple reminders of things to do, but by filling in fields such as Status, Priority, and % Complete, and by adding notes to the body of each task, you can use tasks to keep track of your progress in different activities. By filling in

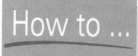 **Display and Use the TaskPad**

Perhaps because the Calendar and Tasks list are so closely related, Outlook allows you to see your tasks in Calendar view. The *TaskPad* is an optional pane that can appear on the right side of the Calendar view. When the TaskPad is visible, it shows by default a Calendar for the current month, as well as a list of tasks.

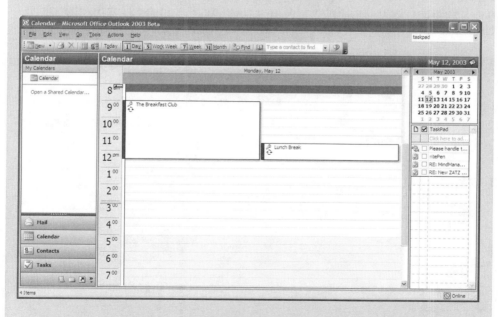

The TaskPad comes in particularly handy when you want to schedule Calendar time for a task. With the TaskPad visible, all you need to do is find the date and time on the Calendar where you want to work on the task and drag

11

> the task from the TaskPad into the appropriate location on the Calendar. Adjust the start and end times as necessary and you're done.
>
> To open the Taskpad if it is not visible, click View | TaskPad. You must be in Calendar view to do this.

the information on the Details tab, you can even use your tasks to track billable hours and mileage. And you can go one step further.

When you assign tasks to people, you can have Outlook automatically track the progress of those tasks and send you status reports on them. If you think back to when you were learning about assigning tasks, you had the option of selecting or unselecting the Keep an Updated Copy of This Task on My Task List check box and the Send Me a Status Report When This Task Is Complete check box. Setting these check boxes for tasks you assign is the secret to tracking their progress.

The Keep an Updated Copy of This Task on My Task List check box does exactly that. When you select this option, you can still see the task in your Tasks list. Instead of the usual clipboard with a checkmark icon used for regular tasks, tasks that you've assigned to others have a hand holding a checkmarked clipboard.

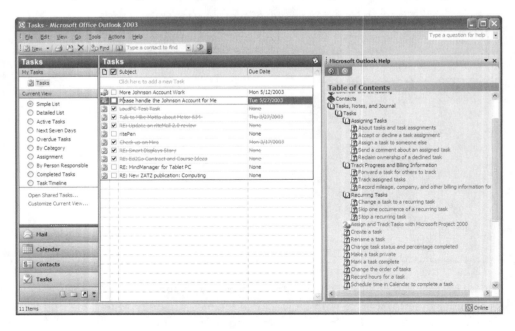

Whenever the person who is working on the task changes its status and saves the task on their machine, their copy of Outlook sends a message to Outlook on your machine that tells it to update the status of the task in your Tasks list. Similarly, when the person working on the task sets its status to Completed, Outlook sends a message to your machine notifying you that the task is complete. The message looks very much like the one in Figure 11-6.

To make keeping track of the tasks you assign to others even easier, you can use Assignment view to sort tasks based on who they are assigned to. To do this, just click Assignment in the Parent View section of the Tasks pane. To even further sort the tasks you assigned to others, you can click the Owner heading in the Tasks list to sort all the tasks you've assigned by assignee name.

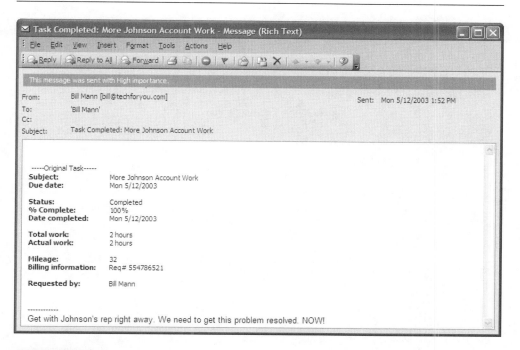

| FIGURE 11-6 | You can tell Outlook to automatically report back to you when tasks are complete. |

NOTE

This chapter has given you the information you need to use tasks and Tasks view effectively, but there are still many more things you can do with tasks. The Outlook 2003 Help system has an extensive section on tasks and task assignments. If you need to do something with tasks that isn't covered in this chapter, the chances are good that you can do it with the aid of the Help system.

Chapter 12

Gather Stray Information with Notes and Shortcuts

How to...

- Navigate the New Notes view

- Work with Notes

- Navigate the Shortcuts Pane

- Work with Shortcuts and Shortcut Groups

The theme of this chapter is keeping track of stuff that doesn't readily fit into other areas of Outlook. While the Mail, Contacts, and Calendar folder are great for tracking and working with messages, contacts, and appointments, you also need to track and work with other kinds of stuff.

Outlook notes are ideal for storing little bits of information that don't otherwise have a home. For example, I have an Outlook note with instructions for updating a friend's web site, and another with the model numbers for the ink cartridges for my wife's printer. Notes work perfectly for information like this.

Outlook shortcuts are great when the information you want to track and work with already exists, and you need a way to find it again. For example, I used to keep track of where stuff was on my hard drive and on the network by storing the path to each item in an Outlook note, but I've done away with the notes. Instead, I created a shortcut directly to the item. It's a much more efficient approach.

This chapter covers notes and shortcuts. Each feature is relatively simple, and by the time you read these few pages you'll have all the information you need to put notes and shortcuts to work for you.

Navigate the New Notes View

Like the other new views in Outlook, the new Notes view is a two-panel view, with the Notes pane on the left and notes on the right, as shown in Figure 12-1. Thanks to the new design, you can see more notes than you could in previous versions of Outlook.

The Notes pane follows the same form as the Navigation pane of the Tasks and Contacts folders. The Notes pane has four main sections, starting from the top:

■ **My Notes** gives you access to all your notes, whether local to your PC or shared by others.

■ **Current View** lets you easily switch between different Notes views.

■ **Links** contains links to Notes view features such as opening shared Notes folders, sharing your own notes, and customizing the current view.

NOTE   *The exact links that appear in this section vary, depending on whether Outlook is connected to Exchange, is connected to SharePoint, or is being used standalone.*

■ **Buttons** on the bottom of the pane work just as they do in every other Navigation pane. Click any button to open its associated folder.

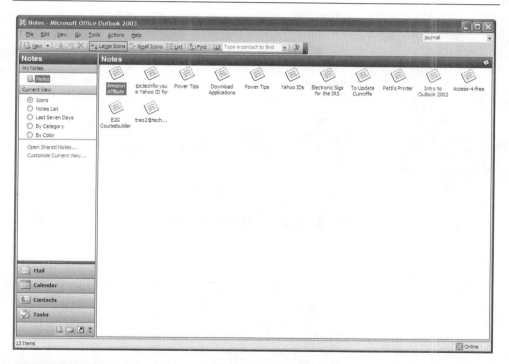

12

FIGURE 12-1   The new Notes view lets you see more of your notes collection than ever before.

Work with Notes

There really isn't much to working with Notes: you can create them, open or close them, and change their basic appearance. That's it. Aside from being a place to store random bits of information, the cool thing about Outlook Notes is that you can leave them open on the desktop. After you create a note, you can just drag it somewhere and drop it. It will stay put until you close the note or close Outlook.

 To open Notes view, choose Go | Notes or click the Notes icon (it looks like a pad of yellow sticky notes) at the bottom of any navigation pane.

Create a Note

To create a new note, choose File | New | Note or, if you're working in Notes view, click the New button on the Standard toolbar. The blank new Note window appears, as shown in Figure 12-2. Not much to it, is there?

 *You can also press* CTRL-SHIFT-N *to open a new Note window.*

After the new Note window appears, type your note into it. You can leave the window open on your desktop as long as you want (as long as Outlook is open).

To close the note, click the note icon in the upper-left corner of the Note window, then click Close. Outlook automatically saves a copy of the note in the Notes folder whenever you change it, so you don't have to worry about explicitly saving the note.

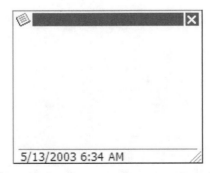

5/13/2003 6:34 AM

FIGURE 12-2   Entering stray information into a blank Note window is easy; just type it in.

That Tablet PCs Have Really Cool Notes?

If you use a Tablet PC, you can use the notes that are part of Outlook, but you have another option as well. Windows XP Tablet PC edition, the version of Windows installed on Tablet PCs, ships with Sticky Notes, a utility that simulates a technologically enhanced pad of paper sticky notes.

When you create a note with Outlook, you type the note into a little box that gets stored in the Notes folder. When you create notes with Sticky Notes, you handwrite your note on the screen as if you were using a physical sticky note. (You can also speak your notes into Sticky Notes.)

If you use a Tablet PC, I recommend trying both kinds of notes and seeing which works best for you.

View or Edit a Note

To view or edit a note, find it in Notes view and double-click it to open it. After the note is open, you can view or edit it as you would any plain-text file. Basic editing commands are available when you click the note icon in the upper-left corner of the Note window, and you can use the up and down arrows on the keyboard to scroll through a note that's too long to fit in the window.

Change the Look of a Note

To help you work with Notes more easily (and perhaps make them a little more fun), Outlook lets you change the color of notes, the fonts in notes, and the size of notes. The controls for manipulating Notes are scattered throughout Outlook. Just follow along and I'll show you what to do.

Change Notes' Default Settings

You can adjust three default settings for Notes: the color, the font, and the size. Follow these simple steps to change notes' default settings:

1. In the Outlook main window, choose Tools | Options.

12

2. On the Preferences tab of the Options dialog box, click Note Options. This opens the Notes Options dialog box, as shown here. You can set the three main characteristics of notes by using this dialog box.

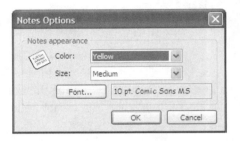

3. Select the new Color and Size you want. These settings will apply to all new Notes that you create, not to existing Notes.

4. Click Font to select a new font for your notes.

5. Click OK to put the changes into effect.

 *The font you select will apply not only to new notes you create, but to notes you open from this point forward. Suppose that a note open on your desktop is written in Arial font and you go into the Notes Options dialog box and select Times Roman. If you create a new note after you change the font, the new note will use Times Roman. If you open an existing note that was created with the Arial font, it will appear in Times Roman. If you close the Arial note that's open on your desktop and then reopen it, it will reappear in Times Roman.*

Change the Color of the Current Note

You can change the color of an existing note in two ways:

■ If the note is closed, right-click it, click Color on the shortcut menu, and choose one of the five color options.

■ If the note is already open, click the note icon in the upper-left corner of the Note window, select Color, and choose one of the colors in the menu that appears.

Show the Time and Date in New and Existing Notes

Notes can show the time and date they were last modified, but they don't do so by default. Follow these steps to make notes display the time and date:

1. Choose Tools | Options to open the Options dialog box.

2. On the Other tab, click Advanced Options. This opens the Advanced Options dialog box, shown in Figure 12-3.

3. In the Appearance Options section, select the When Viewing Notes, Show Time And Date check box.

Navigate the Shortcuts Pane

The Mail pane, Calendar pane, Contacts pane, and so on are all specific examples of Outlook's new Navigation pane. Each of them helps you navigate one of the major folders in Outlook. But what about all the folders that aren't "major" folders like Mail or Calendar? What about all the rest of the information you work with? Shouldn't there be a Navigation pane that helps you with all this stuff? There is. It's called the Shortcuts pane.

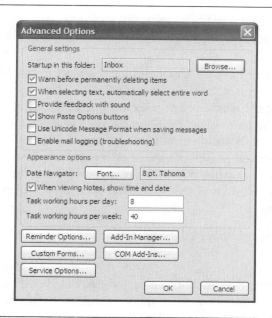

FIGURE 12-3   Use this dialog box to control whether Notes display the date and time they were last modified.

FIGURE 12-4   The Shortcuts pane lets you create links to virtually any information
Outlook can find.

As shown in Figure 12-4, the Shortcuts pane is a place to put shortcuts to virtually
any information. You can create shortcuts to Outlook folders, files on your PC, files
on the network, shared folders, web pages, even applications such as Microsoft Office
Word and Internet Explorer. Using the Shortcuts pane is another way to keep track of
all the diverse bits of information that you use in your day-to-day activities.

 To open the Shortcuts pane, click the Shortcuts button in the Navigation pane.
The Shortcuts button is a white box with a black arrow in it. The Shortcuts pane is
very similar to other versions of the Navigation pane. It is divided into three sections,
starting from the top:

 *You can open the Shortcuts pane from anywhere in Outlook by pressing*
CRTL-7.

- **My Shortcuts** is the default group for shortcuts you create. When you start
  out, the My Shortcuts group contains shortcuts to things such as Outlook
  Update, the Outlook page at the Microsoft Office Download Center web
  site. This section of the Shortcuts pane can also contain groups that you
  create for yourself, such as the group in Figure 12-4.

- ■ **Links** contains links for adding a new shortcuts group (covered later this chapter), and adding new shortcuts.

- ■ **Buttons** on the bottom of the pane work just as they do in other versions of the Navigation pane.

To use one of the shortcuts, click it in the Shortcuts pane. Outlook automatically takes the appropriate action based on the type of item that the shortcut points to. For example, Outlook might start an application, open a window, open a view of an Outlook folder, or open a web page, all right inside the Outlook view pane.

But a Shortcuts pane containing a massive number of shortcuts wouldn't be very useful, and that's where shortcut groups come in. Create groups to organize your shortcuts into logical collections. If you decide to change the organization, you can remove or rename existing groups, as well as move shortcuts between groups, to create an organization that fits your current needs. The rest of this chapter shows how to work with shortcuts and shortcut groups.

Work with Shortcuts and Shortcut Groups

Working with shortcuts and shortcut groups is pretty simple, seeing as there aren't too many things you can do with them. Even so, a few quirks need to be taken into account, and these are covered in the sections that follow.

Create a Shortcut

You can create shortcuts in two ways: with the Add New Shortcut link in the Shortcuts pane, or by dragging and dropping. You use the Add New Shortcut link when you want to add a shortcut to an existing Outlook folder. You use the drag-and-drop method when you want to create a shortcut to anything else.

12

The Shortcuts Pane is Different from Other Panes?

When you click the Mail, Calendar, Contacts, Tasks, or Notes navigation buttons, Outlook displays the associated Navigation pane and opens the relevant folder. When you click the Shortcuts button, on the other hand, the current view stays in place. Only the Navigation pane changes. This way, you can create shortcuts without losing the thread of what you were doing by jumping to a completely different view.

FIGURE 12-5   Add a new shortcut for an Outlook folder by using this dialog box.

To create a shortcut using the Add New Shortcut link, click the link. When you click Add New Shortcut, Outlook opens the Add to Navigation Pane dialog box, as shown in Figure 12-5. Click the name of the folder you want to create the shortcut for. If the folder isn't visible in the main list, open the Folder Name list and look for it there.

When you add a new shortcut in this manner, the shortcut appears in the first shortcut group. If you want to place it in a different group, see "Move a Shortcut to another Shortcut Group" for instructions.

To add a shortcut by dragging and dropping, drag the icon for the document, folder, file, or whatever onto the name of a Shortcut Group and drop it. Outlook creates a shortcut to that item in that group.

Remove a Shortcut

To remove a shortcut from the Shortcuts pane, right-click it and click Delete Shortcut. Deleting the shortcut from the Shortcuts pane does not remove the item that the shortcut points to.

Move a Shortcut to Another Shortcut Group

Moving a shortcut from place to place within the Shortcuts pane is a matter of dragging the shortcut where you want it and dropping it there. As with creating a shortcut by dragging and dropping, you need to drop the shortcut on the name of the group you want to add it to.

Create a Shortcut Group

Create a shortcut group by clicking the Add New Group link. This creates a spot for a new shortcut group in the top section of the Shortcuts pane. Type the name of the new group and press ENTER. Your new group is ready to receive shortcuts.

Rename or Remove a Shortcut Group

To rename a shortcut group, right-click its name, choose Rename Group on the shortcut menu, and then type a new name for the group.

To remove a shortcut group, right-click its name and choose Remove Group on the shortcut menu. Outlook opens a message window asking you to confirm that you really want to remove the group. Click OK to remove the group.

When you remove a shortcut group, you also remove all the shortcuts that are in the group. If you want to retain any of the shortcuts, move them to a new group before you remove the group.

Change the Order of Shortcut Groups

Changing the order of shortcut groups is a clumsy procedure. To do it, you right-click the name of the group you want to move. In the shortcut menu that appears, click Move Up In List or Move Down In List.

TIP   *When you need to do a lot of rearranging of shortcut groups, renaming an existing group and dragging shortcuts between groups is sometimes more efficient than rearranging the existing groups one step at a time.*

12

Chapter 13

Track What You've Done with Journal

How to...

- Navigate the New Journal View
- Work with Journal

Journal is a tool for tracking activities related to a particular contact, as well as tracking when you worked on documents. It displays the information it records in a timeline or a list, and you can open the documents or Outlook items associated with Journal entries.

Journal isn't one of the more popular Outlook folders. As a matter of fact, in Outlook 2003, Journal is turned off by default. Even so, if you work on multiple projects and charge clients by the hour, or if you want an easy way to keep track of what you worked on yesterday, last week, or last month, Journal could be the tool for you. This short chapter walks you through the information you need to put Journal to work.

Navigate the New Journal View

The new two-pane Journal view will surely look familiar. On the left side is the Journal pane with the usual sections and features. The right side is where Journal

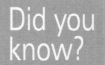

About Windows Journal on the Tablet PC?

Here's a situation sure to cause some confusion: If you are a Tablet PC user and also have Outlook installed, you have two different kinds of Journal. Outlook Journal, the thing we're talking about in this chapter, is a part of Microsoft Office Outlook. Windows Journal, on the other hand, is an application for taking handwritten notes. It comes installed on Tablet PCs as part of Windows XP Tablet PC Edition.

Most of us Tablet PC users use Windows Journal a lot more than we use Outlook Journal. So if you're talking to Tablet PC users and they mention the word "Journal," odds are good that they're *not* talking about the subject of this chapter at all.

entries appear. Depending on the view you choose, entries appear in lists that are grouped in various ways, or are interspersed on a timeline that reflects when they occurred.

By default, Journal is turned off in Outlook 2003, so it doesn't appear among the buttons at the bottom of the Navigation pane. You can open the Journal view by choosing Go | Journal at any time. However, if you plan to use the Journal, a better choice is to add the Journal button to the set of buttons at the bottom of the Navigation pane. I've provided instructions for doing so later in this chapter.

For now, choose Go | Journal to open the Journal view. If this is the first time you've opened Journal, Outlook displays the dialog box shown in Figure 13-1 instead of Journal view.

The point of this dialog box is to let you know that you can track e-mail messages associated with contacts without using the Journal. Given this information, you need to decide whether to actually turn on the Journal. The key question is whether you want to track Office documents and other information related to contacts, or just e-mail messages related to contacts. If you just want to track e-mail messages, click No and don't bother reading any more of this chapter. You don't need it.

On the other hand, if you are considering using Journal to track more than just e-mail messages, click Yes, and read on.

Work with Journal

Since you're still here, I assume that you decided to give Journal a try. If you clicked Yes in the previous dialog box, you should now be looking at the Journal Options dialog box shown in Figure 13-2. This is where you configure Journal to track the information you're interested in.

13

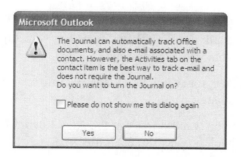

FIGURE 13-1   Do you really need to use Journal? This dialog box helps you decide.

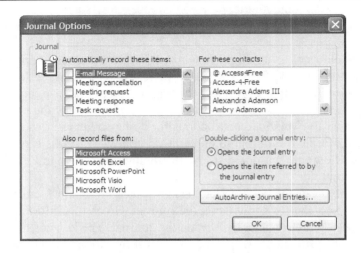

FIGURE 13-2 Tell Outlook what information you want to track in the Journal Options dialog box.

Set Journal Tracking Options

Journal gives you a lot of options, but it doesn't give you real fine-grained control. By that, I mean you can specify which Outlook items and Office files you want tracked for which contacts, but you can't specify one set of things to track for one contact, and a different set for a different contact.

To set the Journal options, follow these instructions:

 You can always get to the Journal Options dialog box from the main Outlook window by choosing Tools | Options and, in the Contacts section of the Preferences tab, clicking Journal Options.

1. In the Automatically Record These Items list, select the check box next to each item type that you want to track.

2. Select the contacts for which you want this information tracked in the For These Contacts list.

3. Select the files you want to track in the Also Record Files From list by selecting the check box next to each file type.

NOTE   *When Journal tracks a file type, the entries aren't associated with a particular contact.*

4. In the Double-clicking a Journal Entry section of the dialog box, select the appropriate response.

5. Click AutoArchive Journal Entries if you want Outlook to archive the entries that Journal creates. You can get more information on autoarchiving in Chapter 17.

6. Click OK.

Add the Journal Button to the Navigation Pane

If you're going to use Journal regularly, you might as well follow these steps to add a button for it to the Navigation pane:

1. Click the Configure Buttons button on the lower-right corner of the Navigation pane.

2. In the menu that appears, choose Navigation Pane Options to open the Navigation Pane Options dialog box, shown in Figure 13-3.

3. Select the Journal check box and click OK. The Journal button will now be visible in the navigation pane.

Manually Record Items and Files

You can also record Journal entries manually. You might do this to get finer control over what gets recorded in Journal or to record things such as telephone calls that Journal can't record automatically.

A standard Journal entry is an Outlook item or one of the Microsoft file types that Journal recognizes. To manually record a standard Journal entry, follow these steps:

1. In the Outlook main window, choose File | New, then click Journal Entry. This opens a blank Journal Entry similar to the one shown in Figure 13-4.

13

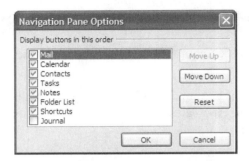

FIGURE 13-3   The Navigation Pane Options dialog box controls which buttons appear at the bottom of the Navigation pane.

SHORTCUT   *You can also open a new blank Journal Entry by pressing* CTRL-SHIFT-J.

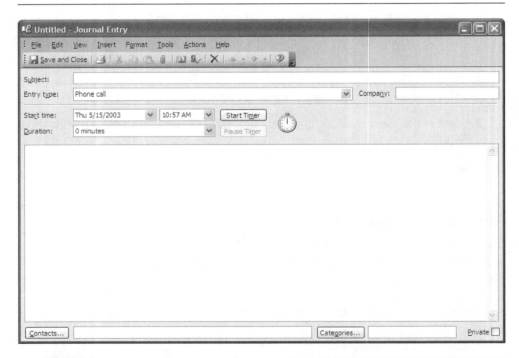

FIGURE 13-4   Use a blank Journal Entry dialog box to manually create entries.

2. Enter a description of the entry in the Subject box.

3. In the Entry Type list, choose the type of entry you want to create.

4. Add any other information as necessary, and then click Save and Close.

A nonstandard Journal entry is *not* an Outlook item or one of the Microsoft file types that Journal recognizes. Follow these steps to manually record a nonstandard Journal entry:

1. Find the file you want to record.

2. Drag the file onto the Journal button of the Navigation pane and drop it there. Outlook opens a new Journal entry with Document as the Entry Type, and a shortcut to the file in the body.

3. Fill in the Subject field with a descriptive name (Outlook puts the file name here when it creates the entry), and enter any other necessary information.

4. Click Save and Close to record the entry.

Open and Modify Journal Entries

Unless you changed the settings in the Journal Options dialog box, you can open a Journal entry simply by double-clicking it. You can also open a Journal entry by right-clicking it and then clicking Open Journal Entry on the shortcut menu.

After a Journal entry is open, you can modify it in any way you wish. For example, you can change the subject, the entry type, the start time, and the duration.

 Because entries in Journal are arranged in a timeline, changing the Start Time fields for a Journal entry moves an entry around within Journal.

When you are tracking billable hours on a project, Journal's built-in timer can be very useful for recording how long you work on a task. By opening the appropriate Journal entry and clicking Start Timer when you begin work and Pause Timer when you finish work, you can keep a running tally of the amount of time you spend on a particular Journal entry.

See the Journal Entries Related to a Particular Contact

If you want to see all the Journal entries for a particular contact, there are a few ways to go about it. You can see all your Journal entries in Journal view. You can

13

also organize entries in various ways, one of which is by contact. When organized by contact, each contact's entries are grouped together, but they're still spread across the timeline.

An easier way to see all the Journal entries for a particular contact is to start in the Contacts folder. Follow these steps:

1. Open the contact for which you want to see Journal entries.

2. In the Contact dialog box, select the Activities tab.

3. In the Show list, select Journal. After a bit of buzzing and whirring, Outlook displays all Journal entries related to this contact. In Figure 13-5, a couple of e-mail messages have been recorded in the Journal.

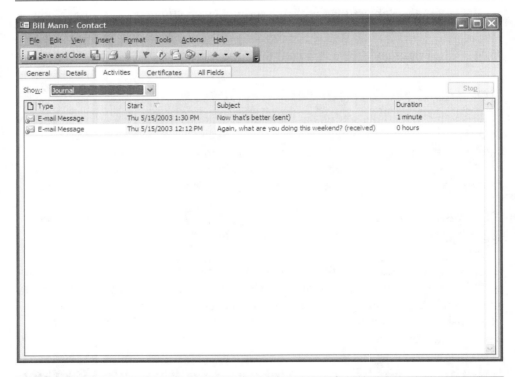

FIGURE 13-5   Viewing Journal entries in the Contact dialog box is the best way to see a single contact's entries.

Part IV

Customize and Manage Outlook 2003

Chapter 14

Take Advantage of Search Folders

How to...

■ Understand Search Folders

■ Use the Default Search Folders

■ Create Your Own Search Folders

■ Save Searches as Search Folders

■ Customize a Search Folder

Search folders are a new feature in Outlook 2003. If you've used this or previous versions of Outlook for a while, you'll probably recognize this situation: You receive an e-mail message from your boss that includes instructions for two different tasks. Being the efficient worker that you are, you have separate folders in Outlook for each of those tasks. Where do you store the message? It pertains to two projects, so it belongs in two different folders. In the bad old days of Outlook 2002, I dealt with the problem by making two copies of the message and putting one in each folder, but there are real problems with that approach. Each duplicate message means another item for Outlook to manage and a little bit more disk space chewed up. Even worse, with multiple copies of the same message, it's very easy to get out of synchronization.

What if you need to do something with the message after you put multiple copies in different locations? You either need to let the copies differ, or you need to remember where each copy of the message is and make the same changes to each one. Even something as simple as deleting an old message becomes a headache when multiple copies are scattered around different folders.

This is where search folders come in. Search folders are an elegant solution to the problem of what to do with items that need to be in multiple locations. As their name implies, search folders are also a great way to find stuff. This chapter explains what search folders are, how they work, and how you can best take advantage of them.

Understand Search Folders

Search folders look like other folders, but they are not the same. Search folders are actually the results of searches conducted on e-mail messages in some or all of the folders in your Outlook mailbox. As Figure 14-1 shows, the contents of a search folder appear to be e-mail messages, but they really are not. The contents of the search folder are actually views of messages that match certain search criteria.

The messages themselves are still in whichever folder you or Outlook stored them in. Neither you nor Outlook has to move them into the search folder. Here, then, is the solution to the problem of one message that needs to go in two locations. Thanks to

| FIGURE 14-1 | The contents of a search folder may look like regular messages, but they're not. |

search folders, there are many ways to address that particular scenario. Suppose you want to keep all e-mail messages from your boss in a single folder called Boss Messages. You could create a search folder for each project, and after you get things set up properly, Outlook would automatically display all messages dealing with each project in the appropriate search folder. The single message could be in a single Boss Messages folder, while appearing in two search folders simultaneously.

Not only do search folders display the results of a search on the e-mail messages in Outlook, they display *live* search results. Every time you open the search folder, Outlook repeats the search. This makes search folders incredibly powerful. The contents of a search folder are always up to date and, assuming you've set them up properly, show only the messages you want to see.

Outlook 2003 comes with a set of default search folders, as well as a set of templates for creating your own. You can even create completely custom search folders. Learning to use search folders can make a significant difference in the efficiency of your work in Outlook. We will start things off with the default search folders.

14

Use the Default Search Folders

Outlook comes with three default search folders that are set up and operating right out of the box. The three folders are

- For Follow Up
- Large Mail
- Unread Mail

In general, you can treat these folders like any other Outlook folder. However, each has some unique characteristics of its own, as described in the next three sections.

Use the Unread Mail Folder

The Unread Mail Folder is a search folder that shows you all the unread e-mail messages anywhere in the Outlook mailbox. As you can see in the Mail pane shown in Figure 14-2, the Unread Mail folder appears in the Favorite Folders section of the pane as well as in the All Mail Folders section.

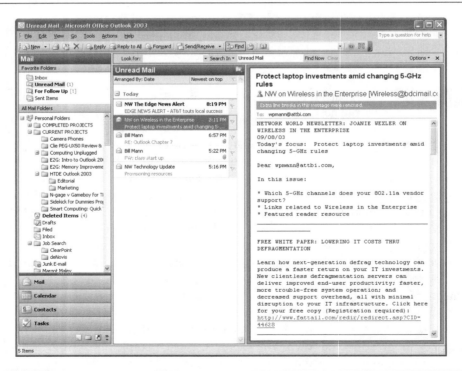

FIGURE 14-2 To find unread mail anywhere in your Outlook mailbox, just open the Unread Mail search folder.

By default, the Unread Mail folder organizes unread messages by the folder they are stored in. That way, if you store messages related to specific projects or subjects in specific folders, you can easily deal with all unread messages related to each project or subject without having to hunt for them.

Use the For Follow Up Folder

The For Follow Up folder is like an automatic To Do list, at least when it comes to e-mail messages. Every flagged e-mail message stored anywhere in your Outlook mailbox automatically appears in the For Follow Up folder.

As Figure 14-3 shows, the For Follow Up folder appears in the Favorite Folders section of the Mail pane as well as the All Mail Folders section. By default, the For Follow Up folder arranges flagged messages by flag color. That is, all the messages with blue flags are grouped together, as are all those with the other color flags. If you use a consistent color scheme to flag messages (everything to do with Project X is red, for example), this grouping scheme gathers together related information automatically no matter where the messages themselves are stored.

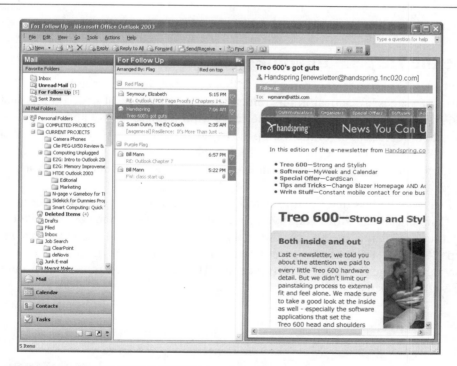

14

FIGURE 14-3   The For Follow Up folder gathers together all messages that have been assigned Quick Flags.

The For Follow Up folder does some neat tricks that can really help you get your work done quickly. When you're done working on a flagged message, you need only click its flag to mark it as complete as well as mark the message's date and time of completion. Because it is no longer flagged, the newly completed message automatically disappears from the For Follow Up folder.

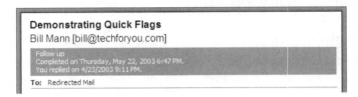

The other neat trick that the For Follow Up folder can do is quickly convert the flags on messages from one color to another. To do that, you need merely drag the message from its current group into the new group. Doing so automatically changes the color of the message flag, both in the For Follow Up folder and in the folder where the message actually resides. Converting flags from one color to another really simplifies life when you realize that you misclassified a message. Just drag it where it needs to be and Outlook takes care of the rest.

Use the Large Mail Folder

The Large Mail folder is a search folder that contains, not surprisingly, large e-mail messages. To appear in this folder, a message must be at least 100KB (100 Kilobytes). As Figure 14-4 shows, the Large Mail folder does not appear in the Favorite Folders section of the Mail pane by default. To reach it, you need to look in the All Mail Folders section of the Mail pane. As you can also see in the figure, the Large Mail folder normally organizes messages by size, using groups such as Large, Very Large, and Huge.

I have to confess that I don't see too much use for the Large Mail folder in most circumstances. However, if you're running out of disk space or your .PST file is getting very large, the ability to identify and perhaps delete large messages, or strip off their attachments (as described in Chapter 24), can be useful. For more on deleting messages in search folders, see the "How to Delete Search Folders and the Messages in Them" box.

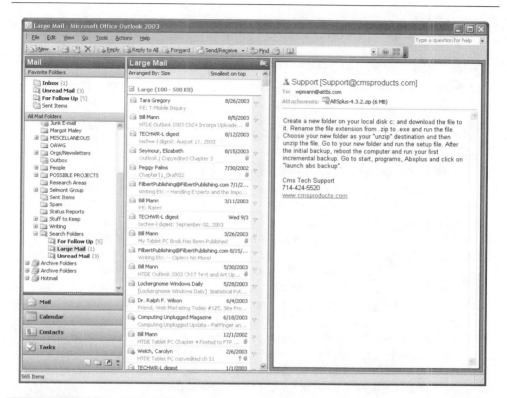

FIGURE 14-4   The Large Mail folder lets you find your largest messages almost instantly.

Create Your Own Search Folders

The default search folders—Unread Mail, For Follow Up, and Large Mail—in Outlook give you a good feel for what you can do with search folder technology. But there's a lot more you can do, and Microsoft was thoughtful enough to give normal users like you and me the tools we need to create our own search folders.

You can create your own search folders in two ways. One is to use one of the thirteen or so pre-defined search folder templates included with Outlook. The other is to create a completely custom folder. The following sections walk you through each approach.

14

Delete Search Folders and the Messages in Them

While search folders act in many ways like regular folders, one way in which they differ has to do with deleting messages. Normally when you delete a folder, you also delete all the messages inside it. Not so with search folders. Because a search folder contains only the results of searches, there are no messages in them to be deleted. When you delete a search folder, it goes away, but none of the messages you saw in the search folder are affected in any way.

Here's how to delete the messages in a search folder: right-click the message and choose Delete on the shortcut menu that appears. You can also open a message and click the Delete button or press CTRL-D. But beware! When you delete a message in a search folder using one of these techniques, you're not deleting the message in the search folder. You're deleting it from the real folder it is stored in, as well as every search folder it appears in.

If you repeat this process with every message in the search folder, you can delete every message that meets the search criteria for the search folder, wherever the messages are stored in the Outlook mailbox.

If what you really want is a particular message to stop appearing in a particular search folder but still reside in its real folder and any other search folders that show it, you need to do something else. You need to either change the search folder's search criteria (you'll learn how to do this later in this chapter), or change the message so that it no longer matches the search criteria.

Start from a Predefined Search Folder

Outlook comes with over a dozen predefined search folder templates, grouped into three broad categories: Reading Mail, Mail from People and Lists, and Organizing Mail. Some templates offer customization options so you can further tweak the behavior of the search folder you create. Follow these steps to create a new search folder based on one of the predefined search folder templates:

1. Starting in Mail view, choose File | New | Search Folder. This opens the New Search Folder dialog box, shown here. You can create a new search folder using predefined folder templates, or strike out on your own and create a custom search folder.

You can also open the New Search Folder dialog box by pressing CTRL-SHIFT-P.

2. Select one of the templates from the Select a Search Folder list. Selecting certain of the templates causes options to appear under the Customize Search Folder heading in the dialog box.

3. Select options to meet your objectives in creating this search folder if any options are visible below the Customize Search Folder heading.

4. The Search Mail In list at the bottom of the New Search Folder dialog box lists all the mailboxes that Outlook has access to. If you wish to have the search folder search a different mailbox than the default mailbox (Personal Folders), select it from this list.

5. Click OK to activate the new search folder.

Create a Custom Search Folder

While Outlook comes with plenty of predefined search folder templates, you may still feel the need to create a search folder from scratch. Follow these steps:

1. Starting in Mail view, choose File | New | Search Folder. This opens the New Search Folder dialog box, shown in the preceding illustration.

14

 *You can also open the New Search Folder dialog box by pressing CTRL-SHIFT-P.*

2. Select Create a Custom Search Folder in the Select a Search Folder list. This causes a text box and a button to appear beneath the Customize Search Folder heading.

3. Click Choose to open the Custom Search Folder dialog box, shown in the following illustration. Use this dialog box to name your custom search folder.

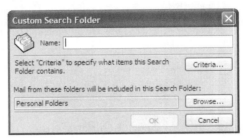

4. Click Criteria to open the Search Folder Criteria dialog box, shown in the following illustration. The Search Folder Criteria dialog box lets you create complex and highly targeted searches.

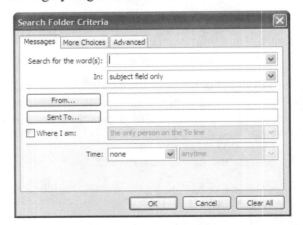

5. The Search Mail In list at the bottom of the New Search Folder dialog box lists all the mailboxes that Outlook has access to. If you wish to have Search Folder search a different mailbox than the default mailbox (Personal Folders), select it from this list.

6. Click OK to activate the new search folder.

Save Searches as Search Folders

Knowing how to use Outlook's Find and Advanced Find features can really help you out as the number of items you store in Outlook grows. If you frequently search for certain types of e-mail messages, you can create a custom search folder that automatically finds those types of messages every time you open it.

NOTE   *Chapter 17 includes complete instructions on using Find and Advanced Find.*

How you create a custom search folder from search results depends on whether you are turning the results of a Find or an Advanced Find into a search folder. The following two sections walk you through each process. Turn to Chapter 17 if you need help using Find and Advanced Find to conduct a search.

Create a Custom Search Folder from Find Results

Creating a custom search folder from the results of a Find search is a quick and easy process. You might want to do this if you frequently search for the same word or phrase in your e-mail messages. To turn the results of a Find into a custom search folder, follow these steps:

1. Enter your search term into the Find text box. If the Find text box isn't visible, press CTRL-E.

2. Conduct your search by clicking Find Now.

3. When the search results appear, choose Options | Save Search As Search Folder. As shown in the illustration, this opens a Save Search As Search Folder dialog box, where you can name your search.

Save Search As Search Folder [X]

Type a name for the new Search Folder:

OK   Cancel

14

4. Enter a descriptive name for your search and click OK. Outlook adds your new search to the Search Folders folder in the All Mail Folders section of the Mail pane.

Create a Custom Search Folder from Advanced Find Results

Creating a custom search folder from the results of an Advanced Find search is a little more complicated than creating a folder from the results of a Find search. Advanced Find offers so many more capabilities than Find. You can use this kind of search when you seek anything more complicated than just a simple word or phrase.

To turn the results of an Advanced Find into a custom search folder, follow these steps:

1. Open the Advanced Find dialog box and create your search.

SHORTCUT *You can press* CTRL-SHIFT-F *to open the Advanced Find dialog box.*

2. Click Find Now to conduct your search. The results appear in a list at the bottom of the dialog box, as shown in the illustration. You can turn the results of a search in the Advanced Find dialog box into a search folder, potentially saving yourself lots of time in the future.

3. In the Advanced Find dialog box menu bar, choose File | Save Search as Search Folder. The Save Search as Search Folder dialog box appears.

4. Enter a descriptive name for your search and click OK. Outlook adds your new search to the Search Folders folder in the All Mail Folders section of the Mail pane.

Customize a Search Folder

You can customize any existing search folder, including the For Follow Up, Large Mail, and Unread Mail default search folders. To customize an existing search folder, follow these steps:

1. In the Mail pane, right-click the search folder you want to customize.

2. Choose Customize This Search Folder on the shortcut menu. This opens a Customize Search Folder dialog box.

3. Change the folder name if you wish.

4. If the Criteria button is active, you can click it to change the search criteria using a dialog box.

5. To change the list of folders searched by this search folder, click Browse. This opens the Select Folder(s) dialog box shown in the following illustration. You can get very specific search results by limiting the set of folders that the search folder you create will search. For example, you can create a search folder that only displays flagged messages for particular project or a particular subject. You can narrow or expand the range of a search folder's results by selecting the appropriate folders to search in this dialog box.

14

Chapter 15

Customize the Outlook 2003 User Interface

How to…

- Use and Customize Outlook Today
- Customize Menus and Toolbars
- Customize the Navigation Pane

As you've seen throughout the book, the Outlook user interface is very flexible. This chapter covers three more areas where you can customize this interface to suit yourself.

Outlook Today is a view that combines elements from Mail, Calendar, and Tasks to give you a quick overview of your day. You can make Outlook Today appear whenever you start Outlook, and you can customize the way it presents information to make it even more useful.

Outlook toolbars and menus are designed to help you be productive and efficient. In this chapter, you'll learn a few ways to customize them to even better match the way you work.

Similarly, the Navigation pane is well designed for its tasks, but you may want to make a few changes of your own. The last part of this chapter shows you how.

Use and Customize Outlook Today

Outlook can contain vast amounts of information, organized by type (e-mail, appointments, and so on). But sometimes, all you may want is to know what's on tap for today. It can be really useful to see all your appointments and tasks for the day gathered in one spot. Likewise, knowing how many unread messages are in your Inbox, and how many drafts you're working on, can really help you get organized for your day.

Outlook Today (see Figure 15-1) is a single view that can show you all these things. You can use it to get a quick preview of your day, and you can set Outlook to automatically open in this view. Even better (and particularly relevant for this chapter), you can customize Outlook Today to make it more fun and more useful for you.

Switch to Outlook Today View

With just a few clicks, you can make Outlook Today appear whenever you need to get an overview of your day. The Outlook Today button appears on the Advanced toolbar. Follow these steps to switch to Outlook Today view.

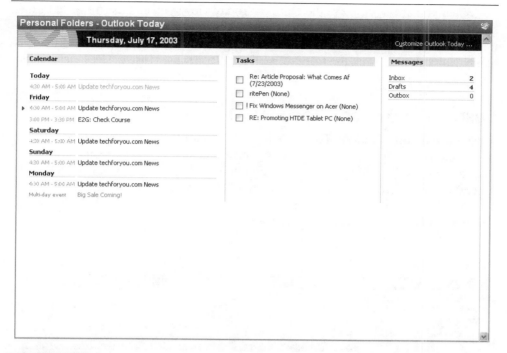

FIGURE 15-1   The Outlook Today view gathers the day's key information into a single view.

1. In the Outlook main window, right-click in the empty space next to the menu bar or the Standard toolbar. This opens a shortcut menu listing additional toolbars.

2. Click Advanced to make the Advanced toolbar appear.

 3. On the Advanced toolbar, click the Outlook Today button shown at left. This opens the Outlook Today view, seen here.

NOTE   *Later in this chapter, you'll learn how to customize toolbars. If you find Outlook Today useful, you may want to consider adding the Outlook Today button to the Standard toolbar to give you even quicker access. See "How to Add the Outlook Today Button to the Standard Toolbar" for the specific steps.*

15

When you are working in the Outlook Today view, you can use a subset of the capabilities of each of the other views without leaving Outlook Today. Click any item to view it. Mark tasks complete by setting the check box to the left of the task name. You can also click the titles of each area (Calendar, Tasks, Messages, and so on) to go to the standard view for that type of information.

Customize Outlook Today

You can customize Outlook Today to display more of the information you want to see, organized in the way you want it organized, in any of several visual styles. The following topics address customizing Outlook Today. To customize Outlook Today, you work from the Customize Outlook Today view shown in Figure 15-2. To make this pane appear, you first need to open Outlook Today, then click Customize Outlook Today in the Outlook Today view.

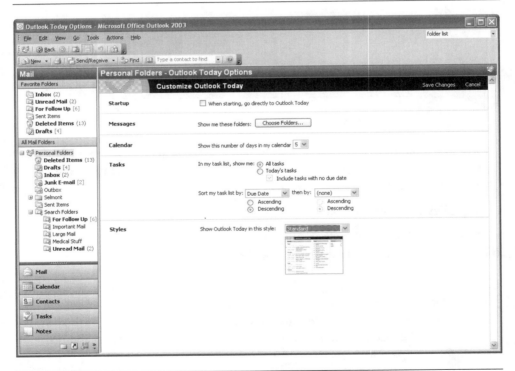

FIGURE 15-2   Customize the Outlook Today view with the options in this dialog box.

Make Outlook Today Appear Whenever You Start Outlook

If you turn off your computer at night or close Outlook when you're away from your computer, one of the best ways to use Outlook Today is to set it to appear automatically whenever you start Outlook.

To set Outlook Today to appear whenever you start Outlook, follow these steps:

1. Open the Customize Outlook Today view.

2. Select the When Starting, Go Directly To Outlook Today check box.

3. Click Save Changes.

Determine Which Message Folders Outlook Today Will Show You

By default, Outlook Today displays the number of unread messages in the Inbox, along with the total number of messages in the Drafts and Outbox message folders. You can configure Outlook Today to display similar information for any message folders. Just follow these steps:

1. In the Messages section of the Customize Outlook Today view, click Choose Folders. This opens the Select Folder dialog box shown in Figure 15-3.

2. In the Folders list of the Select Folder dialog box, choose the folders you would like information on. You aren't limited to choosing folders that

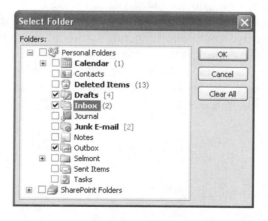

| FIGURE 15-3 | Use this dialog box to choose which message folders Outlook Today will display information about. |

15

contain messages: you can have Outlook Today display information about the Calendar, Contacts, Journal, even the Deleted Items folder.

3. Click OK, then Save Changes to return to the main Outlook Today view.

Configure the Outlook Today Calendar and Tasks Sections

The Calendar section of the Customize Outlook Today view allows you to specify the number of days of calendar information to be displayed.

The Tasks section of the Customize Outlook Today view allows you to specify which tasks will appear and the order in which they will be sorted. Select the options you want and click Save Changes to put them into effect.

Set the Outlook Today Style

Outlook Today can display its information using one of the five provided styles. There isn't a lot of variety here, but it's probably worth spending a few minutes trying out each style for yourself.

Customize Menus and Toolbars

Most of the controls you'll commonly use for Outlook are accessible through the menu bar or one of the toolbars. You click the button or menu item name to issue the command. Since most menus and toolbars have far more commands than most people use on a regular basis, Microsoft designed them to automatically alter their contents depending on how you use them. Office moves the commands you use most frequently to the tops of menus or makes them visible on the toolbar.

Menu commands that you use infrequently (or not at all) eventually disappear from view. They're still there, but they've been moved out of sight to reduce the clutter on the screen. To see the hidden commands, click the double down arrows at the bottom of the menu, or hover the mouse pointer over the menu for a moment. This opens the full menu.

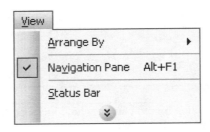

Toolbar buttons can work similarly. By default, Outlook will move those buttons you use most frequently toward the left of the toolbar, while hiding the less frequently used ones. To see the hidden buttons, click the toolbar options button at the right end of the toolbar. This opens a menu containing all the buttons that are not currently visible for that toolbar.

Change the Way Outlook Reconfigures Its Menus and Toolbars

While some people like the way Outlook (and the other Office applications) menus and toolbars reconfigure themselves depending on what you do, others dislike that behavior. You can change the default behavior of menus and toolbars by following these steps:

1. In the main Outlook window, click Tools | Customize to open the Customize dialog box shown in Figure 15-4.

2. On the Options tab, make any changes you wish to the Personalized Menus and Toolbars options. Some of the options may or may not be available depending on which other options are selected.

15

FIGURE 15-4   The Options tab of the Customize dialog box lets you control how menus and toolbars behave.

3. Click Reset Menu And Toolbar Usage Data if you want Outlook to start sorting options from scratch depending on how often you use them.

4. Click Close to put the changes into effect.

Choose Which Toolbars Appear

You can control which toolbars appear. Which toolbars are available varies depending on which applications and Windows features you have installed, but you can select from all the available ones easily. Follow these instructions:

Some applications that work with Outlook add optional toolbars to the Outlook interface.

1. Just as you did when you made the Advanced toolbar appear, right-click a blank spot adjacent to the menu bar or a visible toolbar. A shortcut menu appears, listing all the available toolbars.

2. On the shortcut menu, click the name of the toolbar you want visible. If a toolbar is already visible, there will be a check mark next to its name. Click it again to make it disappear.

3. As soon as you click the name of the toolbar, the menu disappears, and Outlook displays the toolbar.

Add Items to Menus and Toolbars

Many times, the buttons or menu options you want to use appear on the menu bar or the Standard toolbar. But what if you make frequent use of menus and buttons that are not normally found in these places? One option is to simply make all the toolbars you need visible all the time. But if you use only a few buttons from a toolbar, it seems a waste of screen space to have the entire toolbar visible all the time.

An alternative approach you can take when you need access to only one or two items from a different toolbar or menu is to add the items to the menu bar or the Standard toolbar. That way, they are readily available without wasting a lot of screen space. The following sections show you how to add a button to a toolbar, and how to add commands to menus.

NOTE   *For even more options, see the Add a Button, Menu, or Command topic in the Outlook help system.*

Add Buttons to a Toolbar

Adding buttons to the Standard toolbar is one good way to deal with the situation where you need access to only one or two buttons from a toolbar that isn't normally visible. Follow these steps to see how it is done in general, and read the "How To Add the Outlook Today Button to the Standard Toolbar" box for a useful specific example:

TIP   *This approach will work with any of the toolbars you can display in Outlook.*

1. If it isn't already visible in the Outlook main window, click View | Toolbars and select the toolbar you want to modify so that it appears in the Outlook window.

2. On the toolbar, click the Toolbar Options arrow.

3. In the menu that appears, click Add Or Remove Buttons. This opens another menu listing all the toolbars currently visible.

4. Click Customize to open the Customize dialog box shown in Figure 15-5.

5. In the Categories list on the Commands tab, select the category that contains the button you want. You may need to do a bit of poking around before you find the right category.

6. In the Commands list for the category you selected, find the button you want to add to the toolbar.

7. Drag the button from the Commands list to the exact location where you want it to appear in the toolbar.

8. Click Close when done.

15

FIGURE 15-5   Use the Commands tab of the Customize dialog box to add buttons to toolbars.

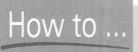 **Add the Outlook Today Button to the Standard Toolbar**

If you like to use Outlook Today, I seriously recommend that you add the Outlook Today button to the Standard toolbar (remember that it normally appears on the Advanced toolbar). Follow these steps to do it:

1. If it isn't already visible in the Outlook main window, click View | Toolbars and select the Standard toolbar so that it appears in the Outlook window.

2. On the Standard toolbar, click the Toolbar Options arrow.

3. In the menu that appears, click Add Or Remove Buttons. This opens another menu, this one listing all the toolbars currently visible.

4. Click Customize to open the Customize dialog box shown in Figure 15-5.

5. In the Categories list on the Commands tab, select the Advanced category.

6. In the Commands list for the category you selected, find the Outlook Today button.

7. Drag the Outlook Today button from the Commands list to the exact location where you want it to appear in the Standard toolbar.

8. Click Close when done.

Add a Command to a Menu

Just as you can add buttons to toolbars, you can add commands to menus. This is analogous to adding a button to an always-visible toolbar to save time and screen space. Make sure the menu you want to add a command to is visible, then follow these steps:

1. In the Outlook main window, click View | Toolbars | Customize to open the Customize dialog box.

2. On the Commands tab of the Customize dialog box (see Figure 15-6), select the category containing the command you want to add to the menu.

3. Drag the command from the Commands list to the menu. Do not release the mouse button. After a moment, the full menu should appear.

4. Point to the spot in the menu where you want to insert the command, then release the mouse button.

5. Click Close in the Customize dialog box.

Animate Outlook Menus

Here's a way to add a bit of fun to your use of Outlook. When you click a menu item on the menu bar, the way the menu itself appears is animated. You can easily change the animation. It won't transform your use of Outlook or anything like that,

15

FIGURE 15-6   Use the Commands tab of the Customize dialog box to add commands to menus.

but it can add a touch of variety to your work. Follow these instructions to change the menu animation:

1.   In the Outlook main window, click Tools | Customize. This opens the Customize dialog box.

2.   On the Options tab of the Customize dialog box, open the Menu Animations list and select an animation to use.

Customize the Navigation Pane

Throughout this book, you've learned ways to add folders to the Navigation pane, change views, manipulate the buttons at the bottom of the pane, and otherwise customize it for your work. There are, however, a few additional Navigation pane customizations we haven't talked about yet. In particular, you can add or remove the large buttons (they look like bars) at the bottom of the Navigation pane, as well as change their order. You can also control whether the Current View section appears, or hide the entire Navigation pane.

Add or Remove Buttons

If you don't ever use one of the major components of Outlook (say you never use Journal), there's little point in having a button for it taking up space in the Navigation pane. It takes only a few clicks to remove Navigation pane buttons (and only a few clicks to restore them too). Follow these steps to see for yourself:

1. In the Navigation pane, click Configure Buttons to open the Configure Buttons menu.

2. In the Configure Buttons menu, click Add Or Remove Buttons. This opens a menu containing all the Navigation pane buttons. The icons for the buttons that are visible in the Navigation pane are highlighted.

3. Click the icon for a button to add it to or remove it from the Navigation pane. The menu closes and the button appears or disappears.

4. Repeat as necessary to display only the buttons you want to see.

Change the Order of Buttons

The order of the buttons in the navigation pane is easy to change. Just follow these steps:

1. In the Navigation pane, click Configure Buttons to open the Configure Buttons menu.

2. Click Navigation Pane Options to open the Navigation Pane Options dialog box shown in Figure 15-7.

3. To change the order of the buttons, select the name of the button you want to move, then click the Move Up or Move Down button appropriately.

4. Click Reset if you want to restore the buttons to the default order.

15

NOTE *You can add or remove buttons using this dialog box too. Select or clear the check box next to the name of a button to make it appear or disappear in the Navigation pane.*

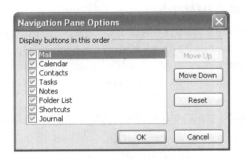

FIGURE 15-7   Use this dialog box to change the order of buttons in the Navigation pane, or to restore them to their original order.

Show or Hide Current View

When the Calendar, Contacts, Tasks, Notes, or Journal pane is visible, the pane normally includes a Current View section, a list of the possible views. If you primarily use a single view for one or more of these panes, or you want to eliminate a little bit of visual clutter, you can hide the Current View section. Here's how:

1. With the pane you wish to modify visible, click View | Arrange By.

2. In the menu that appears, click Show Views In Navigation Pane. This will hide the Current Views section if it is currently visible, or show it if it is currently hidden.

Show or Hide the Entire Navigation Pane

If you need the maximum amount of room on the screen for the view you're working in, you may want to hide the Navigation pane (at least temporarily). Showing or hiding the Navigation pane is a two-click process: click View | Navigation Pane. Figure 15-8 shows the Outlook Today view with the Navigation pane hidden.

 *You can also show or hide the Navigation pane with the* ALT-F1 *keyboard shortcut.*

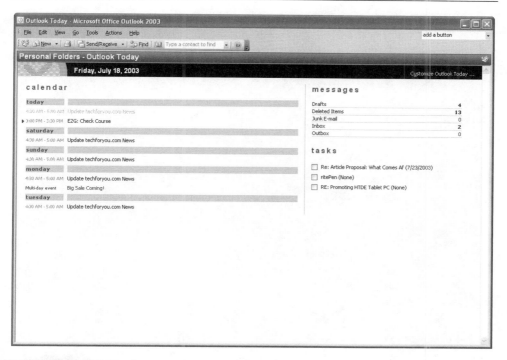

FIGURE 15-8   Hiding the Navigation pane gives you a lot more room for the view on the screen.

15

Chapter 16

Create Custom Views and Print Styles

How to...

- Customize Views
- Customize Print Styles

One of the nice things about Outlook is its customizability. This chapter looks at two particular areas of customization: views and print styles.

You already know a lot about views. Views are the way Outlook organizes the information it presents to you. Throughout this book, you've seen the default views for the various Outlook folders, and you've tried out some of the other views available in the folders.

When you print an item or a group of items in Outlook, their appearance on the paper is determined by the *print style* Outlook uses to print them. A print style is a combination of paper and page settings that control the format of an item or items you print. Print styles control characteristics such as the font used, the layout of the items on the page, the appearance of the header and footer on each sheet, and so on. Every item and view has one or more print styles associated with it.

Customize Views

You can customize views in a few different ways. Without making any changes to an existing view, you can change the information that appears in the view by applying a filter to it, or by altering the way the items in the view are grouped, sorted, or arranged. Going a step further, you can create custom views based on one of the five view types that Outlook supports. See the "Did You Know What the Five View Types Are?" box for more on the five view types.

Change the Information That Appears in an Existing View

Changing the information that appears in an existing view is an easy way to make views more useful. The ability to filter (show only items that meet certain criteria), sort, and group (cause related items to appear together) items makes it much easier to find and work with the items you need. Arrangements (predefined ways of grouping and sorting together) take this one step further, allowing Outlook to do things like arrange your messages by conversation or importance.

Did you know?

What the Five View Types Are?

Outlook 2003 comes with five basic view types. They are:

- ■ **Table**   Shows items organized by rows and columns. Each row contains the information about one item. Each row can contain a single line of text or multiple lines. This is the most versatile view.

- ■ **Timeline**   Shows items as icons arranged from left to right on a scale that displays time. Primarily useful for viewing Journal items.

- ■ **Day/Week/Month**   Shows items on a calendar, as if in a day planner. Most useful for viewing meetings, appointments, and events.

- ■ **Card**   Shows items as if they were individual business cards or file cards, and arranges them in alphabetical order. Most useful for viewing contacts or other items that can sensibly be organized alphabetically.

- ■ **Icon**   Shows items as icons arranged in a grid. Double-clicking an icon opens that item. Most useful for viewing notes.

The following sections show you how you can take advantage of filtering, sorting, grouping, and arrangements.

Filter a View

A *view filter* lets you make Outlook display only the items that match criteria you specify. You could filter the messages in the Inbox by someone's name, for example. Doing this causes Outlook to display only the messages that have the right name in them. When you apply a filter to a folder, the words "Filter Applied" appear in the left corner of the Outlook status bar (assuming it is visible). When you disable the filter, all the other items in the folder reappear.

To apply a filter to a view (or turn off a filter that's already applied to the view), follow these steps:

1. Select the folder where you want to use a filtered view.

2. On the Outlook toolbar, click View | Arrange By, then click Custom. This opens the Customize View dialog box.

16

3. Click Filter to open the Filter dialog box shown in Figure 16-1.

4. Create your filter by entering the appropriate criteria on the tabbed pages of the Filter dialog box.

5. To turn off a filter, click Clear All.

Sort a View

When you sort a view, you tell Outlook to arrange the items in ascending or descending order. You can sort any view other than time-based ones like the Timeline or Day/Week/Month view. Further, you can sort on any visible field.

To sort a view, follow these steps:

1. Select the folder you want to sort.

2. On the Outlook toolbar, click View | Arrange By, then click Current View. This opens a menu of the views that are possible for this folder.

3. Select a view that displays items in a table, as icons, or as cards.

4. On the Outlook toolbar, click View | Arrange By, then click Custom. This opens a Customize View dialog box.

5. Click Sort to open the Sort dialog box shown in Figure 16-2.

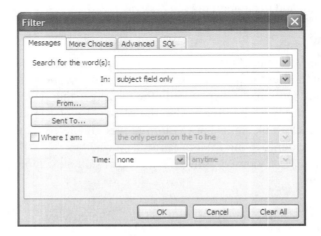

FIGURE 16-1   Control which items appear in a view by setting appropriate filters.

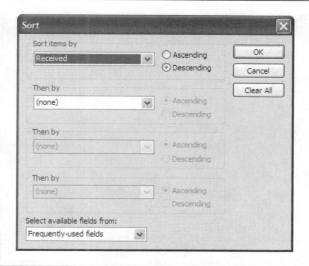

FIGURE 16-2   This dialog box helps you to sort items within a view.

6.   Choose the first field to sort by in the Sort Items By list box. If the field you want to sort by does not appear in the list, select a different field set from the Select Available Fields From list.

7.   Click Ascending or Descending to specify the sort order.

8.   If you wish to sort by additional fields, follow the same steps in the Then By lists in this dialog box.

Group a View

When a set of items has something in common, Outlook can group them for you. By default, many of the views in Outlook automatically group items by preset criteria. You can open or close a group by clicking the plus or minus sign before the group's name. You can also ungroup items, or create your own custom groupings.

   To create your own group, follow these instructions:

1.   In the Outlook toolbar, click View | Arrange By, then click Custom.

2.   In that Custom dialog box, click Group By. This opens the Group By dialog box shown in Figure 16-3.

16

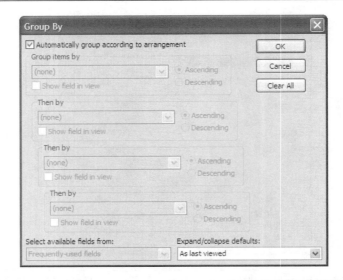

FIGURE 16-3   This dialog box allows you to set the criteria for grouping items.

3. Choose the first field to group by in the Group Items By list box. If the field you want to group by does not appear in the list, select a different field set from the Select Available Fields From list.

4. Click Ascending or Descending to specify the grouping order.

5. If you wish to sort by additional fields, follow the same steps in the Then By lists in this dialog box.

If you want to ungroup items instead of creating a new group, click View | Arrange By, then click Custom. In that Custom dialog box, click Clear All to eliminate the existing groups.

 *If the view you are working in has an active arrangement, the groups that are defined by that arrangement will still be in effect. The next section includes information on dealing with arrangements.*

Use an Arrangement

An *arrangement* is a table view of a folder, with predefined grouping and sorting. Outlook comes with 13 predefined arrangements, which are available in table-based views. By default, each of the groups in an arrangement starts out fully expanded, except for the groups in the Conversation arrangement, which start out collapsed.

You cannot create your own arrangements, but you can create custom views with their own grouping and sorting that will function the same way as an arrangement.

To use an arrangement, follow these steps:

1. Select the folder containing the items you want to view in an arrangement.

2. Choose a table-based view of the folder by clicking View | Arrange By | Current View and then selecting one of the views from the menu that appears.

3. Click View | Arrange By, then select one of the 13 standard arrangements from the menu that appears.

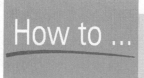

See the "How To Change Arrangements in Mail Views" box for an easier way to go when you want to arrange your e-mail.

How to ... Change Arrangements in Mail Views

When you work in a Mail view, there's a quick way to see what arrangement is active and to change arrangements. The key is in the Inbox pane.

If you look at the top left of the Inbox pane, you can see text that says "Arranged By:" followed by the name of the current arrangement. Click that text and Outlook displays a list of the available arrangements for you to choose from. It couldn't be much simpler.

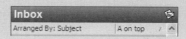

Create Custom Views

If you find that you like to set up certain views certain ways, and you find yourself spending time setting up the same combination of view, filters, sorts, and so on, you might want to create your own custom views. You can define one or more custom views for any folder and make them available in the menus as if they were members of the default set of views.

The sections that follow show you how to define custom views for particular folders and make them appear along with the default views. Along the way, I'll show you the dialog box where you'll do the actual creation of custom views. It'll be up to you to create the custom views that do what you need.

You can define your custom views in two ways: from scratch, or by modifying an existing view. Each approach is described here.

Define a New Custom View from Scratch

Defining a custom view from scratch could be your best approach if the view you want differs sharply from any of the available views. Here's how you go about it:

1. Click View | Arrange By. In the menu that appears, click Current View, then click Define Views to open the Custom View Organizer dialog box shown here. Use this dialog box to manage the views associated with a particular folder.

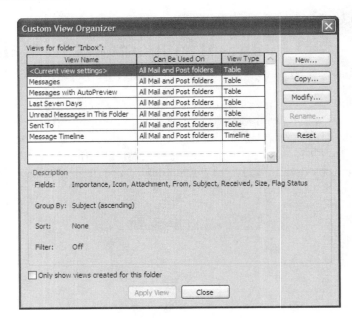

2. In the Custom View Organizer, click New to open the Create A New View dialog box shown in this illustration. Set the basic type for your new view as well as where it can be used in this dialog box.

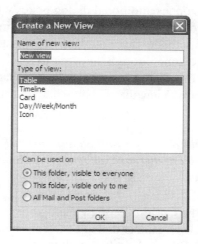

3. In the Create A New View dialog box, enter the name of your new view. In the Type Of View list, select one of the available basic types. In the Can Be Used On section of the dialog box, set one of the options to determine how widely available your new view will be. Click OK to open the Customize View dialog box shown here. Use this dialog box to configure your new custom views.

4. The Customize View dialog box is the place where you do the real work of setting up your view the way you want it. Depending on which basic view you selected, any or all of the buttons in this view will be active. Clicking any of the buttons opens additional dialog boxes where you can make the kinds of changes described next to each button. Since you've probably got some definite ideas about what you want your custom view to look like (or you wouldn't have gone through the work to reach this step), I'll leave it up to you to explore this dialog box and make the changes you want. Click OK in the Customize View dialog box when you're done making changes to the view.

 *If you create a multiline view and include several display fields in that view, you may need to increase the number of lines displayed in order to see all of your fields.*

5. When you leave the Customize View dialog box, Outlook takes you back to the Custom View Organizer dialog box. You should see your new custom view in the Views For Folder table, with the Can Be Used On and View Type settings you selected.

6. If you want to put your new view to work right away, click Apply View at the bottom of the Custom View Organizer dialog box. Click Close when you're done with this dialog box.

Define a New Custom View Based on an Existing View

Defining a new custom view based on an existing view is generally faster and easier than defining a new custom view from scratch. Here are the steps to follow:

1. Click View | Arrange By. In the menu that appears, click Current View, then click Define Views to open the Custom View Organizer dialog box shown earlier.

2. Select the view you want to base your new view on, then click Copy. This opens the Copy View dialog box shown in the following illustration. Create a copy of a custom view if you want the view to be usable in another place.

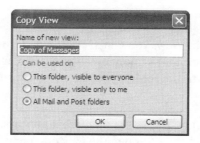

3. In the Copy View dialog box, enter the name of your new view. In the Can Be Used On section of the dialog box, set one of the options to determine how widely available your new view will be. Click OK to open the Customize View dialog box shown earlier.

4. In the Customize View dialog box, click the various buttons to open dialog boxes where you can change every aspect of the view you copied. Repeat until you've made all the changes you want. Click OK in the Customize View dialog box when you're done making changes to your copy of the view.

5. When you leave the Customize View dialog box, Outlook takes you back to the Custom View Organizer dialog box. You should see your modified view in the Views For Folder table, with the Can Be Used On and View Type settings you selected.

6. If you want to put your new view to work right away, click Apply View at the bottom of the Custom View Organizer dialog box. Click Close when you're done with this dialog box.

Rename a Custom View

While it is of course always best to give a custom view the perfect name when you create it, that doesn't always happen. If you decide you need to rename a view, here's what you need to do:

1. Click View | Arrange By. In the menu that appears, click Current View, then click Define Views to open the Custom View Organizer dialog box.

2. In the Views For Folder list, select the view you want to rename, then click Rename. This opens the Rename View dialog box.

3. Enter the new name of the view and click OK.

16

Use a Custom View in Another Place

When you create a custom view, you can specify which folders it is visible in. If you decide you want to use that same view in another place, or make it visible to other people with access to the folder, you can do so by copying the view. These steps show you how:

1. Click View | Arrange By. In the menu that appears, click Current View, then click Define Views to open the Custom View Organizer dialog box.

2. Select the view you want to use in another place, then click Copy. This opens the Copy View dialog box shown earlier.

3. Enter a new name for the copied view, then select one of the options in the Can Be Used On section of the dialog box. The new view becomes available in the folders you selected, and appears on the Current View menu for those folders.

Customize Print Styles

While Outlook comes with a set of predefined print styles (see the "Did You Know What the Default Print Styles Are?" box for more information) that are well matched to its items and views, you may find reason to customize print styles by modifying existing ones or creating your own styles. The rest of this chapter gives you the information you need to do exactly that.

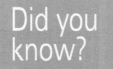

What the Default Print Styles Are?

Outlook 2003 comes with several predefined print styles. Which of these styles is available to you at any given time is determined by the type of Outlook item you're working with and the view you're working in. The main print styles are

- **Memo**   Shows each item, one after the other.

- **Table**   Shows all items in a list. The fields that are currently visible in the view appear in the table.

- **Daily**   Shows one day per page, with Tasks and Notes also visible. Each day is displayed from 7 AM to 7 PM.

■ **Weekly**   Shows one week per page. No Tasks and Notes areas are included.

■ **Monthly**   Shows one month per page. No Tasks and Notes areas are included.

■ **Tri-Fold**   Shows one day, one month, and the TaskPad. They're evenly spaced to allow you to fold the page into three equal sections.

■ **Calendar Details**   Shows all selected Calendar items, and also the body of each item.

Modify an Existing Print Style

The easiest way to customize a print style is to modify an existing one. Here's how you do it:

1. Switch to the Outlook view associated with the print style you want to change. For example, if you want to change the way the Weekly print style looks, you would first get into a Calendar view.

2. Click File | Print to open the Print dialog box shown here. Select the print style you want to modify in the Print dialog box.

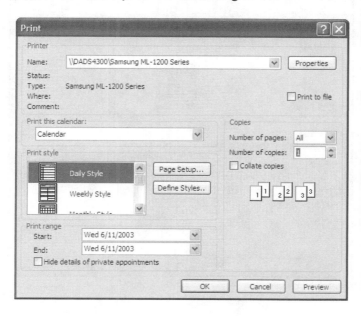

3. In the Print Style section of the dialog box, select the print style you want to use as the basis for your new style, then click Define Styles. This opens the Define Print Styles dialog box shown in the illustration. Choose a print style to work with in this dialog box.

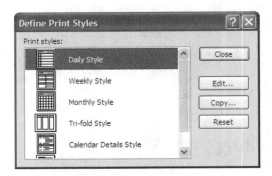

4. Click Edit to open the Page Setup dialog box shown in Figure 16-10. The specific options available in this dialog box vary with the print style you selected. For many of the options, you can get a basic idea of the way they affect the page layout by watching the way things change in the small Preview window, as seen here.

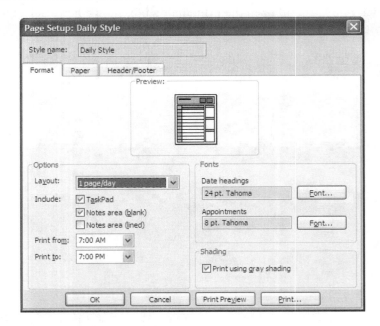

Create a New Print Style

If you're looking for a little more adventure, consider creating a new print style instead of just modifying an existing one. These instructions will get you started:

1. Open the view you want to create a print style for.

2. Open the folder containing the items you want to use the print style with.

3. Click File | Print to open the Print dialog box.

4. In the Print Styles list, select the print style you want to use as the basis for your new style, then click Define Styles to open the Define Print Styles dialog box.

5. Click Edit to open the Page Setup dialog box. Enter the name for your new style in the Style Name box, then make your changes to the base style. You can use the Preview to get a basic idea of what your new layout looks like, and Print Preview to see exactly what it would look like if you clicked Print right now.

Delete or Reset a Print Style

You can delete any modified print style when you no longer need it. You cannot delete the default print styles. You can, however, reset the default print styles to their original settings if that suits your purposes. The process is mostly the same for doing either; it consists of these steps:

1. Click File | Print to open the Print dialog box.

2. In the Print Styles list, select the print style you want to change, then click Define Styles to open the Define Print Styles dialog box.

3. If you want to delete a modified print style, select it in the Print Styles list. Click Delete.

TIP *The Reset button in the dialog box changes to a Delete button when you select a modified print style.*

4. If you want to reset all the default print styles, select any default print style and click Reset. You can't reset default print styles individually.

16

Chapter 17

Search for, Manage, and Archive Items

How to...

- Search for Items
- Learn Ways to Manage Items
- Learn Ways to Archive Items
- Come Up with an Item Management and Archiving Strategy

Once upon a time (not really very long ago), people faced the problem of too little information. Today, the problem is reversed. Gathering information isn't a problem. We're practically drowning in the stuff. Finding, managing, and saving the information you need is the problem.

This chapter helps you to find, manage, and archive (save) information stored in Outlook items. These capabilities work together in Outlook 2003. Outlook's powerful search capabilities make it practical to manage information better while still being able to find it when you need it. At the same time, the ability to archive old information makes it easier to search and manage by moving old stuff someplace out of the way, but still where you can get it easily if you need it. After looking at these capabilities, the chapter ends with a short discussion of the things you need to consider when coming up with a strategy for managing and archiving Outlook items.

Search for Items

The longer you use Outlook, the more stuff you accumulate. E-mail messages, contacts, tasks, notes, all seem to pile up incredibly quickly. I typically have several thousand Outlook items of all sorts stored away. It's great to be able to keep all this information and have it right there when you need it. The trick is finding the right item in that vast pile. Storing related items in the same folder can help, as can Outlook's rules for automatically filtering information, but they're not enough. Sometimes you just need to run a search.

Outlook offers two search tools: Find, and Advanced Find. Find is for basic keyword searches using words or phrases you enter. Advanced Find is for everything else. The next two sections explain how to use these two tools.

Use Find for Simple Searches

Find is the tool to use for simple searches. The Find tool is part of the Find bar, which, when active, appears above the View pane. The Find bar includes several text boxes and buttons. If it isn't visible, click Find on the toolbar to open it. Since the Find bar isn't a toolbar, you can't open it by right-clicking in the Menu bar as you can a toolbar.

SHORTCUT *You can also open the Find bar with the* CTRL-E *keyboard shortcut.*

Create and Run a Search with Find

To use the Find bar to search in the current folder, enter a word or phrase into the Look For text box and click Find Now. If you want to rerun a search that you conducted recently, click the down arrow on the right side of the Look For text box to see a list of recently used search terms.

To search in a different folder than the one that's open right now, follow these steps:

1. Click Search In and select the folder you want from the list that appears.

2. If the folder you want to search isn't in the list, click Choose Folders. This opens the Select Folder(s) dialog box shown in Figure 17-1, where you can specify the folder you want searched.

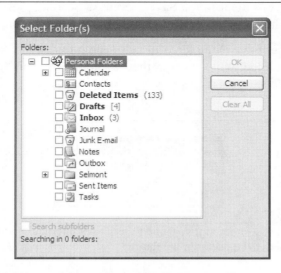

FIGURE 17-1   The Select Folders dialog box lets you specify which Outlook folders will be searched when you click Find Now.

17

3. If you want your search to include any subfolders of the folders you selected, set the Search Subfolders check box. Click OK to return to the main Outlook window, and click Find Now in the Find bar to launch the search.

Turn a Search into a Search Folder

If you find that you frequently search for the same words or phrases, you should consider creating a search folder for that search. As you learned in Chapter 14, search folders are virtual folders that represent the results of searches. Every time you open a search folder, Outlook runs the search that goes with it. Using search folders can save you all sorts of time and effort, even on simple searches. Here's how you turn the results of a search conducted with Find into a search folder:

1. Run your search using Find.

2. Make sure that the search results are plausible to you. You need to be careful to create the search you really want, and get it right, right now. Once you create a search folder, you're unlikely to go back and check to see if the search is set up properly in the future. So make sure to check your spelling and the folder being searched.

3. When you're convinced that the search is set up correctly, click Options on the Find bar.

4. On the Options menu, click Save Search As Search Folder. This opens the Save Search As Search Folder dialog box shown in Figure 17-2.

5. Enter a descriptive name for your new search folder, then click OK. The new search folder will appear in the Navigation pane along with your other search folders.

FIGURE 17-2   Choose a descriptive name for each search folder you create if you want them to be useful in the future.

Use Advanced Find for Serious Searching

If you need to find an item that contains a particular word or phrase, Find should work just fine for you. But if you need to do more sophisticated searches, or need to search on something other than a word or phrase, Advanced Find is what you need.

Advanced Find lets you search on dates or file sizes, or find tasks with a particular word or phrase in the Subject field. You can save searches that you find particularly useful, and search multiple folders simultaneously. The ability to search multiple folders simultaneously is particularly useful once you start actively managing your Outlook items with rules.

In this book, we're going to cover only some of the more commonly used capabilities of Advanced Find, and leave exploring the rest to you. It really is an amazingly powerful tool that you'll find more uses for the more you use it.

Create and Run a Search with Advanced Find

While Find appears as part of the Find bar, Advanced Find has its own dialog box. To open the Advanced Find dialog box, go to the main Outlook window and click Tools | Advanced Find. Figure 17-3 shows the Advanced Find dialog box.

The Advanced Find dialog box is crowded and complicated. The good thing is that you'll seldom need to use more than a few of the search criteria you can set here. To help you get oriented, the following list describes several of the major elements of the Advanced Find dialog box:

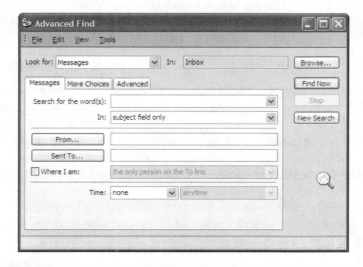

FIGURE 17-3   The Advanced Find dialog box is a busy and complicated place.

17

- **Look For list** The Look For list is where you specify the type of Outlook item you want to search for. By default, the dialog box opens with an object type that is appropriate to the current Outlook folder. You can search for one particular type of item at a time or search all types simultaneously. The type of item you specify in this list also determines the types of search criteria the dialog box presents to you. For example, when the item type in the list is Messages, the first tabbed page in the dialog box shows common search criteria related to e-mail messages. Switch to Contacts, and the name of the first tabbed page presents search criteria that are appropriate for searching for contacts.

- **In list** The In list is where you specify the folder or folders you want Outlook to search. By default, the In list is set to the current Outlook folder. You can also specify the folder or folders to be searched by clicking the Browse button.

- **Tabbed pages** The three tabbed pages in the Advanced Find dialog box let you set the search criteria you want to use. As I mentioned a little earlier, the first tabbed page changes to present criteria that are appropriate to the type of item selected in the Look For list. The second and third tabbed pages also change to present criteria relevant to the item type. This makes it pointless to try to describe in detail what you'll find on each page. The best I can tell you is to work your way through the pages from left to right. They're arranged from the most basic criteria to the most complex. Other people may have had different experiences, but I've seldom needed to use the criteria on the More Choices page, and I almost never go to the Advanced page.

- **Find Now button** The Find Now button launches your search.

- **New Search button** The New Search button clears all your search criteria, enabling you to start designing a new search with a more or less clean slate.

When your search is ready, click Find Now to launch it. The results appear in a list that opens at the bottom of the dialog box. If you think the search you just created will be useful in the future, you can save it or convert it into a search folder.

NOTE *For help in deciding when to save a search instead of creating a search folder for that search, as well as tips for where to save your searches, see "Come Up with an Item Management and Archiving Strategy" later in this chapter.*

Save Searches

If you create a search that you think you'll want to use again, you can save it. To save a search, click File | Save Search in the Advanced Find dialog box. This opens the Save Search dialog box shown in Figure 17-4. Use this dialog box to give your saved search a name and select the folder where you'll store it. Saved searches end with a .oss file type.

Use Saved Searches

To use a saved search, you need only open it, then run it as if you had just set it up. To open a saved search, click File | Open Search in the Advanced Find dialog box. This opens the Open Saved Search dialog box. This dialog box is the same as the Save Search dialog box, except that now you're using it to find saved searches. Locate the saved search you want to use, then double-click it to load it.

When you load the saved search, all the search criteria that you saved originally are restored. You can either run the search immediately by clicking Find Now, or make any necessary changes to the saved criteria, then run the search.

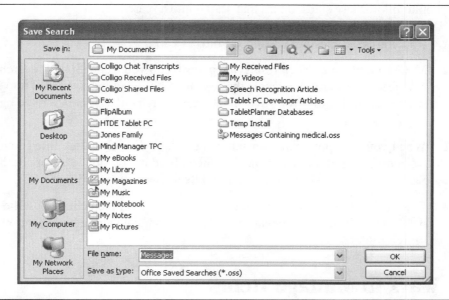

FIGURE 17-4   You may want to have a strategy for where you save searches before you see this dialog box.

Delete Saved Searches

The process for deleting a saved search is very similar to that for loading one. You start by clicking File | Open Search in the Advanced Find dialog box to open the Open Saved Search dialog box. Locate the saved search you want to delete, then right-click it. In the shortcut menu that appears, click Delete.

Turn a Search into a Search Folder

If you find yourself re-creating the same search over and over in Advanced Find, you should seriously consider creating a search folder for that search. The more complex and time-consuming a search is to set up, the more you will benefit from creating a search folder.

For help in deciding when to create a search folder instead of just saving a search, see "Come Up with an Item Management and Archiving Strategy" later in this chapter.

Of course, if you know you'll never run the same search again, creating a search folder is pointless, but if you think you will run a complex search more than once, you should follow these steps to turn that search into a search folder:

1. Run your search using Advanced Find.

2. Make sure that the search results are plausible to you. As with basic searches, you need to be careful to create the search properly before you turn it into a search folder. Be sure you have all the right search criteria set before going any further.

3. When you're happy with your search criteria and results, click File | Save Search As Search Folder in the Advanced Find dialog box. This opens the Save Search As Search Folder dialog box shown earlier in Figure 17-2.

4. Enter a descriptive name for your new search folder, then click OK. The new search folder will appear in the Navigation pane along with your other search folders.

Learn Ways to Manage Items

While search folders and regular searches make it easier to find what you're looking for in Outlook, they're not a total solution. There was a time when I kept *all* my relevant e-mail messages in the Inbox. Anything that I thought might be useful stayed there until AutoArchive swept it into an archive after three months.

NOTE   *AutoArchive is covered later in this chapter.*

That approach was workable when I received only a few e-mail messages a day. My Inbox might contain hundreds of messages, but a quick visual search or a search with Find or Advanced Find would quickly turn up the messages I needed.

But as e-mail became more common, that system became unworkable. For one, my Inbox would regularly contain over 2000 messages. Even with Find or Advanced Find, finding anything in that mess took a while. Searches might turn up dozens of matches that I would have to look through to find the information I needed.

The answer to the problem was to create a system of folders to hold related messages (and other Outlook items as necessary).

Create Folders to Manage Items

In Chapter 5, you learned how to automatically manage e-mail messages by applying rules to them. Perhaps the most common use of those rules is to move e-mail messages into folders. Now it's time to learn how to create those folders.

NOTE   *For help in deciding what folders to create and what to store in them, see "Come Up with an Item Management and Archiving Strategy" later in this chapter.*

To create a new folder, follow these steps:

1. Click File | New, then Folder. This opens the Create New Folder dialog box shown in Figure 17-5.

2. Enter the name for the folder, making sure to choose a name that will remind you of what is in the folder later on.

3. In the Folder Contains list, select the type of Outlook items that you plan to store in the folder.

4. In the Select Where To Place The Folder list, select the name of the folder that you want to contain your new folder. For example, select Inbox if you want the new folder to appear as a subfolder of the Inbox.

FIGURE 17-5   Creating new folders in Outlook makes it possible to manage your information more efficiently.

Learn Ways to Archive Items

Eventually, you'll need to do something with old Outlook items. When you reach the point where you have hundreds, even thousands of items in individual folders, it just becomes too cumbersome and time-consuming to do anything with them. There are several ways to tackle this problem, each with its own advantages and disadvantages.

You can set aside some time every so often to go through folders and delete old items you don't need anymore. The advantage of this approach is that you're in control of every item. The disadvantages of this approach are that it is time-consuming, and even if you do get rid of items you don't need, your folders are likely to keep growing, just a bit more slowly than if you didn't delete old items.

Another approach is to manually delete old items you don't want, and put old items you do want into a different folder for storage. This has the same advantage as the first approach but doesn't eliminate its disadvantages, as moving the old files into yet another folder just shifts the problem to a different spot. Plus, moving the items into some "old stuff" folder makes it harder to find the items when you do need them.

A better approach is to have a file outside of Outlook that can easily store old stuff while still being able to find and retrieve it easily when you do need it. The ideal external storage would compress Outlook items to save disk space and would be accessible from outside Outlook. That way, you could back up this old information on another machine or some long-term storage device.

Of course, Outlook does support exactly this approach. The outside file is an Outlook data file. Data files have a file extension of .pst (which is why people often refer to these files as "PST files"). Data files are flexible, and you can use them at least three different ways.

The simplest way is to drag items into the data file when you want to store them. You can also use the copy or move command as you normally would in Outlook. This approach lets you store the items (or at least copies of the items) somewhere safe, without having to think about organizing them. You will still have the problem of finding the items you want when you need them, but at least they're not cluttering your regular Outlook folders.

The next way to use a data file is to export entire folders into it. This preserves the organization of the folders you export, but you can export only one folder (and its subfolders) at a time. You also end up backing up all the items in the folder, not just the old ones. Plus, you still have the original items in their original Outlook folders, meaning you still need to clean out the folders manually.

The third approach is the best. You can use AutoArchive to automatically archive items that are over a certain age. Items that get archived are removed from the Outlook folders they were in, so your folders get cleaned up automatically. AutoArchive organizes the contents of the data file the same way your regular Outlook folders are organized, so you can actually find things you store in the data file.

> **NOTE** *If you use Outlook at work, your Outlook items may be affected by corporate retention policies. These can limit the length of time you can store items. Corporate retention policies are imposed by the network administrator or IT department, and override any AutoArchive settings you enter.*

Archive Items Automatically

You need to understand a few things before working with AutoArchive. First, it treats Contacts differently than any other items, by ignoring them completely. While it might sound strange at first, it actually makes perfect sense once you

17

think about it. You certainly don't want AutoArchive moving your contacts around on you.

When it comes to the other Outlook items, AutoArchive is interested only in old items and expired items. Old items are items that have been unchanged long enough to be archived. By default, items in the Inbox, Calendar, Tasks, Notes, Journal, and Drafts folders are old after six months without changes.

You can choose to have AutoArchive delete old items, or move them to an archive data file. By default, AutoArchive will move old items to the data file instead of deleting them.

Expired items are items (old meeting requests, for example) that are no longer valid after a date you specify. I've found the expired items features of AutoArchive to be of little use. This chapter concentrates on handling old items.

When Outlook runs AutoArchive for the first time, it creates a default archive data file named Archive.pst. This data file appears in the Outlook File List with the name Archive Folders. If you open Archive Folders in the File List, you'll find that AutoArchive moves items into folders with the same names and organization as your regular Outlook folders. As far as you can tell from within Outlook, working with the items in archived folders is the same as working with items in your regular folders.

There are two types of AutoArchive settings: global settings and per-folder settings. Global settings apply to all folders and are the easiest way to set up autoarchiving. Per-folder settings apply to a specific folder. When you set per-folder settings for a folder, they override the global settings. So for example, if your global settings say to archive items every two months, but you want one particular folder to be archived every week, you can accomplish that by changing the per-folder settings in that folder, thereby overriding the global settings.

Configure AutoArchive Global Settings

To configure AutoArchive, you set its global settings. To do this, follow these instructions:

1. Click Tools | Options to open the Options dialog box.

2. On the Other tabbed page of the Options dialog box, click AutoArchive to open the AutoArchive dialog box shown in Figure 17-6.

3. Before you can do anything in the AutoArchive dialog box, you need to set the Run AutoArchive Every X Days check box. This activates all the other AutoArchive controls and options as shown in Figure 17-6.

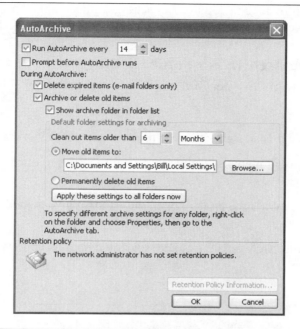

FIGURE 17-6   Use the AutoArchive dialog box to set global archiving settings and to activate AutoArchiving.

4. Begin by setting the value in the Run AutoArchive Every X Days field to match the frequency with which you want archiving to occur. By default, Outlook runs AutoArchive every 14 days.

5. Set the Prompt Before AutoArchive Runs check box. AutoArchive can take a while, particularly the first time around. When AutoArchive is running, it definitely slows down your machine. I suggest you watch how long it takes to run on your computer a few times, then decide if you still want Outlook to prompt you before it runs.

6. Fill in the rest of the settings as you wish. I do recommend setting the Show Archive Folders in Folder List check box, and archiving old messages rather than deleting them (by selecting Move Old Items To and entering a path to the location where the archive will be stored). If this is the first AutoArchive folder you've created, you can use the default settings for the location.

17

7. When you're done making global settings, click Apply These Items To All Folders Now. Your global settings should now be in effect.

Configure AutoArchive Per-Folder Settings

To configure AutoArchive per-folder settings for a particular folder, follow these steps:

1. In the Folder List, right-click the folder you want to work with.

2. In the shortcut menu that appears, click Properties to open the Properties dialog box.

3. Click the AutoArchive tab to open the AutoArchive tabbed page shown in Figure 17-7.

4. On the AutoArchive tabbed page, select the options you want to apply to this folder.

FIGURE 17-7   Use this tabbed page to set AutoArchive values for a particular folder.

Come Up with an Item Management and Archiving Strategy

Coming up with an item management and archiving strategy is a practical and sensible goal. With so much information flowing contained in the e-mail messages and other items stored in Outlook, knowing how to find, manage, and archive items will pay off over time. And coming up with a strategy isn't that hard. The things to consider are

- How you tend to use Outlook items

- How you organize your daily work

- What your company's policies are with regard to data retention

The way you use Outlook items can have a big impact on what you need to do as far as management and archiving. If you get a lot of information by e-mail and keep that information in Outlook, you need a management and archiving strategy. If, on the other hand, you don't get a lot of important information by e-mail, and you don't tend to keep the information you do get in Outlook (some people like to print their important messages, for example), then you can probably skip the strategy.

The way you organize your daily work primarily determines the folders, rules, searches, and search folders you need to create. The goal is to make your information easy to find when you want it, while minimizing the amount of work you need to do personally to get it arranged that way.

Your company's data retention policies (if it has them) provide the boundaries within which you can manage and archive items. These policies can either be the kind of rules you find written in a manual somewhere, or they can be rules actually enforced by the Exchange server. For example, one company I did some work for instituted a policy barring the retention of more than 5MB worth of items on the Exchange server, and barring any storage of items locally on your PC. This required everyone on staff to change the way they handled Outlook items, typically eliminating most folders and all AutoArchiving in order to comply with the rules.

Decide on an Archiving Strategy

Coming up with an archiving strategy is relatively simple. The strategy really has three parts: do you archive, how often do you archive, and which folders do you archive?

17

How to ... Decide Between Searches and Search Folders

Outlook provides you with two similar ways to find information: searches and search folders. So which should you to use when? Here are some rules of thumb:

- When you expect to use the same search repeatedly, consider creating a search folder. It's easier to conduct a search using a search folder (just open the folder), which saves you time.

- When you're creating lots of searches, consider saving searches you won't use as frequently instead of turning them into search folders. Search folders are easy to get at in the All Mail Folders section of the Mail pane, but if you create lots of them, that area is going to become very cluttered. By saving less frequently used searches as saved searches instead of search folders, you reduce the clutter in the Mail pane.

Here's a related tip. If you end up saving a lot of searches, you might want to consider storing them in project-specific or person-specific folders. Since the Save Search dialog box works the same as any other saved dialog box, you can create new folders to store your saved searches in, right from the dialog box.

NOTE *I'm assuming that you will use AutoArchive instead of manually archiving your files. Manual archiving just takes too long.*

In most cases, archiving your files makes sense. You can have AutoArchive run as frequently as you want, but the default of every 14 days is probably just fine. So are the default settings, which call for AutoArchiving everything but Contacts. Unless, of course, your company has retention policies that conflict with the advice I'm giving you. Corporate retention policies always win, especially when they're set by the network administrator and are enforced by Exchange.

Deciding which folders to archive can take a little thought, although if you stick with the default (archiving everything except Contacts), you can hardly go wrong. If you don't want to archive everything, I suggest you concentrate on the Inbox, and the folders of your current projects. That should give you a good balance between archiving everything in sight, and risking losing important information.

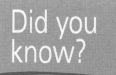

Where to Look for Retention Policies?

There's an easy way to tell if your copy of Outlook is subject to data retention policies put in place by the network administrator. You can check for yourself in the AutoArchive dialog box. To get there, click Tools | Options, then the Other tabbed page. On the Other tabbed page, click AutoArchive to open the AutoArchive dialog box.

Look at the bottom of the dialog box, in the section named Retention Policy. If your network administrator has put formal retention policies in place, they will show up here.

AutoArchive

☑ Run AutoArchive every 14 ⇅ days
☐ Prompt before AutoArchive runs
During AutoArchive:
   ☑ Delete expired items (e-mail folders only)
   ☑ Archive or delete old items
      ☑ Show archive folder in folder list
      Default folder settings for archiving
      Clean out items older than 6 ⇅ Months ▾
      ⦿ Move old items to:
         C:\Documents and Settings\Bill\Local Settings\   [Browse...]
      ○ Permanently delete old items
      [Apply these settings to all folders now]

   To specify different archive settings for any folder, right-click
   on the folder and choose Properties, then go to the
   AutoArchive tab.
Retention policy
   The network administrator has not set retention policies.

   [Retention Policy Information...]
                        [OK]   [Cancel]

Chapter 18

Attend to Your Security

How to...

- Deal with Junk E-Mail
- Improve Security with Digital Certificates
- Deal with Attachments
- Avoid Macro Viruses

It's unfortunate, but in any area where there are people, there are troublemakers. The online world is no different. As the most popular e-mail program in the world, Outlook is a prime target for online troublemakers. Over the years, Microsoft has added a number of features to Outlook to make it more secure against attacks and invasions of privacy. This chapter covers the key security (and privacy protection) features of Outlook 2003.

Deal with Junk E-Mail

Junk e-mail (also known as spam) has become a major problem for e-mail users the world over. Depending on whose statistics you care to believe, up to half of all e-mail messages sent in the first half of 2003 were junk e-mail. Despite new state and federal laws in the United States and elsewhere, the flood of spam continues to grow.

Outlook 2003 has new features designed to reduce the amount of junk e-mail that actually makes it into your Inbox. Specifically, Outlook 2003 provides a sophisticated junk e-mail filter, along with a set of lists that determine whether messages from specific addresses or domains should be blocked by the filter or not. Here's some more information on each of the components of the new junk e-mail handling system:

- **The Junk E-Mail Filter** This filter relies on sophisticated algorithms to identify messages that are likely to be junk. It takes into account factors like the time of day the message was sent and the actual contents of the message. This approach is more flexible and potentially much more powerful than older approaches, which relied on specific rules.

- **The Safe Senders List** This list is a place to specify particular senders as people you trust. By doing so, you tell the junk e-mail filter never to block messages from these senders. Note that you don't have to add people to this list to receive mail from them. Instead, add someone to this list if they are accidentally blocked by the junk e-mail filter.

■ **The Blocked Senders List**   This list is the place to specify that e-mail from certain senders is always to be treated as junk.

■ **The Safe Recipients List**   This list is a little less obvious. You use it to tell Outlook that any e-mail sent to the recipients in this list is not to be treated as junk. You might want to add the addresses of your favorite mailing lists to the Safe Recipients list. That would keep Outlook from blocking any e-mail messages sent to the list and then forwarded to you.

Use the Enhanced Junk E-Mail Filter

By default, the junk e-mail filter is active, and set to the lowest of its three security levels. On the Low setting, the filter catches only the most obvious junk e-mail messages and will likely let some junk messages get through to your Inbox. The good thing about this setting is that it is unlikely to block messages you should be receiving. You can adjust the way the junk e-mail filter does its work, and make changes to the Safe Senders, Safe Recipients, and Blocked Senders lists, using the instructions that follow.

Adjust the Junk E-Mail Filter Settings

To adjust the e-mail filter settings, follow these instructions:

1. In the Outlook main window, click Tools | Options. On the Preferences tabbed page of the Options dialog box, click Junk E-Mail. This opens the Junk E-Mail Options dialog box shown in Figure 18-1.

2. On the Options tabbed page of the Junk E-Mail Options dialog box, set the level of junk e-mail protection you want. Choose between Low Protection, High Protection, and Trusted Lists Only.

NOTE   *If you select the No Protection option, you effectively turn off the junk e-mail filter.*

3. Tell Outlook what to do with junk messages. Normally, Outlook puts suspected junk e-mail messages in a Junk E-Mail folder. If you're really comfortable with the way the junk e-mail filter is working, you can tell Outlook to eliminate junk messages instead of storing them in the Junk E-Mail folder by setting Permanently Delete Suspected Junk E-Mail Instead Of Moving It To The Junk E-Mail Folder.

18

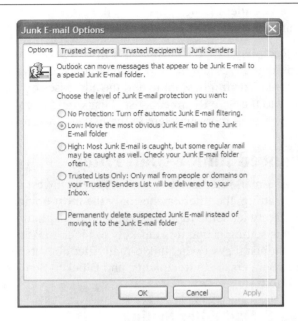

FIGURE 18-1   Adjust your junk e-mail filter settings using this dialog box.

How to ... Keep Spam from Coming in the First Place

While Outlook is good at fighting spam once it arrives, another way to cut down on it is to prevent spammers from sending it to you in the first place. While it's impossible to prevent everyone from sending you junk e-mail, there are steps you can take to reduce the amount that gets sent to you in the first place. Here are some of the best:

■ **Never reply to junk e-mail** Some junk e-mail messages arrive complete with instructions on how to opt out of future mailings. While this sounds like a good idea, don't do it. In reality, when you follow the opt-out instructions, you may or may not be removed from that junk mailer's list. But in almost all cases, your e-mail address will be sold to other junk e-mailers. By replying to the message, you've shown that yours is a valid and actively used e-mail address. This information is quite valuable to junk e-mailers, and you'll likely get barraged with even more spam than before.

■ **Alter your e-mail address when you post it in public**   By changing your e-mail address slightly whenever you post it on a web site, a newsgroup, or a mailing list, you can thwart some of the software that's used to automatically harvest e-mail addresses for the spam senders. One simple approach is to replace the @ sign in your e-mail address, like this: bill@techforyou.com becomes bill (at) techforyou.com.

■ **Create a disposable e-mail address**   You can easily create a disposable e-mail address on one of the web e-mail services. If you use this disposable address when registering software or filling out forms on web sites, most of the spam that you get will go to that address. When the address becomes too much of a target for junk e-mailers, you just close it and open a new disposable address. If you use this approach, you can save your main e-mail address for close friends or other people that you trust.

Nothing you can do as an individual will protect you from all junk e-mail. But following the suggestions, and using Outlook's junk e-mail handling capabilities, you should be able to greatly reduce the amount of junk e-mail you have to deal with.

Work with the Lists

All three of the junk e-mail-related lists work the same way. You can follow these basic instructions to work on any of them. In step 2, just choose the appropriate tabbed page for the list you want to work on. For simplicity, these instructions deal with the Safe Senders list:

1. In the Outlook main window, click Tools | Options. On the Preferences tabbed page of the Options dialog box, click Junk E-Mail. This opens the Junk E-Mail Options dialog box.

2. On the Safe Senders tabbed page of the Junk E-Mail Options dialog box (shown in Figure 18-2), use the Add, Edit, and Remove buttons to manage any names in the list.

18

FIGURE 18-2   Use this dialog box to add, edit, or remove members of the Safe
Senders list.

3. If you have an ASCII text list of senders you want to add to the Safe
Senders list, click Import From File and select the appropriate text file.
Using the Export To File button, you can similarly export your current list
of Safe Senders to an ASCII text file.

4. To ensure that all your Outlook Contacts are automatically trusted (even
though they don't appear in the Safe Senders list), make sure that the Also
Trust E-Mail From My Contacts check box is set.

> NOTE   *The Also Trust E-Mail From My Contacts check box appears only on the
> Safe Senders tabbed page.*

Block and Unblock External HTML Content

Some spammers send HTML e-mail messages using objects called *web beacons*.
By default, Outlook 2003 blocks most external HTML content, which prevents
web beacons from functioning. The exception is messages from members of the

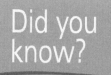

Antivirus Software Is Crucial?

While Outlook 2003 has several capabilities designed to provide you with better security than previous versions, they're not enough. You need antivirus software too. The manufacturers of antivirus software, companies like Symantec and McAfee, go to great lengths to keep up with the ever-changing designs of viruses and other harmful programs that are out in the world. If you install antivirus software and keep it up to date, you'll do much to protect the security of your computer.

If your PC is connected to the Internet through a broadband connection, I suggest you investigate products like McAfee VirusScan online, a subscription service that delivers the latest updates to your PC as soon as they're available.

Safe Senders and Safe Recipients lists. External HTML content from people on these safe lists is allowed to function normally.

 For more information on what web beacons are and how they work, please read the following sidebar, "Did You Know about Web Beacons?"

Enable or Disable External HTML Blocking

While the default setting for Outlook 2003 is to automatically block the downloading of external HTML content, there may well be situations where you don't want that to happen. If you want to allow automatic downloads from certain senders or domains, you can easily do so by adding those senders or domains to the Safe Senders list.

You can change the default settings to control whether or not Outlook automatically downloads content for all HTML messages by following these directions:

1. In the main Outlook window, click Tools | Options to open the Options dialog box.

2. On the Security tabbed page shown in Figure 18-3, click Change Automatic Download Settings in the Download Pictures section. This opens the Automatic Picture Download Settings dialog box.

18

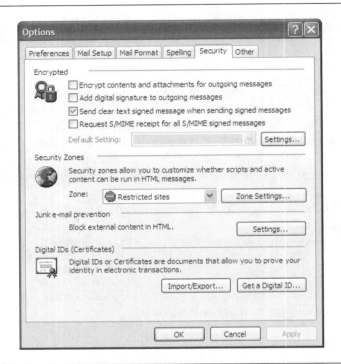

FIGURE 18-3 The Security tabbed page of the Options dialog box provides access to many of the key security features in Outlook 2003.

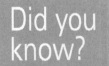

About Web Beacons?

Web beacons, also known as web bugs, are usually tiny images, 1 pixel by 1 pixel, that are transparent or the same color as the background of the web page or e-mail message they're part of. We'll concentrate here on how they work when included in HTML e-mail messages.

Some HTML e-mail messages include images in the body of the message itself. Others include links to the images, which reduces the size of the e-mail message. Web beacons typically link to a different web server than the rest of the images in the message. Prior to Outlook 2003, when you opened a message containing a web beacon, your e-mail program automatically loaded the image for the web beacon from its web server, same as any other image. When that happened, the web server was able to gain all sorts of information from your computer.

Spammers use web beacons to determine if someone opens the e-mail message the spammer sent to them. If the spammer's web server detects your computer trying to download the web beacon that was included in the message they sent to you, they know that your e-mail address is an active one. Then the flood of spam really begins, since your address is now known to be a good one.

3. In the Automatic Picture Download Settings dialog box shown in Figure 18-4, select or clear the check boxes to alter the external content behavior the way you wish.

View Blocked External HTML Content

Another way to deal with external content in HTML e-mail messages is to allow Outlook to block it, then manually choose the items you want to see. When Outlook blocks an external image, it displays a box with a red X where the image would have been. When Outlook blocks external content in this way, a message appears in the InfoBar to explain what happened, as you can see in Figure 18-5.

FIGURE 18-4   Use this dialog box to control how Outlook handles external content in HTML e-mail messages.

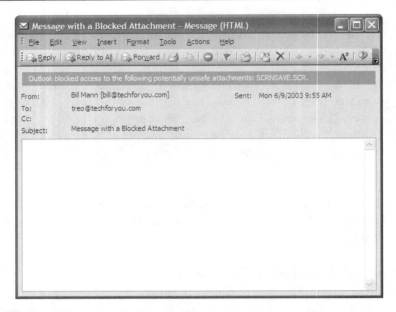

FIGURE 18-5   When Outlook blocks external content in an HTML message, it tells you what it did with a message in the InfoBar.

There are two ways to see the blocked items. One is to right-click the blocked item, then in the shortcut menu that appears, click View Source.

The other way to see the blocked content is to click the InfoBar. When you do that, a shortcut menu appears. Click Download Pictures to see the blocked content.

Apply Parental Controls to the Research Library

The new Research Library is a powerful tool. But since it gets information from a variety of sources, it's possible that it will display material that's not suitable for children. If children are using your copy of Outlook, you may want to activate the Parental Controls feature of the Research Library. The following instructions show you how it's done:

 *To use the Research Library in Outlook 2003, you need to be reading an e-mail message.*

1. Open an e-mail message. In the message, click Tools | Research to open the Research Library.

2. At the bottom of the Research Library pane, click Research Options. This opens the Research Options dialog box.

3. Click Parental Control to open the Parental Control dialog box shown in Figure 18-6.

4. To activate parental controls, set the Turn On Content Filtering To Make Services Block Offensive Results check box.

5. If you want to limit searches to only services that can block offensive content, set the Allow Users To Search Only The Services That Can Block Offensive Results check box.

6. If you want to keep others from changing the parental control settings, enter a password.

Improve Security with Digital Certificates

Digital certificates (also called digital IDs) are files that can be attached to e-mail messages (and other things) to provide security. Outlook can use digital certificates to *digitally sign messages* and to *encrypt messages.* A message that has been digitally signed can be shown to have been created by you (or at least on your computer), thereby protecting against someone impersonating you when sending e-mail messages. A message that has been encrypted has been changed so that only the intended recipient (or someone using their computer) can read it.

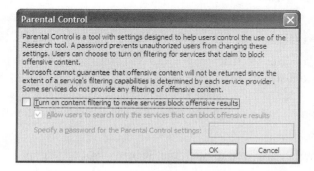

FIGURE 18-6   Use the Parental Control dialog box to block offensive content from appearing in the Research Library.

18

Digital certificates are provided by organizations known as *certificate authorities (CAs).* A certificate authority is a known and trusted organization that provides a means to validate each certificate it issues, and presumably will not share your certificate with anyone else. The process for getting a digital certificate varies depending on whether or not Outlook is connected to an Exchange server. If your computer is connected to Exchange, your company probably already has a policy on the use of digital certificates. You should contact your network administrator for further information.

Get a Digital Certificate When Microsoft Exchange Is Not Involved

To get a digital certificate when Microsoft Exchange is not involved, follow these steps:

1. In the Outlook main window, click Tools | Options to open the Options dialog box.

2. Click Security to open the Security tabbed page shown earlier in Figure 18-3.

3. In the Digital IDs (Certificates) section of the dialog box, click Get A Digital ID. This opens your web browser to a page in the online Microsoft Office Assistance Center. This page, shown in Figure 18-7, provides you with links and instructions for getting a digital certificate.

4. Choose a certificate authority, and follow the instructions to get your digital certificate.

Configure Outlook to Use Your Digital Certificate

Once you have a digital certificate, you need to configure Outlook to use it. To do this, follow these instructions:

1. In the main Outlook window, click Tools | Options to open the Options dialog box.

2. Click the Security tab to open the Security tabbed page.

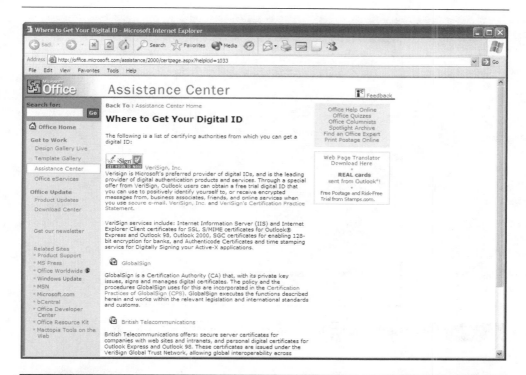

This web page will help you find a certificate authority and get yourself a digital certificate.

3. On the Security tabbed page, click Settings. This opens the Change Security Settings dialog box shown in Figure 18-8.

4. In the Security Message Format list, select S/MIME, since this is the format used for sending certificates on the Internet.

5. In the Certificates And Algorithms section of the dialog box, you can specify the signing certificate and the encryption certificate you want to use. In either case, click Choose next to the certificate type, then select the certificate from the list in the Select Certificate dialog box that appears.

18

FIGURE 18-8 Use this dialog box to specify the digital certificate you want to use.

When you send or receive an e-mail message containing a certificate, Outlook indicates this by adding a red ribbon to the envelope icon used to indicate an e-mail message in the Inbox pane, as well as in the header of the message itself.

When you open a message that has been signed, you will see some additional information in the message header, as Figure 18-9 shows. This information tells you who signed the message.

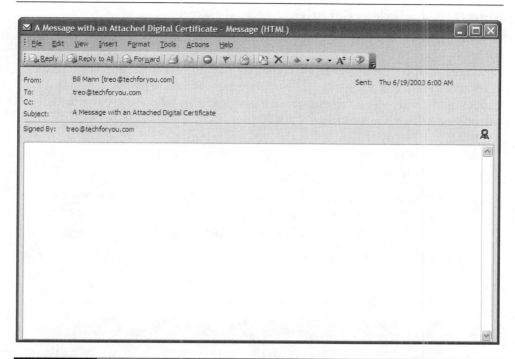

FIGURE 18-9   A digitally signed message includes information about the signer in its header.

Automatically Include a Certificate in Every Message

If a lot of your communications require digital signatures or encryption, you may want to configure Outlook to always use your digital certificates and automatically attach a copy to each message you send. These steps show you how:

1. In the main Outlook window, click Tools | Options to open the Options dialog box.

2. Click the Security tab to open the Security tabbed page.

3. On the Security tabbed page, click Settings. This opens the Change Security Settings dialog box.

4. In the Certificates And Algorithms section of the dialog box, set the Send These Certificates With Signed Messages check box.

18

Manually Include a Certificate in a Message

If your messages don't usually need to be digitally signed or encrypted, you're probably better off manually including a certificate when necessary. Because messages with certificates look different than regular messages, and because the certificates are included as attachments, they can confuse people who aren't expecting digitally signed or encrypted messages. Here's how you can manually include a certificate in a message:

1. In the message window, click Options to open the Message Options dialog box shown in Figure 18-10.

2. Click Security Settings to open the Security Properties dialog box for the message. As Figure 18-11 shows, this dialog box lets you enable or disable digital signatures or encryption for the message it belongs to.

3. Set the relevant check boxes to apply encryption and a digital signature to the message as appropriate.

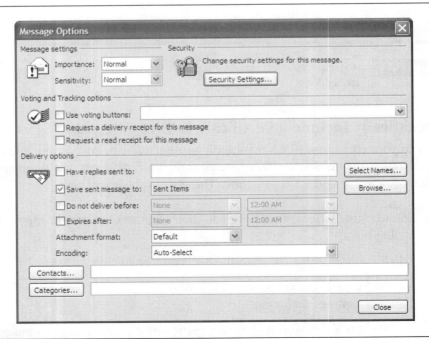

FIGURE 18-10   Use this dialog box to set options for a specific message.

FIGURE 18-11   The Security Properties dialog box allows you to control the use of certificates in a specific message.

Deal with Attachments

For a few years now, one of the primary ways people attack computers has been through e-mail attachments. Many viruses travel disguised as pictures or screen savers, or other types of files attached to innocuous-looking e-mail messages. When the recipient tries to open the attachment, the virus goes to work, wreaking havoc. While it is well known that viruses travel this way, many times every day, someone somewhere tries to open an unexpected e-mail attachment and creates a major headache for themselves, their co-workers, the corporate IT staff, and often every person in their Outlook Address Book.

How Outlook Protects You Against Bad Attachments

In an attempt to protect you from such threats, Outlook takes a brute force approach: it prevents you from receiving a wide range of e-mail attachments. It does this by looking at the file extension of each attachment, and blocking those that Microsoft (or your IT department) has decided pose a risk.

18

This approach may be effective, but it may also require you to change the way you do your work. Many people are used to e-mailing various files back and forth in ways that may no longer be possible. Microsoft Office System documents, things like Word or Excel files, get through just fine. But other commonly used files types, such as batch files (.bat file extension), screen savers (.scr file extension), and help files (.hlp file extension) are blocked. If you sometimes send these kinds of files around, you'll have to change your ways.

When you receive a message that contains an attachment Outlook doesn't like, the attachment seems to disappear. You have no access to it at all, and the only way to know it was ever there is to look at the InfoBar in the message. As Figure 18-12 shows, the InfoBar contains a message telling you that Outlook has blocked access to the potentially unsafe attachments, and lists the names of those attachments.

Outlook recognizes two kinds of potentially dangerous file attachments: Level 1 and Level 2. Level 1 attachments are file types could conceivably carry viruses or other dangerous content. Outlook blocks you from even seeing any attachments that are on the Level 1 list. By default, Outlook comes with a list of about 40 file extensions that are treated as Level 1. To see the entire list of extensions that are

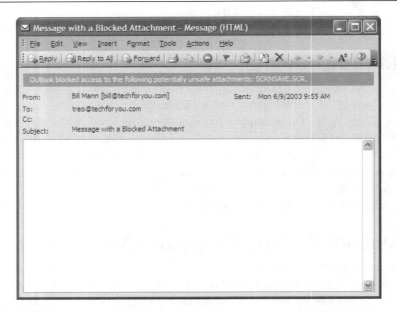

FIGURE 18-12   The message InfoBar will tell you if Outlook has blocked any attachments that it deems "potentially unsafe."

blocked by default, open the Outlook help system and search for the word "attachments." In the results list that appears, click Attachment File Types Blocked By Outlook to see the appropriate help topic.

The Level 2 list is empty by default. Network administrators can add file extensions to the Level 2 list, as well as convert Level 1 file extensions into Level 2 file extensions. Outlook doesn't completely block Level 2 files, but you cannot open them from within Outlook. Instead, you must save the file to your hard drive before opening it. Doing this gives your antivirus software a chance to scan the file before you open it.

> NOTE   *If you are connected to Microsoft Exchange, your e-mail administrator can change the security level of file types. Contact the administrator for more information.*

Working Around Attachment Blocking

While Outlook 2003 is set up to prevent you from circumventing its attachment blocking (you could circumvent attachment blocking in the previous version of Outlook), there are still some things you can do to get your attached files through. Either one of the following techniques will get the job done, at the cost of some additional work for both sender and recipient:

- Add a dummy file extension to your attachments. Say you want to send a file with a .hlp extension as an attachment. Outlook would normally block that. But if you change the extension to something like .hlp_dummy, Outlook will let that through. The recipient can then save the file without the _dummy part of the extension, and all will be well.

- Use a file compression or packaging tool on your attachments. Attached files with extensions like .zip are not blocked by Outlook. If you use a program like WinZip to compress and package the files you want to send in an attachment, they'll get past the attachment blocking. Then all you need to do is be sure the recipients have the tools and information needed to restore the files to their original forms.

Avoid Macro Viruses

Outlook can also protect your computer from macro viruses. A computer program like Microsoft Office Word consists of a set of instructions that are executed by the

Windows operating system. Macros are sets of instructions that are executed by programs like Microsoft Office Word. Macro viruses are harmful macros that can be attached to Microsoft Office Word documents, Microsoft Office Excel spreadsheets, and many other types of files.

Since a macro contains instructions for the program that opens the file containing it, the programs that read the macros can do only certain things with them, which should prevent any problems. However, it's possible to write macros that defeat the built-in security of the program viewing them, thereby allowing the macro to act like a virus.

Once launched, a macro virus can cause strange behavior on your PC, infect other files, even tell Outlook to mail the infected document to every one of your Contacts, thereby spreading the infection. The Melissa virus, which infected millions of computers in 1999, is a well-known example of a macro virus.

To protect you against macro viruses, Outlook defaults to a high macro security level. In this state, Outlook will not execute the macros in any file unless the developer of the macro is in a list of trusted sources, and the macro itself is digitally signed with the developer's digital ID.

The only problem with this is that many, if not most, of the legitimate macros in use are not digitally signed and aren't in anyone's trusted sources list. If you're in a position where you need to run macros like this within Outlook, you'll need to change macro security settings to accommodate the way you actually work.

To Change Outlook's Macro Security Level

It takes only a few moments to change the macro security level. But don't do it unless it is really necessary. Microsoft set the security level to High for a reason. However, if you're running an antivirus program, that should catch macro viruses for you, making it much safer to reduce the security level. Here are the steps to follow:

1. In the main Outlook window, click Tools | Macro. In the menu that appears, click Security to open the macro Security dialog box shown in Figure 18-13.

2. On the Security Level tabbed page, set the security level you want to use.

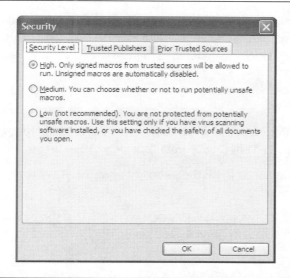

FIGURE 18-13   Use this dialog box to adjust Outlook's macro security level.

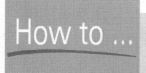 **Prevent Outlook from Attaching Personal Information to Documents**

Did you know that Outlook adds personal information to certain types of documents when you attach them to an e-mail message? Well, it's true. In order to facilitate the merging and tracking of changes, Outlook attaches personal information to the documents you're sending, perhaps including your name or e-mail address.

NOTE *Outlook adds personal information to Word, Excel, and PowerPoint documents.*

Depending on what you're doing, or who is receiving the attached documents, this could be a real problem. Here are the steps you need to follow to prevent Outlook from attaching personal information to documents that you e-mail:

1. In the Outlook main window, click Tools | Options to open the Options dialog box.

2. On the Preferences tabbed page, click the E-Mail Options button. This opens the E-Mail Options dialog box.

3. Click Advanced E-Mail Options to open the Advanced E-Mail Options dialog box.

4. In the When Sending A Message section of the dialog box, clear the Add Properties To Attachments To Enable Reply With Changes check box.

NOTE *There are also steps you can take to remove personal information from Office documents before you attach them to an e-mail message. Check the help system for the application you're using to create a document for more information.*

Part V

Go Further with Outlook 2003

Chapter 19

Take Advantage of the Research Pane

How to...

- Understand the Research Pane
- Use the Research Pane
- Configure the Research Pane

It is sometimes necessary to do research while working in Outlook. You might, for example, receive a message containing a word whose meaning you're unsure of. Under the right circumstances, you might also find that you need access to an encyclopedia, stock information, a thesaurus, or various other sorts of information. If you work at a large company, you might need access to information stored on the company intranet, or receive a message from a co-worker who speaks a different language than you do.

Formerly, in all these situations, you would have to open a Web browser, start an online dictionary or encyclopedia, or otherwise leave Outlook to find the information you needed. In Office System 2003, Microsoft has addressed this issue by creating the Research pane, which allows you to get the information you need without leaving Outlook. This chapter introduces the Research pane and shows you how to configure and use it.

Understand the Research Pane

The Research pane (shown in Figure 19-1) is a new feature integrated into all Microsoft Office System 2003 applications. Using the Research pane, you have access to a wide collection of information sources (called *Research services*) all without leaving the Outlook window. Research services can reside on the Web, on your company intranet, or on your own PC.

What's So Great about the Research Library?

Because the Research pane is integrated into Outlook, you can do your research without opening a different application or leaving Outlook. The information resources available in the Research pane can be Web services, intranet pages, or certain information local to your PC.

The integration of the Research pane into Outlook has other benefits too. Starting a search of the Research Library can be as simple as holding down the ALT key and clicking a word. Information you find in the Research Library can easily be cut and pasted into your message. And depending on the Research

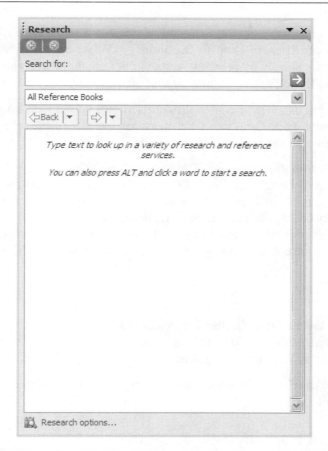

FIGURE 19-1   The Research pane lets you conduct research without ever leaving the Outlook window.

service you're working with, you may see Smart Tags that provide sophisticated additional capabilities beyond just cutting and pasting.

> TIP   *You can find out more about using Smart Tags in Chapter 25.*

What Services Are Available?

The Research pane comes with free access to several useful Research services right off the bat. These break down into three broad categories: reference books, research sites, and business and financial sites.

19

Reference Books

- **Microsoft Encarta English Dictionary** You can look up words in this dictionary simply by pressing ALT and clicking the word. The Reference pane will also support additional dictionaries when they become available.

- **A thesaurus** The included thesaurus allows you to look up synonyms and easily insert them into your messages in place of the selected word. Non-English thesauri are also available.

- **Translation dictionaries** The Research pane can work with bilingual dictionaries installed on your PC to provide quick translations of words or phrases. It can also call out to machine translation sites on the Web, which can translate words, phrases, paragraphs, or an entire message. These services are great for employees of multinational corporations, or anyone who has to exchange e-mail messages with someone who speaks a different language.

Research Sites

- **Microsoft Encarta English Encyclopedia** You use this service to get access to the tens of thousands of articles in the Encarta Encyclopedia. These articles also contain links to additional relevant information on MSN.

- **MSN Search** This service allows you to search the Web using the MSN search tool.

Business and Financial Sites

- **MSN Money Stock Quotes** This service provides basic information about publicly traded companies.

 The exact names, quantities, and types of Research services available are subject to change. The ones described here are the ones that were available when I wrote this chapter.

The design of the Research pane doesn't limit the number of Research services that you can use. Beyond the free services that you can use right out of box, there are premium services such as eLibrary, Factiva, and Gale that provide even more specialized or valuable information for a fee. If the Research pane becomes a

You Can Create Your Own Research Services?

If you or someone in your organization knows how to develop web services, you can create your own Research services. This would allow people to connect to your service just as they do to any other Research services. Guidelines for creating your own Research service are far outside the scope of this book, but you can easily get information you need off the Web.

If you go to the MSDN web site (msdn.microsoft.com) and search for Research Task Pane, you'll find multiple articles on building and customizing Research services.

popular tool for Office System 2003 users, I expect many more Research services will become available.

Use the Research Pane

The first thing to know about using the Research pane in Outlook is that it's available only in certain situations. You need to be composing or reading an e-mail message or working in a Task window to open the Research pane. This makes sense, since you're unlikely to be doing much research while editing a Contact or reading a Calendar entry.

Research a Single Word

As I mentioned before, using the Research pane can be as easy as pressing ALT and clicking a word in a message. This is all you need to do when you're researching a single word. To try this approach, select a Task or an e-mail message so that the message or Task appears in the View pane, as shown in Figure 19-2.

Now press ALT and hold it, while clicking a word in the e-mail message or Task. After a moment or two, the Research pane appears. At the top of the pane is the Search For box, which contains the word you ALT-clicked. Directly below the Search For box is a list that contains the names of all the Research services that Outlook searches.

Below the Search For area is the space where Outlook displays the results of its research. This area may already contain the results of that research. If it does not, click the arrow button to the right of the Search For box to initiate the research.

19

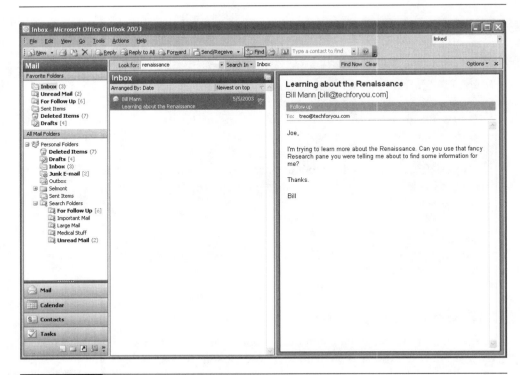

FIGURE 19-2   You need to have an e-mail message or a Task visible in the View pane to open the Research pane in Outlook.

By default, Outlook searches for your word in all of its reference books (but not in reference sites or business and financial sites). Exactly what information appears depends on what Outlook found during the research. Figure 19-3 shows a typical set of search results.

> **TIP**   *The same* ALT-*click technique works if you are viewing an e-mail message or Task in its own window.*

Besides the dictionary definition (if it was found), the Research pane provides a section for each reference book or site that it searched, as well as a section containing additional links to resources you can explore if the research didn't turn up the information you need. Typically, the dictionary section will be expanded and all other sections collapsed. To expand a collapsed section, click the + to the left of its name as you would to expand a folder in Outlook's Folders list.

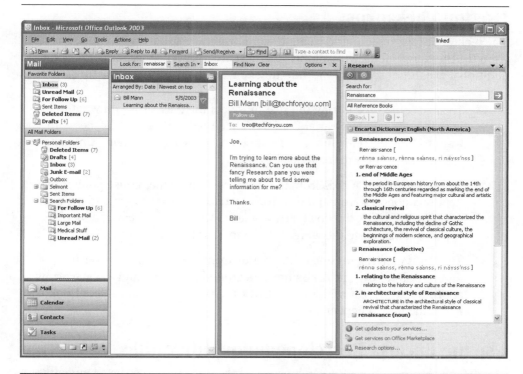

FIGURE 19-3   When activated, the Research pane appears automatically.

Research Phrases

Researching phrases is similar to researching single words with one difference: you can't use the ALT-click shortcut to open the Research pane. Here's what you can do instead:

1. Make the e-mail message or Task visible either in the Preview pane or in its own window.

2. Select the phrase you want to research.

3. Right-click the phrase. In the shortcut menu that appears, click either Look Up or Translate, depending on the task you want to accomplish. This opens the Research pane with the phrase in the Search For box. If the results of the research are not already visible in the pane, click the arrow button to the right of the Search For box to initiate the research.

19

Use the Thesaurus

The techniques for researching a single word or phrase will normally return results from the thesaurus along with all the other research. But the thesaurus has some additional capabilities you might want to take advantage of. Try these tips:

- To save some time during the search, select the thesaurus you want to use in the list below the Search For box. Then press ALT and click the word you want to look up. This limits the search to the thesaurus, saving time and eliminating clutter in the Research pane.

- To use one of the words from the thesaurus, hover the mouse pointer over it. A box appears around the word, and a down arrow appears to the right of the word. Click the down arrow and select Copy in the menu that appears. Then paste the word into the message or Task.

- To find synonyms for one of the words from the thesaurus, hover the mouse pointer over it. A box appears around the word, and a down arrow appears to the right of the word. Click the down arrow and select Look Up in the menu that appears.

Use the Encarta Encyclopedia or Other Sites

The default searches on the Research pane search all the resources listed under the heading of Reference Books in the list below the Search For box. This does not include the Encarta Encyclopedia or any of the other sites listed under the Research Sites or All Business And Financial Sites headings. To search one of the sites, select it in the list below the Search For box, then perform your search.

Reuse Search Results

The Research pane retains the results of searches that you've conducted since you last started Outlook. To see the results of the previous searches, find the Back button directly above the window containing search results. Click Back to step backward through earlier searches. Similarly, when the Search button (the one directly to the right of the Back button) is active, you can use it to scroll forward through searches.

Configure the Research Pane

You can configure the Research pane by clicking Research Options at the bottom of the pane. This opens the Research Options dialog box shown in Figure 19-4.

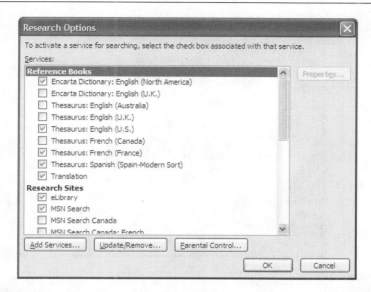

FIGURE 19-4   Use the Research Options dialog box to manage Research pane services.

This dialog box lets you enable or disable services as well as add new ones, update or remove existing ones, or examine the properties of particular services. And if children use your computer, there's a parental control option you may find very useful.

Examine Research Service Properties

If you would like to learn more about any of the Research services, you can do so by selecting the service on the Services list and clicking Properties to open the Service Properties dialog box. Figure 19-5 shows the Service Properties dialog box for the Encarta English Dictionary.

Using this dialog box, you can find the full name of the service and its provider, a description of the service, the copyright notice, its content category, even the path to the service if it's not local to your PC.

Add, Update, or Remove Research Services

The Research Options dialog box is also the place to add, update, or remove Research services. Follow these steps:

1. In the Research Options dialog box, click Add Services to open the Add Services dialog box.

19

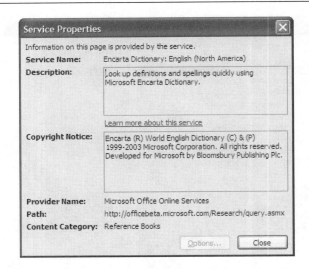

FIGURE 19-5   Get background information about a service using the Service Properties dialog box.

2. Enter the path to a server containing Research services into the Address box of the Add Services dialog box, then click Add. This opens the Microsoft Office Online Services Setup dialog box shown in Figure 19-6.

3. Set the check box to the left of each service you want to add in the dialog box Services list, then click Install to add the services.

Apply Parental Controls

One problem with research on the Internet, even with a tool like the Research pane, is that not all of the contents your search may uncover will be suitable for people of all ages. To help prevent unpleasant situations, the Research pane includes a parental control feature. With a few clicks, you can enable this feature. When active, the parental controls communicate with the Research services and direct them to filter the results they return. While filtering like this is not 100 percent effective, activating the parental controls should greatly reduce the amount of inappropriate information returned by searches.

To activate parental controls, go to the Research Options dialog box and click Parental Control. This opens the Parental Control dialog box shown in Figure 19-7.

Use this dialog box to add Research services to your Research pane.

If the parental controls are disabled, the only option you have available is to set the Turn On Content Filtering To Make Services Block Offensive Results check box. If you do set that option, two additional options become enabled.

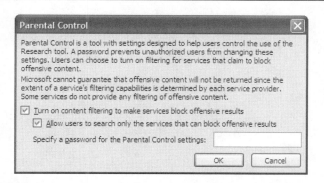

Activate parental controls when you want Outlook to try to prevent offensive content from appearing in search results.

If you want to limit users to only searching services that block offensive materials, set the Allow Users To Search Only the Services That Can Block Offensive Results check box.

To prevent other people from changing the parental control settings, you can also specify a parental controls password in this dialog box. Click OK to put the changes into effect.

Chapter 20

Use Handwriting with Outlook 2003

How to...

- Understand How Handwriting Works with Outlook
- Use Handwriting Recognition with Outlook
- Use Ink with Outlook

Our computers are designed to receive information from us and to be controlled by us with typed text and mouse clicks. Yet throughout history, our primary means of communication have been spoken and written. So it should be no surprise that researchers have been working hard to give our computers the ability to work with spoken and written information and commands. In recent years, they've had some significant success in understanding and solving the problems inherent in these technologies. At the same time, the power of personal computers has increased to the level where it is possible to do basic handwriting and speech recognition on a typical PC.

Recent versions of Microsoft Windows (including Windows XP) have optional features that provide basic handwriting and speech recognition. Recent versions of Outlook (and other Office System programs) have the ability to work with handwritten and spoken information in ways that make it worthwhile for you to investigate.

This chapter covers the use of handwritten input and handwriting recognition in Outlook 2003. Chapter 21 covers spoken input and speech recognition. If you are looking for alternative ways to enter commands and information into your PC, or if you just want to learn more about the ways we may all interact with our computers in the future, these two chapters should prove interesting to you.

Understand How Handwriting Works with Outlook

Outlook works with handwriting in two ways. One way is through *handwriting recognition*. Handwriting recognition means converting handwritten input into typed text, and inserting that typed text into an Outlook item.

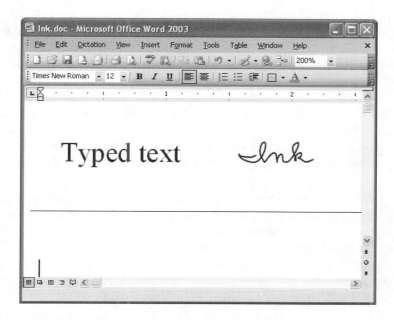

The other way you can use handwriting with Outlook is by treating it as *ink*. When you treat handwriting as ink, what you write is converted into an object that shows your handwriting exactly as you wrote it instead of converting it to typed text.

Each approach to using handwriting has advantages and disadvantages. When you use handwriting recognition, your handwriting get converted to typed text that Outlook can use the same as if you typed it on the keyboard. But handwriting text, then converting it to typed text is a slower, more error-prone process for most people than simply typing the text on the keyboard. Handwriting recognition is most practical for people who have difficulty using a regular keyboard, or in situations where using the keyboard is impractical.

Using ink to represent handwritten input has the big advantage of looking like your handwriting. In many circumstances, a handwritten note (or the computerized equivalent thereof) has far more power, expressiveness, and personality than a typed message. But since Outlook treats ink as a graphical object instead of typed text, you can't use inked input for things like addressing a message or setting the time and date of a meeting.

Understand Handwriting Recognition with Outlook

When doing handwriting recognition, Outlook relies on a *handwriting recognition engine* to recognize your handwriting and convert it into typed text that gets

20

entered into the active Outlook item. A handwriting recognition engine is a language-specific piece of software that can convert handwritten input into typed text. Windows XP and later versions come with five handwriting recognition engines: Simplified Chinese, Traditional Chinese, English, Japanese, and Korean.

This chapter addresses the English handwriting recognition engine. If you are going to use one of the East Asian handwriting recognition engines, please refer to the About Handwriting Recognition in East Asian Languages topic in the Outlook help system.

Once you have a handwriting recognition engine installed and active, you can enter your handwriting using a dedicated writing tool such as a pen stylus and writing tablet or a graphics tablet; you can also use your mouse. You enter your handwriting with the help of the Writing Pad or Write Anywhere, two features that get installed when you install a handwriting recognition engine. These features appear on the *Language bar,* a toolbar of language-related features that appears when you are working in an application that supports language-related features.

NOTE *Some computers come with a handwriting recognition engine preinstalled and activated. See the "How to Determine if a Handwriting Recognition Engine Is Installed" box for tips on how to find out if an engine is already installed on your computer.*

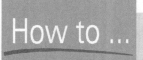 **Determine if a Handwriting Recognition Engine Is Installed**

If your computer already has a handwriting recognition engine installed, you won't need to install one yourself. Here are some ways you can figure out if an engine is already installed:

- Look for the Language bar. If you're working in Outlook or another Office System application, and a little toolbar appears on the screen with buttons for the Writing Pad or Write Anywhere, a handwriting recognition engine is installed and active.

- Check the Text Services settings. In the Regional and Language Options section of the Control Panel, open the Language tab. Under

Text Services and Input Languages, click Details. In the Text Services And Input Languages dialog box that appears, look under Installed Services. If Write Anywhere or Writing Pad appears, a handwriting recognition engine is installed and active.

If a handwriting recognition engine is installed and active, but you still don't see the Language bar, click Language Bar in the Preferences area of the Text Services and Input Languages dialog box. In the Language Bar Settings dialog box that appears, select Show The Language Bar On The Desktop to make the bar visible.

20

Understand Using Ink with Outlook

When you use ink to enter handwriting into Outlook, whatever you wrote appears as a graphical object that looks like your handwriting. For example, suppose I write the word "ink" in cursive on the Writing Pad. (Don't worry about the details of doing this right now. They're explained later in the chapter.) If I am working in handwriting recognition mode (called Text mode on the Writing Pad), a moment after I stop writing, the word "ink" appears in typed text in the Outlook item I'm working on.

If, however, I'm using the Ink mode on the Writing Pad, what appears in the Outlook item might look something like Figure 20-1, with a replica of my actual handwriting appearing in the item.

Use Handwriting Recognition with Outlook

To use handwriting recognition with Outlook, you must have a handwriting recognition engine installed as described in the "How to Install Handwriting Recognition" box. You also need the Language bar running, with either the Writing Pad or Write Anywhere active. Let's make sure you have these items set up first.

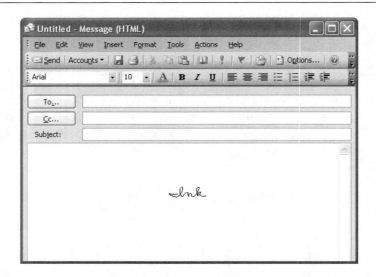

FIGURE 20-1   With Outlook 2003, you can treat your handwriting as ink, and insert handwritten content into items without first converting it to typed text.

 **Install Handwriting Recognition**

Handwriting recognition isn't automatically installed on most systems, so you'll probably have to do it yourself. Fortunately, it isn't hard to do. I've provided the instructions for doing so on a Windows XP machine.

> **NOTE** *If you want to use handwriting recognition and your computer runs Windows 2000, you should search the Windows help system for a topic named Install Handwriting Recognition. That will walk you through the steps.*

To install handwriting recognition on a non–Tablet PC computer running Windows XP, follow these steps:

> **TIP** *If you're using Outlook 2003 on a Tablet PC, you have a completely different set of built-in handwriting tools at your disposal. For more information, check your Tablet PC help system, or see my book,* How to Do Everything with Your Tablet PC *(McGraw-Hill/Osborne, 2003).*

1. Click Start | Control Panel to open the Control Panel dialog box.

2. Click (or double-click as appropriate) Add Or Remove Programs to open the Add Or Remove Programs dialog box.

3. In the Currently Installed Programs list, click Microsoft Office 2003 (the name will vary slightly depending on which version of Office you have installed), then click Change. This opens a Windows Installer wizard.

4. Select Add or Remove Features, then click Next.

5. In the Custom Setup screen that appears, set the Choose Advanced Customization Of Applications check box, then click Next. This opens the Advanced Customization screen.

6. In the Choose Update Options For Applications And Tools box, click the plus sign next to Office Shared Features to expand that area.

7. Click the plus sign next to Alternative User Input to expand that area.

8. Click the down arrow next to Handwriting to see the available handwriting options.

9. Click Run From My Computer then Update to install handwriting recognition.

To Set Up the Language Bar, Writing Pad, and Write Anywhere

If you have a handwriting recognition engine installed, you should have the Language bar, Writing Pad, and Write Anywhere already set up. The easy way to tell is to open Outlook and look for a small toolbar, either floating in the upper right-hand corner of the screen or perhaps docked in the Windows Taskbar. Figure 20-2 shows the Language bar docked in the Windows Taskbar. The Language bar can be docked here or float freely on the screen.

When you look at the preceding illustration, you can see that the Language bar has several icons on it. Which icons appear will depend on the language-specific features you have selected, as well as the active application. The rightmost icon in Figure 20-2 is the Write Anywhere icon. Click this, and you can write anywhere on the screen.

To the left of the Write Anywhere icon is the Handwriting icon. This icon appears when you have multiple handwriting-related text services installed and active. Click it to see a list of the available handwriting features. In this instance, the Writing Pad icon appears in this list, so I know that the Language bar, Writing Pad, and Write Anywhere are all available for use.

If you don't see the Language bar, or the Language bar doesn't include the Writing Pad and Write Anywhere, you need to set them up.

This procedure assumes that you already have the handwriting recognition engine installed.

1. In the Windows Control Panel, click the Regional And Language Options icon. This opens the Regional And Language Options dialog box.

The Regional And Language Options icon will appear directly in the Control Panel if your Control Panel is set for Classic view, or it will be in the Date, Time, Language, and Regional Options category if your Control Panel is set for Category view.

2. On the Language tab of the Regional And Language Options dialog box, click Details. This opens the Text Services And Input Languages dialog box shown in Figure 20-2.

3. Look at the list in the Installed Services section of the Settings tab. Under either the Advanced Text Services heading or the Handwriting Recognition heading (depending on which version of Windows you are running), you

FIGURE 20-2   Use the Text Services and Input Languages dialog box to ensure that handwriting recognition features are installed and that the Language bar is active.

20

FIGURE 20-3   Use the Add Input Language dialog box to add handwriting-related text services.

should see Write Anywhere, the Writing Pad, and perhaps some other handwriting-related text services.

4. If Write Anywhere and Writing Pad do not appear in the Installed Services list, select Advanced Text Services or Handwriting Recognition, then click Add. This opens an Add Input Language dialog box similar to the one in Figure 20-3.

5. Depending on the version of Windows you are running, either the Handwriting Recognition check box or the More Text Services check box will be active. Select the check box to activate the list of text services that appears directly below it.

6. Select the service you want to add, then click OK to activate it.

7. Repeat steps 4–6 as necessary until all the services you want to add are activated.

To Make the Language Bar Appear

It's possible that even with everything set up properly, the Language bar still doesn't appear. It is possible to set the Language bar to not appear on the desktop. Follow these steps to ensure that the Language bar is configured to appear:

1. Navigate to the Text Services And Input Languages dialog box (follow steps 1 and 2 of the preceding procedure).

2. In the Preferences section of the Settings tab, click Language Bar. This opens the Language Bar Settings dialog box shown in the illustration. Use this dialog box to ensure that the Language bar is visible when active.

3. Select the Show The Language Bar On The Desktop check box. This will cause the Language bar to appear at appropriate times.

Apply Handwriting Recognition with the Writing Pad

The Writing Pad (see Figure 20-4) provides a defined space for you to enter handwriting. To perform handwriting recognition using the Writing Pad, make sure the Text button is set (it looks like the key for the letter *T* on your keyboard), then write on the line in the open space on the left side of the Writing Pad.

A moment after you stop writing, the handwriting recognition engine converts your handwritten text into typed text and inserts it into the active Outlook item (or any Office System document) at the location of the cursor.

The Writing Pad includes a toolbar with a number of special icons that help you enter and correct text. By default, this toolbar appears on the right side of the Writing Pad and allows you to do things like insert a tab or a space. Other icons help you to correct or erase text you just entered, and you can expand the Writing Pad (by clicking the ">>" symbol) to get access to cursor control buttons, a Drawing Pad (if installed), and an on-screen keyboard.

On the left side of the Drawing Pad title bar is a down arrow. Click that to open a menu of additional handwriting tools and options. The options include the ability to change the width and color of the lines you draw when writing, as well as adjusting some handwriting recognition parameters and configuring the toolbar.

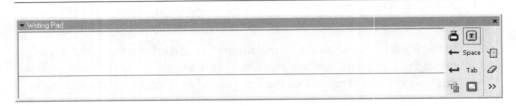

FIGURE 20-4   The Writing Pad provides a defined space for you to enter handwriting.

Apply Handwriting Recognition with Write Anywhere

To use Write Anywhere, you click the Write Anywhere icon in the Writing Pad, or on the Language bar. What you see on the screen is the Writing Pad toolbar that contains all the control buttons. However, when Write Anywhere is active, you can use your writing tool to literally write anywhere on the screen. Whatever you write is captured and passed through the handwriting recognition engine, converted to typed text, and entered at the text insertion point just as if you were working in the Writing Pad. Beware, though. Some people find the Write Anywhere feature disconcerting, as when you use it, you are writing over whatever is on the screen, as you can see in Figure 20-5.

If you don't mind the fact that it looks as if you're writing all over everything on your Windows desktop, Write Anywhere offers you more space and freedom to write than does the Writing Pad.

Use Ink with Outlook

Using ink with Outlook is very much like using handwriting recognition. You work with either the Writing Pad or Write Anywhere, and you have the same options and icons to work with. The difference is that when you want to use ink, you must select the Ink icon, which looks like a little jar of ink and appears in the upper-left corner of either feature's toolbar.

Once you are in ink mode, everything you write on the screen gets converted to an ink object and scaled to fit the size of the text at the cursor location. You can move ink objects around, as well as cut and paste them. Even better, you can resize

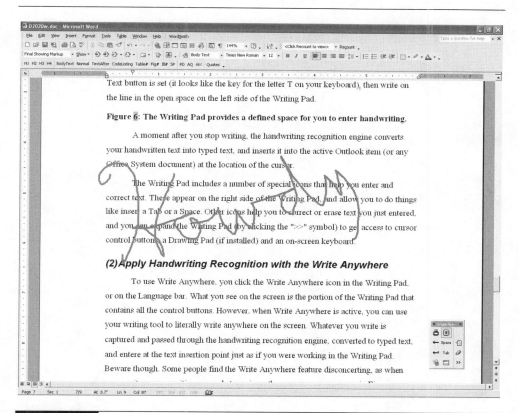

FIGURE 20-5 When you use Write Anywhere, you can literally write anywhere on the screen.

them; make the writing within them bold, or italic, or underlined; change the ink color; and in most ways treat them as normal typed text. You can even search for words that are written in ink, because Windows invisibly converts the ink to typed text in the background.

Chapter 21

Speak to Outlook

How to…

■ Understand How Speech Recognition Works with Outlook

■ Use Speech Recognition with Outlook

Chapter 20 covered handwritten input and handwriting recognition, one of the alternative ways to enter information and commands into your computer. This chapter covers speech recognition, another increasingly popular way to interact with your computer. Recent versions of Microsoft Windows (including Windows XP) have optional features that provide basic speech recognition.

Understand How Speech Recognition Works with Outlook

Using speech recognition with Outlook involves no special Outlook features or capabilities related to speech recognition. You use speech recognition in Outlook the same way you would use it in any other Office System application: you speak, it translates what you said into typed text, then inserts it into the active document or item at the text insertion point.

So if you are already using the Windows speech recognition system with other Office System applications, you already know all you need to know to use it with Outlook. Unless you would like a review of how to use speech recognition in general, you can skip most of this chapter. I do, however, suggest that you read the How To and Did You Know? boxes before moving along.

If you aren't already familiar with using the Windows speech recognition system, this chapter will show you how to install it, train it, and use it, with an emphasis on doing so in Outlook. One thing to note is that talking to a computer is a little different than talking to a person. See the "Did You Know How to Speak to a Computer?" box for some tips on how to speak in a way that is most likely to be understood by your computer.

Use Speech Recognition with Outlook

The speech recognition system in Windows is a language-specific piece of software that can convert spoken input into typed text. Windows XP and later versions come with the ability to recognize several languages, including: Simplified Chinese,

Did you know?

How to Speak to a Computer?

You've known how to speak to other people for a long time now, but did you know how to speak to a computer? No computer is as good at understanding speech as a typical person is: you can shout, whisper, slur your words, talk fast, or talk slow, and most people will understand what you say. You need to speak more consistently for your computer to understand you. Speak in a level tone, not too loud, not too soft, not too fast, and not too slow. Don't pause between words, either.

Traditional Chinese, English, and Japanese. By default, when you install the Windows Speech Recognition system, it is configured to work with the same language the rest of the operating system is working with.

Once you have the speech recognition system installed and active, you can speak to your computer using a high-quality headset microphone (see the Getting Started with Speech Recognition topic in the Outlook help system for more information on system requirements). You control the speech recognition system through the *Language bar,* a toolbar of language-related features that appears when you are working in an application that supports language-related features.

> **NOTE**   *Some computers come with a speech recognition system preinstalled and activated. See the "How to Determine if a Speech Recognition System Is Installed" box for tips on how to find out if this is the case on your computer.*

Speech recognition works in two modes: Dictation and Voice Command. In Dictation mode, whatever you say gets translated into typed text and inserted into the current Outlook item or other document. This mode is what most people think of when they think of speech recognition.

In Voice Command mode, the speech recognition system interprets what you speak as commands. For example, if you're working in an e-mail message in Voice Command mode and you say "Format," the Format menu for the message opens. Or if you have some text selected in a message and you say "Bold," Outlook treats that the same as if you clicked the Bold button on the Formatting toolbar, and makes the selected text bold.

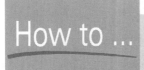

Determine if a Speech Recognition System Is Installed

If your computer already has a speech recognition system installed, you won't need to install one yourself. Here are some ways you can figure out if a system is already installed:

■ Look for the Language bar. If you're working in Outlook or another Office System application, and a little toolbar (the Language bar) appears on the screen with buttons for the Microphone and Tools, a speech recognition system is installed and active.

■ Check the Text Services settings. In the Regional And Language Options section of the Control Panel, open the Language tab. Under Text Services And Input Languages, click Details. In the Text Services And Input Languages dialog box that appears, look under Installed Services. If Speech Recognition appears, a speech recognition system is installed and active.

If a speech recognition system is installed and active, but you still don't see the Language bar, click Language Bar in the Preferences area of the Text Services And Input Languages dialog box. In the Language Bar Settings dialog box that appears, select Show The Language Bar On The Desktop to make the bar visible.

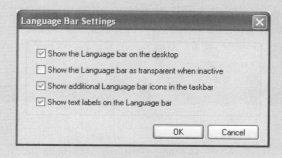

Install Speech Recognition

If the speech recognition system isn't already installed, you will need to do it yourself. This isn't hard and should take only a few minutes. Follow these instructions to install the Windows Speech Recognition system.

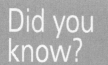

You Can Buy Third-Party Speech Recognition Software?

The speech recognition system that is part of Windows XP is good, but there are more capable systems that you can use if you become serious about using speech recognition. Scansoft, Inc., sells a product called Dragon NaturallySpeaking, and IBM sells one called ViaVoice. I've used both and find that they provide somewhat better recognition accuracy than does the speech recognition system that comes with Windows.

You can get more information about Dragon NaturallySpeaking at http://www.scansoft.com/naturallyspeaking/ and about ViaVoice at http://www-3.ibm.com/software/speech/.

Install Windows Speech Recognition

The Windows speech recognition system is most frequently installed from Microsoft Office Word. However, since we're interested in Outlook here, the following steps show you how to do a custom installation that doesn't require you to use Word:

1. Click Start | Control Panel, then double-click the Add Or Remove Programs icon (if the Control Panel is working in Classic view) or single-click the Add Or Remove Programs icon (if the Control Panel is working in Category view). This opens the Add Or Remove Programs dialog box shown here.

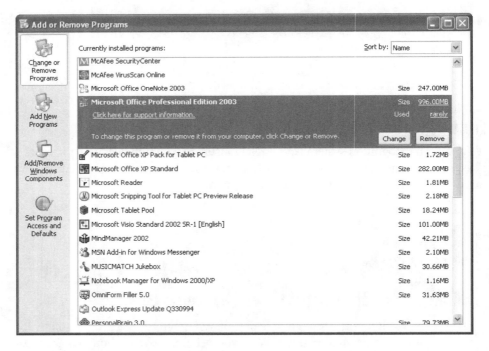

2. Click Change Or Remove Programs if it is not already selected, then select Office 2003 (the exact form of the name will vary depending on the version of Office 2003 you have selected), then click Change. This activates the Windows Installer.

3. In the Microsoft Office 2003 Setup Wizard that appears, select Add Or Remove Features, then click Next. This opens the Custom Setup screen.

4. In the Custom Setup screen shown in the following illustration, select the Choose Advanced Customization Of Applications check box, then click Next.

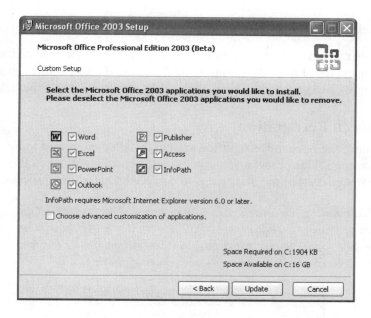

5. In the Advanced Customization dialog box shown in the illustration, in the Choose Update Options For Applications And Tools list, click the plus sign (+) next to Office Shared Features. The Advanced Configuration screen is where you actually tell Windows to install the speech recognition system.

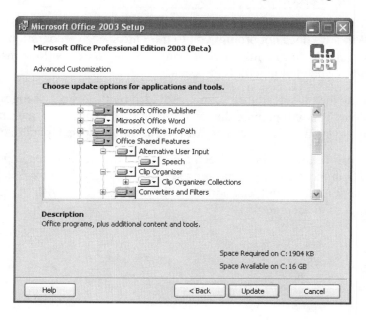

6. Click the plus sign next to Alternative User Input, then click Speech.

7. In the menu that appears when you click Speech, select one of the installation options (Run From My Computer is the option I chose, although any of them will work for you), then click Update to complete the installation.

Train Speech Recognition

Once you have the Speech Recognition system installed, you need to train it for best performance. This process, sometimes called enrollment, takes about 10–15 minutes to complete. Follow these steps to complete the training process:

 If you don't complete the training process when you install speech recognition, you should do so before actually using the system for the first time. If you have not trained the system and you try to use it, a dialog box appears, offering you the option to do so right then.

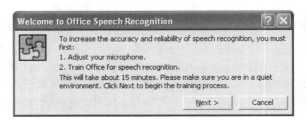

1. If Windows does not prompt you to train the speech recognition system, you can initiate training on your own by going to the Outlook main window and clicking Tools | Speech.

2. Follow the on-screen instructions provided by the speech recognition system. You will prepare the microphone first, then read some sample text to the system so that it can adjust to your unique speech patterns.

3. You can further improve speech recognition accuracy by reading more than one document during the training session. You can also return to training at some other time and read additional documents if you wish to improve recognition accuracy.

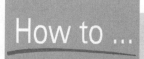 **Improve Speech Recognition Accuracy**

Training the speech recognition system is the primary way to improve recognition accuracy. In general, the more time you put into training the system, the better its recognition accuracy will be. Even so, there are several other things you can do to improve speech recognition accuracy. Here are some of the best ideas:

- Speak in complete phrases or sentences instead of pronouncing each syllable or word separately. Several years ago, speech recognition systems required you to pronounce one word at a time, with a small pause between words. The Windows speech recognition system expects you to speak in full phrases or sentences. Thanks to its understanding of the way people speak and its use of context, the system provides better recognition when you speak in full phrases or sentences. And don't worry if your words don't appear right away. Keep talking—the computer will eventually finish processing what you've already said and your words will appear on the screen.

- Place the microphone in the same location relative to your mouth every time you use speech recognition. The exact position of the microphone can have a significant effect on the accuracy of speech recognition. Try to place the microphone in exactly the same location as it was when you trained the system. And if you move the microphone away from your mouth for any reason, don't forget to put it back in place before resuming dictation.

- Try to work in a quiet place, or at least one that has a consistent level of noise. If your work environment has a variable level of noise, or if you work in multiple different environments, try creating a speech recognition profile for each environment.

Make the Language Bar Appear

It's possible that even with everything set up properly, the Language bar still doesn't appear. Check for the Language bar floating on the screen somewhere, as well as for it to be docked in the Windows Taskbar. It is possible to set the Language bar to not appear on the desktop. Follow these steps to ensure that the Language bar is configured to appear:

1. Navigate to the Text Services And Input Languages dialog box (follow steps 1 and 2 of the previous procedure).

2. In the Preferences section of the Settings tab, click Language Bar. This opens the Language Bar Settings dialog box shown here. Use this dialog box to ensure that the Language bar is visible when active.

3. Select the Show The Language Bar On The Desktop check box. This will cause the Language bar to appear at appropriate times.

Turn on the Microphone

With the Windows Speech Recognition system installed and trained, and the Language bar visible, you're now ready to start working with speech recognition. The first step is to turn on the microphone. You do this by clicking the microphone icon on the Language bar. The Microphone icon looks exactly like a microphone and will likely be labeled as such, as you can see in the following illustration. Click the Microphone icon on the Language bar to turn speech recognition on or off.

Click the Microphone icon on the Language bar to turn speech recognition on or off.

Work in Dictation Mode

21

When the microphone is turned on, additional icons appear on the Language bar. These icons allow you to select Dictation mode or Voice Command mode. If it is not already selected, click the Dictation icon to put the Speech Recognition system into Dictation mode.

With the cursor at the point in an Outlook item where you wish to insert text, begin speaking. While you speak, an unusual-looking dotted underline may appear at the text insertion point. This is nothing to be concerned about. It is merely an indication that the Speech Recognition system is still processing the words you spoke. The dotted lines will disappear and your words appear when the processing is done.

> **CAUTION**   *If the dotted underline that indicates your speech is being recognized is visible on the screen, don't move the mouse or use the keyboard until it disappears. Using the mouse or keyboard interrupts the speech recognition process and prevents your words from being recognized.*

Dictating to the computer will take a little getting used to. For one thing, you need to say the names of any punctuation marks you want to insert. For another, if you are like me, you'll likely find yourself talking to the computer before you turn on the microphone. Or you may forget to turn off the microphone when you aren't talking to the computer, and find that you've accidentally dictated part of a conversation with your friend into that e-mail you're sending to the CEO!

When you are using speech recognition, the Language bar can display helpful messages. For example, if your voice is too low, a message saying "Too soft" may appear in the Language bar. If you are having problems with speech recognition, these messages may hold the solution to the problem.

> **NOTE**   *If you open a help window, or a message appears on the screen while you are using speech recognition, you will need to click in the Outlook window to resume using speech recognition.*

Remember that when you are dictating, you cannot use your voice for things like formatting or giving other commands to Outlook. To do that, you need to switch to Voice Command mode, speak your command, then switch back to Dictation mode. You can switch modes with your voice (switching to Voice Command mode is one of the only commands you can give while in Dictation mode). To switch modes with your voice, pause for a moment, then say "dictation" to switch to Dictation mode, or "voice command" to switch to Voice Command mode.

 *You can reduce the number of times you switch between Dictation mode and Voice Command mode by dictating all your text first, then coming back to it and doing all the editing and formatting at once.*

Correct Speech Recognition Errors

While the Windows Speech Recognition system is vastly more capable than systems available even a few years ago, it is certainly not perfect. No speech recognition system is. This means that you will need to correct recognition errors. There are three ways to do this:

To Dictate Over Recognition Errors

Follow these steps to dictate over speech recognition errors:

1. Use the mouse or keyboard to select the word that was incorrectly recognized. For better results, select one or two words before and after the misrecognized word too.

2. Say the words that you selected. Make sure you pronounce the misrecognized word properly, not the way it appears on the screen.

3. If the selected words are now correct, you're done. If not, repeat steps 1 and 2, or try another correction method.

To Spell Over Recognition Errors

Follow these steps to spell over speech recognition errors:

1. Using the mouse or keyboard, select the misrecognized word.

2. In Dictation mode, pause, then say "spelling mode."

3. Pause again, then spell the word correctly by saying the letters one by one.

To Retype Recognition Errors

Follow these steps to retype speech recognition errors:

1. Using the mouse or keyboard, select the misrecognized word.

2. Type the correct spelling using the keyboard.

Add Words to the Speech Recognition Dictionary

One additional way you can improve speech recognition accuracy is to add words to the speech recognition dictionary. Follow these steps to add a word to the dictionary:

1. On the Language bar, click Speech Tools.

2. In the Speech Tools menu that appears, click Add/Delete Words. This opens the Add/Delete Word(s) dialog box shown in Figure 21-1.

3. Type the word you want to add in the Word box.

4. Click Record Pronunciation, then say the word to add it to the dictionary. You may need to repeat this step several times before the system accepts the word and adds it to the dictionary.

Work in Voice Command Mode

Working in Voice Command mode is quite different than working in Dictation mode. In Voice Command mode, the words you speak are interpreted as Outlook

FIGURE 21-1   Use this dialog box to add words to (or delete them from) the speech recognition dictionary.

and Windows commands as if you had clicked buttons or menu options on the screen. You can select menu items and buttons on menus, toolbars, dialog boxes, and the task pane simply by speaking the name of the item. Just pause slightly then say the name of the item. If you're not sure what name to use for a particular item, hover the mouse pointer over it to see the tool tip, which shows the name of the item.

Don't forget to turn off the microphone when you're not actively talking to your computer. If you don't, it could be very inconvenient if you happen to say something that the computer interprets as an Outlook or Windows command.

Create and Use Additional Speech Recognition User Profiles

A *speech recognition user profile* is a file that contains information about how to recognize what a user says during speech recognition. In most cases, you don't need to worry about these, as the Speech Recognition system creates a profile automatically when you train it. However, if more than one person is going to use speech recognition on your computer, or if you use speech recognition in

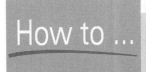 **Make Best Use of Speech Recognition in Outlook**

Between Dictation mode and Voice Command mode, you could theoretically control Outlook with just your voice. However, that isn't really practical in most cases. Unless you need to work exclusively with speech recognition for some reason, you will get the best results if you use a combination of the keyboard, mouse, and speech recognition.

Dictating can be a great way to get words down on paper, and the ability to speak commands instead of clicking them can come in real handy. But navigating to a particular point in a lengthy passage of text is hard with speech, but a snap with the mouse. The keyboard is great for correcting misrecognized words and entering unusual words, symbols, or other text elements that speech recognition is likely to have trouble handling.

environments that have significantly different noise levels, you can create additional speech recognition user profiles for these additional users or environments.

To create a new speech recognition user profile, follow these instructions:

1. Click Start | Control Panel to open the Control Panel.

2. Double-click Speech (if the Control Panel is working in Classic view) or single-click Sounds, Speech, And Audio Devices, then Speech (if the Control Panel is working in Category view). This opens the Speech Properties dialog box shown in Figure 21-2.

3. If it is not already visible, click the Speech Recognition tab.

4. In the Recognition Profiles section of the Speech Recognition tab, click New to open the Profile Wizard.

FIGURE 21-2 Use this dialog box to select the speech recognition profile you want to use.

5. Follow the instructions provided by the wizard to create the new speech recognition user profile.

To choose which profile to use during a speech recognition session, follow these instructions:

1. On the Language bar, click Tools. The Tools menu appears.

2. Point to the Current User option in this menu, then select the profile you want to use.

Chapter 22

Work Smarter with Business Contact Manager

How to...

■ Understand the Reasons for Business Contact Manager

■ Install Business Contact Manager

■ Use Outlook with Business Contact Manager

Business Contact Manager is an Outlook add-in program designed for sales professionals and owners of small businesses who need to work with customers or manage sales opportunities. This chapter provides a basic introduction to Outlook with Business Contact Manager. It is not meant to be a product tutorial or a guide to the ways that you can use Outlook with Business Contact Manager to improve your customer service or increase your sales efficiency. Instead, this chapter gives you the overview you need to decide whether Outlook with Business Contact Manager is worth further investigation.

Understand the Reasons for Business Contact Manager

Organizing and managing customer information is a key to delivering the best service and retaining customers. Tracking sales leads and opportunities allows users to efficiently market their products and target the best sales opportunities.

Many large organizations handle such tasks with complex and expensive multiuser customer relationship management (CRM) applications that are inappropriate for individuals or small companies. But without an integrated solution, the information needed to work with customers or manage sales opportunities tends to be scattered and hard to work with. This is where Outlook with Business Contact Manager comes in.

By adding tools for managing sales opportunities, accounts, and individual contacts into Outlook, Business Contact Manager allows you to find all your relevant information in one place. And because that one place is Outlook 2003, you don't need to learn a separate application for doing the job.

In addition to being a single familiar application in which to manage customer and sales information, Outlook with Business Contact Manager gives you:

■ Easy access to e-mail and print marketing tools

■ Flexible reporting tools that integrate with Outlook and Excel

- The ability to link electronic documents and Outlook items, as well as scanned documents, to accounts

- Activity history for any account, sales opportunity, or business contact

While Outlook with Business Contact Manager can't match the flexibility and power of full-scale CRM applications, it may well be exactly what you need for your own small business or sales efforts.

Install Business Contact Manager

Since Outlook with Business Contact Manager is a tool for individual sales professionals or small business owners, chances are good that you'll need to install it yourself. Fortunately, this isn't hard. Follow these steps to install Business Contact Manager on your computer:

> TIP   *If the Outlook menu contains a Business Tools option, Business Contact Manager is already installed on your computer. You can skip ahead to the section titled "Use Outlook with Business Contact Manager."*

1. Close Outlook 2003.

2. Run the Outlook with Business Contact Manager Setup program. The Setup program may ask permission to install something called .NET Framework. Unless you are certain that this is already installed on your computer, allow the Setup program to install .NET Framework.

3. Reboot your computer if requested.

4. The Setup program now runs the Outlook with Business Contact Manager installer.

5. Once the Outlook with Business Contact Manager installer completes its work, restart Outlook 2003.

6. Business Contact Manager displays the dialog box shown in Figure 22-1, asking if you would like to associate Business Contact Manager with the current Outlook user profile. If you are signing on with the user account you will use to manage customers and sales, click Yes.

FIGURE 22-1 To use Business Contact Manager, you must associate it with your Outlook user account.

7. Outlook with Business Contact Manager displays a dialog box showing the status of the database it is creating to store your business contacts, accounts, and sales opportunities.

8. Once Outlook with Business Contact Manager finishes creating its database, Outlook finishes its startup routine. Assuming the installation went smoothly, when Outlook is in Mail view, you should see the new items shown in Figure 22-2.

Use Outlook with Business Contact Manager

For normal Outlook functions, using Outlook with Business Contact Manager is no different than before. It's only when you make use of the new features like the Business Tools menu that differences appear.

NOTE *See the "Did You Know the Business Tools Menu Simplifies Your Life?" box for more on this powerful way to access Business Contact Manager features.*

New menu   New toolbar

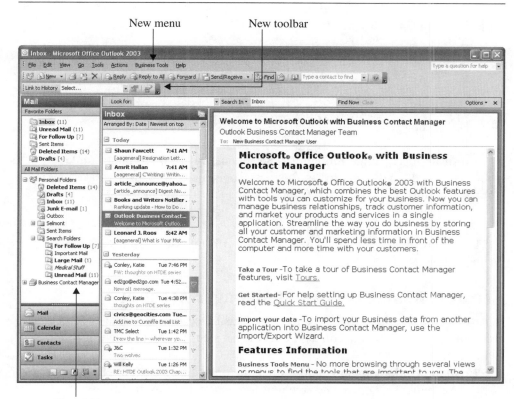

New folders

FIGURE 22-2   Outlook with Business Contact Manager installs several new user interface elements.

The Business Tools Menu Simplifies Your Life?

The Business Tools menu is a central place to gain access to the key Business Contact Manager tools:

- ■ Accounts

- ■ Business Contacts

- Opportunities
- Reports
- Product List
- Business Services
- And more

Instead of searching through various menus and views trying to find the tool you need, go directly to the Business Tools menu whenever you're looking for something on the Business Contact Manager side of Outlook.

The following sections show you how to perform basic Business Contact Manager tasks:

Create a Business Contact Manager Account

Your first step should probably be to create Business Contact Manager accounts for your major customer accounts. Follow these steps to create a new account:

1. In the Outlook main window, click the down arrow next to New, then click Account. This opens the Account form shown in Figure 22-3.

2. Fill in any available account information.

3. Click Save And Close to create the account.

Create a Business Contact

Business Contacts are the contacts you work with at your accounts. You can create a Business Contact from scratch by filling out a form, or by copying a contact from an existing Outlook folder. This makes it easy to transition contacts into Business Contact Manager.

Create a Business Contact from Scratch

To create a Business Contact from scratch, follow these instructions:

1. In the Outlook main window, click the down arrow next to New, then click Business Contact. This opens the Business Contact form shown in Figure 22-4.

2. Enter any available information on the contact into the form.

3. Click Save And Close to create the business contact.

Create a Business Contact from an Existing Outlook Contact

To create a Business Contact from an existing Outlook contact, follow these instructions:

If you follow this procedure, the contact will be moved to the Business Contacts folder you select, and removed from your Outlook Contacts folder.

1. Go to the Contacts view.

2. Select the contact you want to copy into a business contact and drag it to the appropriate Business Contacts folder in the My Contacts section of the Navigation pane.

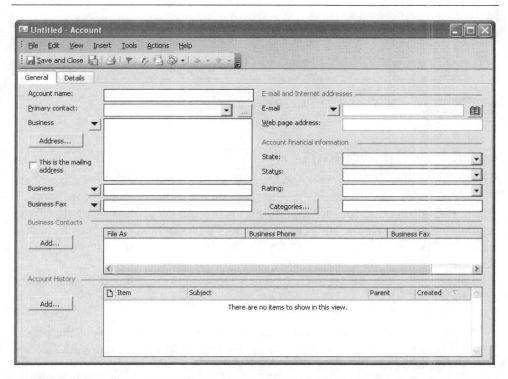

FIGURE 22-3   Fill in this form to create a new Business Contact Manager account.

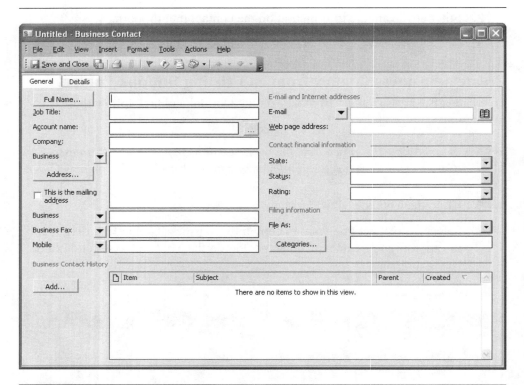

FIGURE 22-4   Fill in this form to create a new Business Contact.

Create an Opportunity

An *Opportunity* is a way to track the progress of a sale through the sales cycle. When you create an Opportunity record, you can link it to Account records and Business Contact records. The Opportunity record can keep a history of all activity related to the Opportunity, and can even contain a product list (see "How to Import a Product List into an Opportunity" for details) that can help you determine the revenue potential of the Opportunity.

Follow these instructions to create a new Opportunity and link it to an Account or a Business Contact:

1. In the Outlook main window, click the down arrow next to New, then click Opportunity. This opens the Opportunity form shown in Figure 22-5.

How to ... Import a Product List into an Opportunity

Follow these steps to import an entire product list into an Opportunity:

1. In the Outlook main window, click Business Tools | Opportunities.

2. In the Opportunities view, double-click the Opportunity you want to add the Product list to.

3. In the Products section of the Opportunity form, click Add. This opens the Add/Edit Product Entry dialog box.

4. In the Add/Edit Product Entry dialog box, click Product List. This opens the Edit Master Product List dialog box.

5. In the Edit Master Product List dialog box, click Import. This activates the Products Import Wizard.

6. Follow the instructions provided by the wizard to import the Product List.

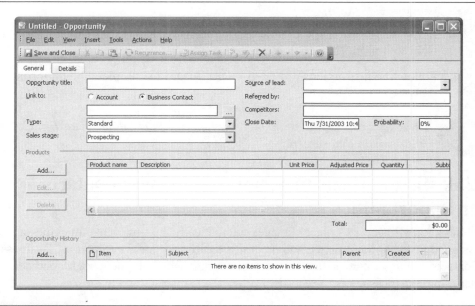

FIGURE 22-5   Create a new Opportunity and track your progress through the sales process using this form.

2. Fill in the basic information about the Opportunity.

3. In the Link To section of the form, select Account to link the Opportunity to an Account, or Business Contact to link it to a Business Contact. Also fill in the Type and Sales Stage fields by selecting the correct options from the pull-down lists.

4. Import a Product List into the Opportunity if appropriate.

5. Click Save And Close to create the new Opportunity.

Import Business Data

If you already have your business data stored in another application, you can probably import it into Outlook with Business Contact Manager instead of manually reentering it. Outlook with Business Contact Manager can import files from Act!, Quickbooks, Excel, Access, and many other applications. Follow these instructions to import your business data from another application:

1. In the main Outlook window, click File | Import and Export, then Business Contact Manager. This starts the Business Data Import/Export Wizard shown in Figure 22-6.

2. Click Import A File, then Next.

3. In the Select The Type Of File To Import list, select the type of file you want to import, then click Next.

4. Follow the instructions provided by the wizard to complete the importing process.

If you are unsure what to do on a particular screen of the wizard, click the Help icon on that screen.

Link History Items to Accounts, Business Contacts, or Opportunities

Outlook with Business Contact Manager automatically links relevant e-mail messages, assigned tasks, appointments, and meetings to the appropriate Accounts, Business Contacts, or Opportunities. In addition, you can manually link phone logs, documents, tasks, and business notes to records. Follow these instructions to do so:

1. In the Business Tools menu, click Accounts, Business Contacts, or Opportunities to open the relevant view.

2. Double-click the Account, Business Contact, or Opportunity you want to add a new History item to.

3. In the History section of the Account, Business Contact, or Opportunity, click Add. In the menu that appears, select the type of item you wish to add to the History.

4. When you're done adding items to the History, click Save And Close.

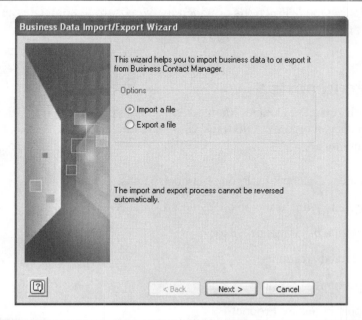

FIGURE 22-6 The Business Data Import/Export Wizard helps you import business data from other applications.

 **Export Business Data**

While you will most likely be importing business data into Outlook with Business Contact Manager, you can also export data for use in another copy of Outlook with Business Contact Manager, or for use in another application. Follow these steps if you need to export data from Outlook with Business Contact Manager:

1. In the main Outlook window, click File | Import And Export, then Business Contact Manager. This starts the Business Data Import/ Export Wizard.

2. Click Export A File, then Next.

3. Select the type of file you want to export data to. If you want to export data to a Word document, select the Comma-Separated Value (.CSV) option. Click Next.

4. Follow the instructions provided by the wizard to complete the importing process.

Generate Reports

Outlook with Business Contact Manager can generate nearly two dozen kinds of reports to help you organize and track your sales and activities. Some of the types you can generate are:

- Business Contacts by Phone Number, Status, or Rating
- Accounts with Associated Business Contacts
- Accounts by Status or History
- Neglected Accounts
- Opportunity Forecast
- Opportunities by Product
- Past Due Opportunities

■ Business Task List

■ Source of Leads

To generate a report, follow these instructions:

1. In the main Outlook window, click Business Tools | Reports.

2. In the menu that appears, select one of the broad categories of reports: Business Contacts, Accounts, Opportunities, or Other.

3. Select the specific report you want from the menu that appears.

Figure 22-7 shows a simple Business Contacts by Status report generated in this manner. The exact form of the reports you generate will of course vary

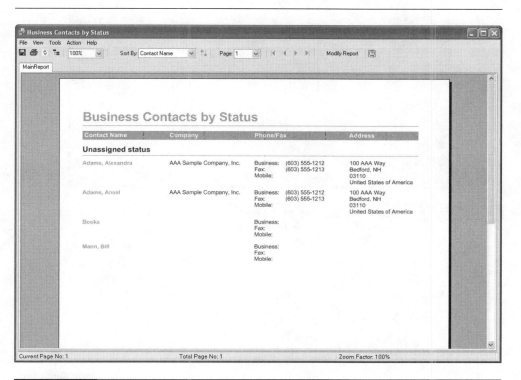

FIGURE 22-7 A simple report generated by Outlook with Business Contact Manager

depending on their content. They will also vary based on how you customize them. As Figure 22-7 shows, a report can be customized by sorting the items in it.

You can also click Modify Report to open the Modify Report dialog box shown in Figure 22-8. Using this dialog box, you can make much more extensive changes to the report, with the exact possibilities depending on the type of report.

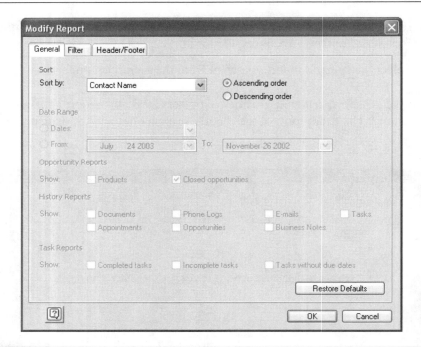

FIGURE 22-8   Use the Modify Report dialog box to make more extensive changes to the reports you generate.

Chapter 23

Work with Exchange Server and Windows SharePoint Team Services

How to…

- Use Outlook with Exchange Server
- Use Outlook with Windows SharePoint Team Services

Throughout this book, we've looked at Outlook primarily as a stand-alone application tapping external services like mail servers, news readers, and instant messaging programs. But especially in a corporate environment, Outlook becomes even more powerful when coupled with Microsoft Exchange Server and Windows SharePoint Team Services.

Microsoft Exchange is a corporate messaging and collaboration server. It helps businesses communicate more efficiently by providing consolidated, reliable, manageable, and secure e-mail services as well as hosting public folders and Outlook private folders.

Collaboration and information sharing are a big part of the future of the Microsoft Office System. Windows SharePoint Team Services provide a central place to access, store, manage, and share information. With Windows SharePoint Team Services, you can create team web sites that serve as the central storage and collaboration area for team resources. With the appropriate permissions, team members can create additional pages within the team site, such as Document and Picture Libraries, lists for Contacts and Tasks, even Discussion Boards, online Surveys, and Web Pages. With these tools, the team can build a site that is customized for its needs, providing access to and storage for only the resources the team needs.

NOTE   *There is also a SharePoint Portal Server, which enables enterprises to manage their own SharePoint Team Services sites. In this book, we're concentrating on SharePoint Team Services, as that is the SharePoint service that directly interacts with Outlook.*

Use Outlook with Exchange Server

Using Outlook with Microsoft Exchange Server is in most ways the same as using it as a stand-alone application. Here are some of the differences you'll notice:

- Setting up an e-mail account looks different and requires the help of your corporate e-mail administrator.

CAUTION   *Most e-mail administrators take a very dim view of employees making any changes or additions to their e-mail accounts and settings. I strongly recommend that you contact your e-mail administrator before trying to set up an e-mail account on an Exchange Server.*

■ You may have access to a set of *Exchange public folders.* These folders are like your personal folders in Outlook, but the public folders reside on the Exchange Server and are meant to be shared among many people.

■ You may have access to an additional address book, the Global Address List (GAL).

■ You may be able to use Cached Exchange Mode to facilitate working in Outlook when you're not connected to the Exchange Server or you have a slow or unreliable connection.

Set up an E-Mail Account on Exchange Server

Setting up an Exchange e-mail account requires that your corporate e-mail administrator create a mailbox for you on the Exchange server and then provide you with the Exchange server name and user name you need to get access to that mailbox. The e-mail administrator should also tell you whether to select or clear the Use Cached Exchange Mode option when creating the account. Once you have that information, you can follow these steps to set up your Exchange e-mail account:

TIP   *Your computer must have an active connection to the Exchange Server computer for you to successfully set up your Exchange e-mail account.*

1. Close Outlook.

2. Navigate to the Mail section of the Control Panel. Click Start | Control Panel | Mail (if your Control Panel is set for Classic view) or Start | Control Panel | User Accounts | Mail (if your Control Panel is set for Category view). This opens the Mail Setup dialog box shown here. Use the Mail Setup dialog box in the Control Panel to create a new Exchange e-mail account.

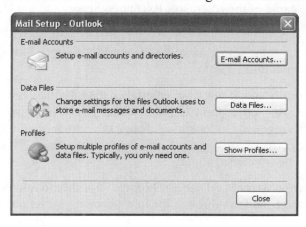

3. In the E-Mail Accounts section of the Mail Setup dialog box, click E-Mail Accounts. This starts the E-Mail Accounts Wizard.

4. Select Add A New E-Mail Account, then click Next to continue. In the Server Type screen, select the Microsoft Exchange Server check box and click Next to continue. This opens the Exchange Server Settings dialog box shown in the illustration. You need to enter the proper Exchange Server name and a user name to get access to your mailbox on the server.

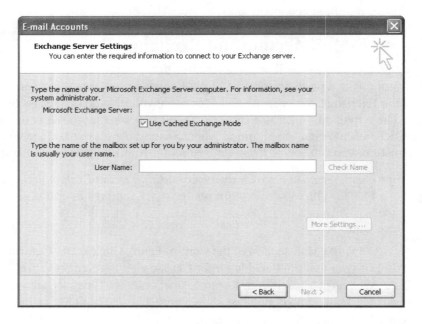

5. Enter the name of the Microsoft Exchange Server and the User Name provided by your e-mail administrator.

6. Select or clear the Use Cached Exchange Mode check box as directed by your e-mail administrator.

7. Click Check Name. If you have entered all the information correctly, Outlook underlines your User Name to indicate that you have a good connection. During this process, Outlook may change the format of your user name to match the correct form of your Exchange mailbox name. This is normal and nothing to be concerned about.

8. Complete the wizard and restart Outlook. You should now have access to the Exchange mailbox through the new account you set up.

Use Cached Exchange Mode

Cached Exchange Mode is a new feature of Outlook 2003. In Cached Exchange Mode, Outlook stores a copy of your Exchange mailbox on your computer. Outlook frequently updates the information in this copy with information taken from the mailbox on the Exchange Server so that you have current information to work with. While Cached Exchange Mode isn't a big benefit if your computer is always connected to the Exchange Server through a standard network connection, it can be extremely useful if you use a laptop or other mobile computer, or your connection to the Exchange Server is slow or intermittent (perhaps you use a dial-up modem to connect from home). See the "Did You Know How Cached Exchange Mode Can Improve Outlook?" box for more information.

Did you know?

How Cached Exchange Mode Can Improve Outlook?

Cached Exchange Mode can greatly improve your Outlook experience if you ever work offline, or if you do not have a solid, fast connection to the Exchange Server at all times. Previous versions of Outlook stored all your Exchange data in your Exchange mailbox on the Exchange Server. If you lost your connection to the Exchange Server, you were out of luck. You couldn't get to any of your data that was stored on the server, and Outlook often crashed in the attempt to reach it.

As you read earlier in this chapter, Cached Exchange Mode involves storing a copy of your Exchange mailbox on your computer, and frequently updating that mailbox to ensure that you have the latest data to work on. Outlook works with the data in the cache, instead of getting it directly from the Exchange Server. This way, if you lose your connection to the Exchange Server when you're using Cached Exchange Mode, you see little difference. You won't be able to send e-mail until you have a connection again, and you won't receive any messages or meeting notices or anything else, but at least you'll be able to work with the Outlook items that were available at the instant you lost the connection.

But Cached Exchange Mode does more than that to improve Outlook performance. Outlook can automatically determine the speed of its connection to the Exchange Server. It uses that information to decide what information to update in the local copy of your mailbox and the copy on the Exchange Server. If you have a fast connection to the server, Outlook updates entire items. If you have a slow connection to the server, Outlook may update only headers.

If you open an item that consists only of the header, Outlook can then download the rest of the item from the Exchange Server (assuming you have a connection at the time). This kind of optimization allows Outlook to make efficient use of the available connection to the Exchange Server, while still providing you with access to your Outlook items.

If you have no connection to the Exchange Server, you can still read and reply to messages, create new items, delete old ones, and so on. What happens when you have a connection again is that Outlook synchronizes the data in your computer's copy of the mailbox with the data in Exchange's copy of the mailbox. This resolves any discrepancies between the two mailboxes. Outlook does this synchronization in the background, and you can continue working while synchronization is taking place.

Your e-mail administrator will need to set up your account to work in Cached Exchange Mode. If this was not done before you created your Exchange e-mail account, you'll need to turn on Cached Exchange Mode yourself. Once Cached Exchange Mode is set up, the next time you have a connection to the Exchange Server, Outlook will download a copy of your Exchange mailbox to your computer.

 The "How to Turn on Cached Exchange Mode in Outlook" box tells how to do this if you need to do so after creating your Exchange e-mail account.

Once Cached Exchange Mode is set up properly, it should be totally transparent to you when you're connected to the same network as the Exchange Server. When you're using a slow connection to the Exchange Server, you should find that Outlook works better than it did before you activated Cached Exchange Mode. And if you're using Outlook without any connection to the Exchange Server, the fact that you're able to work almost as well as if you were still connected should be a great improvement.

Use Outlook with Windows SharePoint Team Services

Using Outlook with Windows SharePoint Team Services depends on the availability of team web sites. These are typically set up by an administrator who then invites team members to join the team site. SharePoint team sites can also include subsites that hold information related to specific meetings.

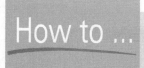

Turn On Cached Exchange Mode in Outlook

Once your administrator sets up your Exchange e-mail account to work in Cached Exchange Mode, you may need to turn on Cached Exchange Mode in Outlook. If so, follow these steps:

1. In the Outlook main window, click Tools | E-Mail Accounts, then select View Or Change Existing E-Mail Accounts. Click Next to continue.

2. In the E-Mail Accounts screen, select your Exchange e-mail account and click Change.

3. In the Microsoft Exchange Server section of the E-Mail Accounts screen, select the Use Cached Exchange Mode check box.

4. Exit Outlook and restart it for the change to take effect.

TIP   *See the "Did You Know How to Get SharePoint Team Services for Your Organization" box for information on how you can get SharePoint Team Services for your organization.*

Did you know?

How to Get SharePoint Team Services for Your Organization?

To get the benefits of Microsoft SharePoint Team Services, your organization can install Microsoft Office SharePoint Portal Server 2003. The SharePoint Portal Server makes it possible to create and manage Windows SharePoint Team Services throughout the enterprise, making them available on your corporate intranet or the Web.

You can also license the Windows SharePoint Team Services through Microsoft Certified Application Service Providers (ASPs) like eInfoSystems.net, or Apptix.net, the ASP that provided the Windows SharePoint Team Services used in this chapter.

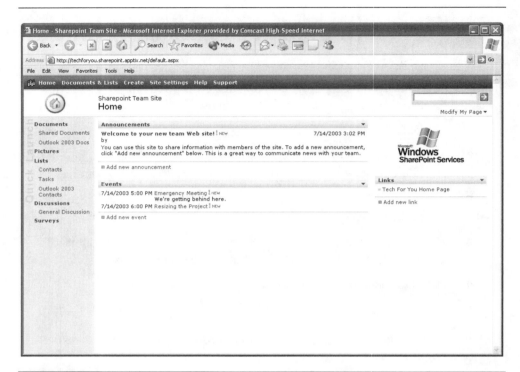

FIGURE 23-1 SharePoint provides convenient places for distributed teams to store and share information, as well as collaborate on projects.

In other words, a team site is a place where you can post announcements and event notifications; list relevant links; share documents, contacts, and task lists; even hold online discussions. Figure 23-1 shows a SharePoint Team Services team site I set up for this book. You can manage and work in a team site with nothing more than your web browser.

While all this SharePoint stuff is cool and clearly has value for teams that must collaborate in online meetings and on projects, you may be wondering what it has to do with Outlook. Well, Outlook 2003 is compatible with Windows SharePoint Team Services. This means that there is some basic level of integration between Outlook and Windows SharePoint Team Services. That integration means you can do these things:

- Link events from a team web site to the Outlook Calendar pane.

- View a team web site's Events list and an Outlook Calendar simultaneously.

- Link contacts from a team web site to the Outlook Contacts pane.

- Import contacts from your Address Book to the team web site.

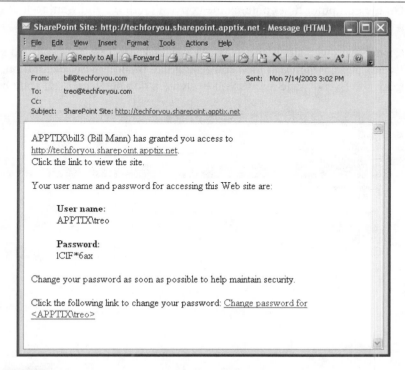

FIGURE 23-2 Windows SharePoint Team Services will send you a message that gives you all the information you need to join a site.

Join the Team Web Site

Before you can take advantage of any of the integrated features I just listed, you need to join the team web site. The most common way for that to happen is for you to receive an e-mail message like the one in Figure 23-2 that invites you to join. Messages like this one are generated automatically when the administrator of the site invites you to join.

Link Events from a Team Web Site to the Outlook Calendar Pane

You can create a new folder on your Outlook Calendar pane that shows the Events list from a team web site. To do this, follow these steps:

NOTE *The link between Outlook and the team site Events is read-only. That means you can view the team site Events, but you cannot change them.*

1. On the computer that contains the copy of Outlook you want to link to the team web page, use Internet Explorer to open the team web site.

2. On the team web site home page, click the Events link. This takes you to the Events page, which will look something like the following illustration. The team site Events page allows you to create a link between itself and Outlook.

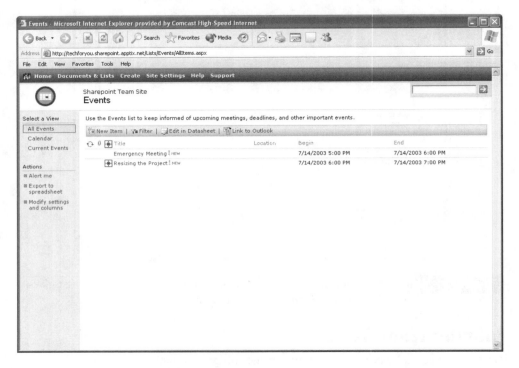

3. Click the Link To Outlook button that appears above the list of events. This opens a dialog box that notifies you that a new folder containing the team site Events list is being added to Outlook. You have the option to accept this or to stop the folder from being added.

4. If you accept the new folder, it is added to the Outlook Calendar pane, as shown here. After you create the link, the team site's Events folder appears on the Outlook Calendar pane.

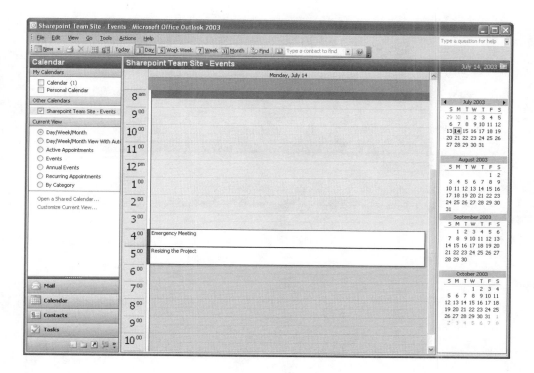

5. Click the Team Site Events folder to view the list of events.

View a Team Web Site's Events List and an Outlook Calendar Simultaneously

Once you establish a link to a team web site Event list, you can treat it just like any other Calendar on your Calendar pane (except that it is a read-only calendar). You can view it simultaneously with other Calendars by selecting the check box next to the calendar name.

Link Contacts from a Team Web Site to the Outlook Contacts Pane

You can create a new folder on your Outlook Calendar pane that shows the Events list from a team web site. To do this, follow these steps:

1. On the computer that contains the copy of Outlook you want to link to the team web page, use Internet Explorer to open the team web site.

2. On the team web site home page, click the Contacts link. This takes you to the Contacts page, which will look something like the following illustration. The team site Contacts page allows you to create a link between itself and Outlook.

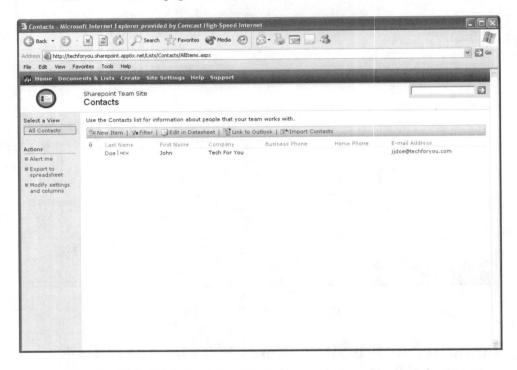

3. Click the Link To Outlook button that appears above the list of contacts. This opens a dialog box that notifies you that a new folder containing the team site Contacts list is being added to Outlook. You have the option to accept this or to stop the folder from being added.

4. If you accept the new folder, it is added to the Outlook Contacts pane, as shown in the illustration. After you create the link, the team site's Contacts folder appears on the Outlook Contacts.

5. Click the Team Site Contacts folder to view the list of contacts.

Import Contacts from Your Address Book to a Team Web Site

A link lets you view contacts that are stored in your team web site. But getting them there in the first place is another story. In most cases, the contacts you want to see in the team web site Contacts list are already stored in the Address Book of someone on the team. Windows SharePoint Team Services allow you to import those contacts to the team web site Contacts page. Follow these steps:

1. While working from a computer that has access to the Address Book containing the contacts you want to import, open the team web site Contacts page.

2. Click Import Contacts. This opens the computer's Address Book with the Select Users To Import dialog box as shown here. Select the contacts you want to import to the team web site Contacts page using this dialog box.

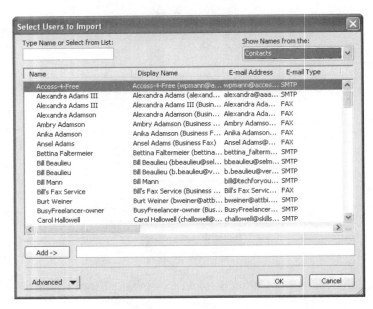

3. Select one or more Contacts, then click Add to add them to the list of Contacts that will be imported to the team web site Contacts page.

4. Click OK to import the Contacts to the team web site.

Chapter 24

Maintain Outlook for Best Performance

How to...

- Maintain Your Data Files
- Do Some General Housekeeping

This chapter describes some maintenance activities you can do to help ensure that Outlook runs quickly and efficiently while consuming a minimum of disk space. Maintaining your data files, repairing them, compacting them, and backing them up is one area where you can do some significant maintenance on your own. But if all your personal folders are stored on the corporate Microsoft Exchange server, you won't have to worry about even these aspects of maintenance.

General housekeeping activities are things that any Outlook user can do, regardless of whether you store your Personal Folders on your own computer or on the corporate server. None of them will make a major improvement in Outlook performance, but they take only a few minutes and can certainly help. Feel free to pick and choose among the activities.

Maintain Your Data Files

If you are using Outlook in the office and it is connected to a Microsoft Exchange server, your personal folders and items are likely stored on the Exchange server and are nothing you need to worry about. If, however, you're not using Exchange, all the information in your personal folders is likely stored on your hard drive, in a data file called Outlook.pst.

NOTE   *See Chapter 17 for more information on Outlook.pst.*

In this case, you should consider doing some basic maintenance on the Outlook.pst data file. Doing so will ensure that Outlook works as efficiently as possible, and help protect you against the catastrophic loss of the items stored in your personal folders. I suggest three activities to keep your Personal Folders file in top shape: repairing it when it gets corrupted, compacting it so that Outlook runs more efficiently and uses less disk space, and backing it up so that you can recover from a disaster.

Repair Your Personal Folders File

While it doesn't happen often, it is possible for Outlook.pst to become corrupted. If that happens, you can use the Inbox Repair tool to try and correct the problem. The Inbox Repair tool (Scanpst.exe) can examine Outlook.pst and make repairs to it.

The Inbox Repair tool is automatically installed along with Outlook. To run the Inbox Repair tool, follow these instructions. The procedure is a little bit complicated, but it certainly beats losing all the items in Outlook.pst.

24

1. Shut down Outlook. You cannot run the Inbox Repair tool successfully if Outlook is running.

2. Run Scanpst.exe. You can find Scanpst.exe at C:\Program Files\Common Files\System\MSMAPI\1033. The 1033 is what is known as a *locale identifier* for the installation of Microsoft Office System applications on your computer. The value 1033 means an English language installation in the United States. If you have a different installation type, your locale identifier will be different.

3. In the Inbox Repair Tool dialog box (shown in the illustration), enter the path to Outlook.pst, or click the Browse button to navigate to it. Use the Inbox Repair tool if your Personal Folders ever get corrupted.

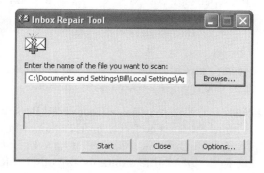

TIP *You can have the Inbox Repair tool create a log of its activities by clicking Options, then selecting the options you want in the dialog box that appears. The log file appears in the same location as Outlook.pst.*

4. Click Start to begin scanning your data file. If problems appear during the scan, the Inbox Repair tool displays a dialog box like the one in the following illustration and prompts you for permission to fix the problems. Click Repair.

5. Once the Inbox Repair tool finishes fixing errors, it displays a message box that tells you when the repairs are complete. Click OK to complete the process.

6. Start Outlook using the e-mail profile associated with the data file you're trying to repair.

7. If the Folder list isn't already visible, click Go | Folder List to open the Folder list (or just use the CTRL-6 keyboard shortcut).

8. Look in the Folder list. You may see a Recovered Personal Folders folder, or a Lost And Found folder. The Recovered Personal Folders folder, if visible, contains default Outlook folders that have been recovered. The Lost And Found folder, if visible, contains any other folders or items that the Inbox Repair tool was able to recover.

9. Move any recovered folders or items to the appropriate locations in the Folder list.

10. Once you have retrieved all the recovered items from them, you can delete the Lost And Found folder and the Recovered Personal Folders folder.

Compact Your Personal Folders File

One surprising thing about the way Outlook stores information in data files is that the files don't automatically get smaller when you remove items from them. Without some sort of intervention on your part, your data files will only get bigger and bigger. To squeeze out the unused space in data files, you must manually compact them.

Compacting a data file reorganizes the information in it, allowing it to shrink to occupy only the amount of space actually needed for the items it contains. Compacting a data file can take several minutes but can free a lot of disk space and perhaps improve Outlook performance.

To compact a data file, follow these steps:

1. Click File | Data File Management to open the Outlook Data Files dialog box shown in the illustration. You should see one or more data file names in the list. You can manage all your Outlook data files from this dialog box.

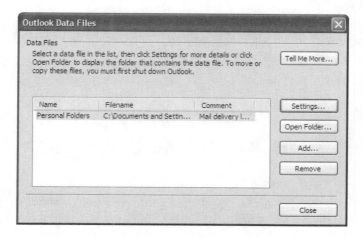

2. Select the data file you want to compact (Outlook.pst should appear in the list with a name of Personal Folders), then click Settings to open a settings dialog box for that data file like the one shown here.

3. Click Compact Now and Outlook will squeeze out the wasted space in your data file.

 *I suggest compacting your data files a few times a year, more frequently if your PC is low on disk space.*

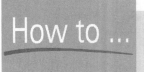 **Password-Protect Your Data Files**

For additional security, you can apply password protection to your data files. You might want to do this to ensure that people with physical access to your computer can't get at your e-mail just by starting Outlook. When you password-protect Outlook.pst, you need to enter that password before Outlook will display any information. Partway through its startup process, Outlook displays the Personal Folders Password dialog box, where you need to enter the correct password for Outlook.pst to complete the startup.

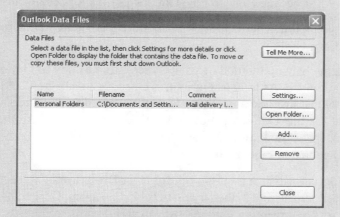

Follow these instructions to set or change password protection on your data files:

1. Click File | Data File Management. This opens the Outlook Data Files dialog box.

2. In the Data Files list, select the data file you want to password-protect. Select the one named Personal Folders to protect your active Outlook items.

3. Click Settings to open the data file's General Settings dialog box.

4. Click Change Password to open the Change Password dialog box.

5. If the data file is already password-protected, enter the old password as well as the new one. If the data file is not password-protected yet, leave the Old Password field blank.

NOTE   *You can tell your computer to remember your data file passwords by setting the Save This Password In Your Password List check box. But do this only if you have your computer user account password-protected and you log out whenever you're going to be away from your machine.*

Back Up Your Personal Folders File

Backing up your Personal Folders file once in a while is a sensible precaution. While the Inbox Repair tool can fix many problems with Outlook.pst, it isn't foolproof. Considering how much information you're likely to have stored away in your Personal Folders after a while, backing it up seems only prudent. Here's how you do it:

1. Figure out where Outlook.pst is stored on your computer. Some of the folders you need to navigate through may be hidden. You can look in Windows help to see how to make hidden folders visible for your version of Windows, but you might need help from your network administrator or someone else who has administrative rights on this computer. If you're not sure how to find Outlook.pst, see the How To Find Outlook.pst box for detailed instructions.

2. Once you know where Outlook.pst is stored, navigate to that folder, then shut down Outlook.

3. Using the backup method of your choice, store a copy of Outlook.pst in a safe place. As long as Outlook is closed, you can copy and paste Outlook.pst just like any other file. But you need to pay attention to the size of the file. Outlook.pst can grow to occupy hundreds of megabytes of disk space, making it impractical to back up on floppy disks or other low-capacity storage media.

4. If Outlook.pst is just a bit too big for any of your available backup options, consider compacting it, then trying to back it up again. Depending on a variety of factors, compacting Outlook.pst can significantly reduce its size.

5. Restart Outlook and resume your work.

Do Some General Housekeeping

Throughout this chapter, you've seen various ways to maintain Outlook for best performance. This last section contains a grab bag of additional things you can do to eke out a little more performance and use a little less disk space with Outlook. There's nothing earthshaking here, just a few tips you might want to investigate. The general housekeeping actions are:

- Retrieve Deleted Items

- Empty the Deleted Items folder

- Empty the Sent Items folder

- Consider removing attachments

Find Outlook.pst

Outlook.pst can be hard to find on your own, especially since it may be located in a hidden folder. Fortunately, Outlook the program can tell you where Outlook the data file is. Just follow these instructions:

1. In the main Outlook window, click Tools | Options to open the Options dialog box.

2. On the Mail Setup tabbed page of the Options dialog box, click Data Files to open the Outlook Data Files dialog box.

3. Your Outlook.pst file should appear in this dialog box with the name Personal Folders. Click Personal Folders and then Settings to open the Personal Folders Settings dialog box.

4. Look at the Filename field. It contains the complete path to Outlook.pst.

Did you know?

Outlook Uses Many Types of Files?

Outlook 2003 creates or uses a large number of data and configuration files that are stored in various locations on your computer. These include the Outlook data files you're reading about right now, Personal Address Book files, Navigation Pane settings, Rules, Print Styles, Stationary, and other assorted file types. To do a comprehensive job of backing up Outlook, you would want to back up all these files too, preferably using a standard backup utility.

To see the types of files Outlook uses, and where it stores all of them, you can use the Outlook help system. Click Help | Microsoft Office Outlook Help. In the Microsoft Office Outlook Help pane, enter **Outlook File Locations** in the Search box, then click the Start Searching button (the green button with the arrow to the right of the Search box).

View the Outlook File Locations help topic. It lists all the data and configuration files Outlook uses, and shows the path to each. Since the paths to some of the files include hidden folders, the help topic also includes instructions on how to make the hidden folders visible under Windows XP and Windows 2000.

24

Retrieve Deleted Items

Outlook provides two ways to retrieve deleted files, one of which is available for any Outlook user, and one of which works only when you're connected to an Exchange server and the feature has been enabled by the e-mail administrator. I cover the first way here. For more on retrieving deleted items when you're connected to an Exchange server, turn back to Chapter 23.

You can retrieve deleted items from the Outlook Deleted Items folder. This folder will either hold deleted items until you manually empty the Deleted Items folder, or delete them every time you exit Outlook, depending on the options you choose.

NOTE *See the "Empty the Deleted Items Folder" topic in the next section for instructions on emptying the folder and on configuring Outlook to automatically empty it for you.*

To Retrieve a Deleted Item from the Deleted Items Folder

To retrieve one or more items from the Deleted Items folder, follow these steps:

1. In the main Outlook window, click Go | Folder List to open the Folder list (or just use the CTRL-6 keyboard shortcut).

2. In the Navigation Pane, click Deleted Items to open the Deleted Items folder. Files that are deleted but can still be retrieved will appear in the folder as shown here. You can instantly retrieve any items in the Outlook Deleted Items folder.

3. Drag the item or items you want to retrieve to the folder you want them in, and you're done.

CAUTION *You can retrieve deleted Tasks that were assigned to someone else, or for which you were receiving status reports, but they will no longer be assigned to the other person and you will no longer receive status reports on them.*

Empty the Deleted Items Folder

Emptying the Deleted Items folder is an easy way to reclaim some disk space. You can do this manually every so often if you like, or you can tell Outlook to empty it for you automatically.

> TIP
>
> *Since the contents of the Deleted Items folder are readily accessible from within Outlook, simply deleting a message from your Inbox doesn't do much to prevent others from seeing it. Anyone with access to your computer for even a moment or two can look into your Deleted Items folder and see what's there. If you want to keep casual snoops from seeing your deleted messages, set Outlook to automatically empty the Deleted Items folder and then manually empty it after deleting any particularly interesting messages.*

24

Automatically Empty the Outlook Deleted Items Folder

To set Outlook to empty its Deleted Items folder automatically, follow these steps:

1. In the main Outlook window, click Tools | Options to open the Options dialog box.

2. On the Other tabbed page of the Options dialog box (see the illustration), set the Empty The Deleted Items Folder Upon Exiting check box. Use this page to tell Outlook to automatically empty its Deleted Items folder whenever you exit the program.

3. Normally, Outlook will notify you before emptying the Deleted Items folder. If you want to eliminate this notification message, click Advanced Options to open the Advanced Options dialog box shown in the following illustration.

Clear the Warn Before Permanently Deleting Items check box to eliminate the warning. You can use the Advanced Options dialog box to eliminate the warning that appears before emptying the Deleted Items folder.

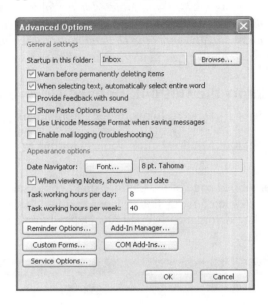

Manually Empty the Outlook Deleted Items Folder

To empty the Deleted Items folder yourself, follow these steps:

1. In the main Outlook window, click Go | Folder List to open the Folder list (or use the CTRL-6 keyboard shortcut).

2. In the Folder list, right-click the Deleted Items folder icon, then click Empty "Deleted Items" Folder in the menu that appears.

Empty the Sent Items Folder

By default, Outlook saves a copy of every e-mail message you send, including all those you copy or forward to someone. These copies go in the Sent Items folder. If you send a lot of e-mail, this folder can quickly accumulate hundreds or thousands of copies of old messages. This uses up disk space, makes your old e-mail readily accessible to anyone with physical access to your computer, makes your Personal Folders file bigger and harder to back up, and generally creates unneeded clutter. It makes sense to occasionally clean out your Sent Items folder.

Remove Items from the Sent Items Folder

You can delete all the messages from the Sent Items folder, or pick and choose the ones you want to keep. Sometimes I find it helpful to retain copies of messages I've sent, particularly if they deal with important or controversial topics. But in general, it's easiest just to delete all the messages in the folder every so often.

 Messages you delete from the Sent Items folder do not go into the Deleted Items folder. Instead they are deleted immediately and permanently. So make sure you don't delete a message you may need again.

24

Follow these steps to remove items from the Sent Items folder:

1. In the main Outlook window, click Go | Folder List to open the Folder list (or just use the CTRL-6 keyboard shortcut).

2. In the Folder list, click Sent Items to open the Sent Items folder. Copies of the messages you've sent since the last time you emptied the Sent Item folder appear here, as shown in the illustration. Copies of all the messages you've sent appear in the Sent Items folder.

3. Select the messages you want to delete from the Sent Items folder. To delete all the files in the Sent Items folder, click Edit | Select All.

4. Click Delete on the Standard toolbar, or use the CTRL-D keyboard shortcut

Consider Removing Attachments

When you receive files as attachments, what do you do with them? If there are ones you don't expect, you probably delete them and the message they came in on. But what if they're attachments you do expect? Do you save the attached file and then use it? If so, you end up with multiple copies of the file. One of them is still attached to the e-mail message it arrived on, and the other is wherever you stored it before you started working with it.

If you want to conserve disk space and lessen the chance of confusion between different versions of the attached file, you should remove the attachment after you've saved a copy of it elsewhere on your hard drive. If you want to try this, it's easy. Here's how you do it:

1. Double-click the message containing the attachment you want to remove so that it opens in a separate window.

2. In the message window, right-click the attachment. This opens the shortcut menu shown in the illustration. Removing attachments from e-mail messages can save disk space and reduce confusion.

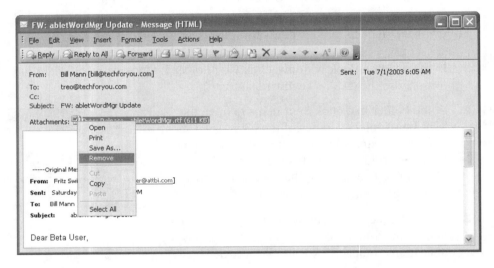

3. Click Remove to remove the attachment from the message.

You have one last chance to recover the attachment if you realize you don't want to remove it. Since you opened the message in its own window, that window remains open after you remove the attachment. When you try to close the message Window, Outlook asks you if you want to save the changes (the changes in this case being the removal of the attachment). If you click NO, Outlook restores the attachment and closes the window, so you don't lose anything.

Chapter 25

Use Outlook with Other Applications

How to...

- Share Information Between Outlook and Other Office System Applications
- Smart Tags Mean Smart Interactions Between Applications
- Learn More Ways to Send Office System Documents

As part of the Microsoft Office System, Outlook is designed to interact smoothly with applications like Word, Excel, Access, and PowerPoint. You've seen examples of this throughout the book, from things like using Word as your Outlook e-mail editor to linking documents to an Outlook Contact.

This final chapter covers some more general ways that Outlook can interact with the other applications in the Office System. The most basic ways involve copying and pasting information between Outlook items and documents created with other applications. These are followed by ways to link documents to Outlook items or embed them within Outlook items.

Smart Tags provide a more sophisticated way for Office System applications to interact. Smart Tags help you work with various types of information in documents, and can activate Outlook to do things like scheduling a meeting on a date that appears in a Word document.

Finally, to aid in collaboration, Office System applications can take advantage of Outlook to mail documents in many ways. You can e-mail documents using a special review format, or even route documents to a list of recipients one after another.

Share Information Between Outlook and Other Office System Applications

You can share information between Outlook and other Office System applications in several ways. You can

- Cut and paste information between documents in different applications
- Drag and drop information between documents in different applications
- Collect and paste multiple items of information into multiple Office System applications
- Link or embed files in an Outlook item

Cut and Paste Information

This is a basic way to share information between Outlook and other Office System applications. Simply select the information you want to move or copy from one document, then cut it (use Edit | Cut) from that location and paste it (use Edit | Paste) in the new location.

Drag and Drop Information

Here you select the information you want to share, then drag it to a new location in the new document. If you drag by holding down the right mouse button, a shortcut menu appears that lets you choose to copy or paste the information as appropriate.

Collect Information to Paste into Office System Applications

If you have only one or two chunks of information you want to move between Outlook and other Office System applications, you can use the standard Windows cut and paste or drag and drop to get the job done. But if you have a lot of stuff to move, you should consider using the Clipboard (shown in Figure 25-1), which allows you to collect up to 24 items and paste them into any Office System application. See the "How to Collect and Paste Between Applications" box for detailed instructions.

FIGURE 25-1 The Clipboard allows you to collect and paste up to 24 items simultaneously.

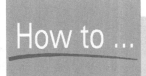

Collect and Paste Between Applications

Follow these steps to collect items that you want to paste into Outlook or copy from Outlook into another application:

1. If the Clipboard isn't visible, click File | Office Clipboard in any open Office System application to open the Clipboard.

2. Select one of the items you want to copy into another application, then click Copy on the Standard toolbar. This adds the item to the Clipboard, where it appears as an icon along with the first bit of the text you copied.

3. Repeat steps 1 and 2 for each item you want to add to the Clipboard. You can collect up to 24 items in the Clipboard.

To paste items from the Clipboard into Outlook or another Office System application, follow these steps:

1. If the Clipboard isn't visible, click File | Office Clipboard in any open Office System application to open the Clipboard.

CAUTION   *The Clipboard may not be available in some Outlook views. In this case, you must use drag and drop or some other technique to paste the item into the view.*

2. Click the spot in Outlook or any other Office System application where you want to paste an item from the Clipboard.

3. Click the item (or items) you want to paste into this location.

4. Repeat as necessary.

   *If you want to paste all the items in the Clipboard to the same location, click Paste All in the Clipboard pane.*

Link or Embed Office System Documents in Outlook Items

The ways of sharing information that we've covered so far in this section have one flaw: they put a copy of the information in a new location, instead of maintaining a direct link to the original file the information comes from. This is important when the information you're interested in can change. If you just copy (or collect) and paste information between documents and the original document changes, the documents you copied the information into won't get changed. That's where linking or embedding documents comes into play.

25

In Chapter 6, you learned about linking Office System documents to an Outlook Contact. You can similarly link part or all of an Office System document to an Outlook item. When you create a link like this, there is a connection between the linked document and the Outlook item. If the original document changes, that change is reflected in the Outlook item that is linked to it.

Complications arise when you plan to share or e-mail Outlook items containing linked documents. Making the link to the original document accessible to people using different computers, different parts of the corporate network, or even different networks altogether requires special steps. See the Link or Embed Files topic in the Outlook help system for more information on how to create linked documents and what you must do to make those links work in various circumstances.

You can also embed a copy of an Office System document into an Outlook item. In this case, the embedded document becomes part of the Outlook item. If you make changes to the embedded document, those changes appear in the Outlook item, but there is no link back to the original document. Again, see the Link or Embed Files topic in the Outlook help system for more information.

Smart Tags Mean Smart Interactions Between Applications

Smart Tags are a feature of Microsoft Office System that first appeared in Office XP. In Office 2003, Smart Tags can appear in Outlook (when you use Word as your e-mail editor), Word, Excel, Access, PowerPoint, and the Research pane. Smart Tags can help you complete common Office System tasks, as well as provide additional control over various automatic features of Office. Of particular interest to us in this book, Smart Tags can cause other Office System applications to interact with Outlook. For example, one Smart Tag option in Word helps you create an Outlook appointment starting with a date in a Word document.

If you're interested in how Smart Tags do what they do, you can find more information in the "Did You Know How Smart Tags Work?" box.

Smart Tags are indicated by a series of purple dots under text in documents, or by a little purple triangle in the lower right-hand corner of Excel spreadsheet cells. When you place the cursor over a Smart Tag, a small button appears on the screen above the tagged text or cell. When you point to this button with the mouse, a small down arrow appears next to it. Clicking this down arrow opens a menu containing the actions provided by the Smart Tag.

The Smart Tag button of most interest when it comes to making Outlook work with other Office System applications is the Smart Tag Actions button. This button, which appears as an *i* inside a circle, inside a square (see the following illustration), offers a range of options that varies with the tagged text or cell. Many of these options involve Outlook.

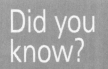

The action that helps create an Outlook appointment from a date in a Word document is a perfect example of Outlook working with another Office System application. Let's walk through that one.

Did you know?   **How Smart Tags Work?**

Smart Tags consist of two small chunks of software (COM DLLs for you programmers out there) that Office System applications use when they are running. The first part of the Smart Tag is the recognizer, software that checks documents for certain text. This can be specific text (the word Microsoft, for example) or a type of text (names or addresses, for example).

The second part of the Smart Tag is the action. The action provides a set of one or more commands that can be executed on the recognized text. These commands are the menu options that appear when you click the down arrow next to the Smart Tag Actions button.

Assuming that your copy of Word 2003 is configured normally, whenever you type a date into a document, Word associates a Smart Tag with that date. If you point at the date with the mouse, the Smart Tag Actions button appears. If you then point to the icon and click the down arrow that appears, you will see a menu similar to the one in the illustration. If you look at the second and third options in that menu, you can see two ways that the Smart Tag Actions button causes Word to interact with Outlook.

The Show My Calendar option opens Outlook in Calendar view and displays your calendar for the particular date associated with the Smart Tag. This is a nice convenience if you want to check your calendar for the day you're writing about.

The Schedule A Meeting option opens a Meeting window, with the start and end dates automatically filled in with the dates associated with the Smart Tag. While you still have to fill in all the rest of the information yourself, using the Smart Tag to get the meeting request started is certainly easier than doing it manually.

Activate Smart Tags in an Office System Application

Smart Tags can help you use other Office System applications with Outlook, but they may not be activated for each of the Office System applications you use. Follow these steps to find out if Smart Tags are active in a particular application and to turn them on if they're not:

1. In the main window for the application you want to check, click Tools | AutoCorrect Options. This opens the AutoCorrect options dialog box for the application.

2. On the Smart Tags tab in the AutoCorrect options dialog box (see Figure 25-2), select the Label Text With Smart Tags check box or the Label Data With Smart Tags check box (depending on which application you're working with). This allows the application to attach Smart Tags to text or data.

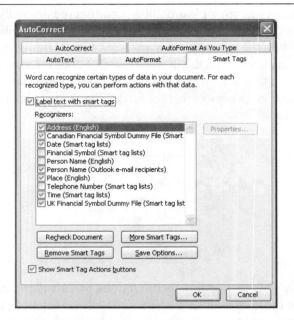

| FIGURE 25-2 | The Smart Tags tab of the AutoCorrect options dialog box in Word is representative of the tabs you will see in other Office System applications. |

3. At the bottom of the Smart Tags tab, select the Show Smart Tag Actions Buttons check box. This allows the Smart Tags icon to appear when you point to text or data with an associated Smart Tag.

Learn More Ways to Send Office System Documents

Back in Chapter 4, you learned how to send Office System documents to recipients as e-mail attachments. But that's only one way to send documents. The Office System applications offer several other methods to send documents from within the individual applications. These methods support such activities as the review of documents by multiple recipients as well as the routing of documents between recipients.

NOTE *The specific methods available in any situation depend on the application you are sending the document from.*

To take advantage of these different methods of sending documents, you use the Send To option in the File menu of any Office System application. When you click File | Send To, the application displays a menu containing all the sending options you can use right now. The following illustration shows a Send To menu with many of the sending options available. The following sections provide more information on some of the most commonly used sending options.

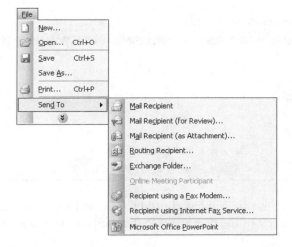

Use the Mail Recipient Option

The Mail Recipient option is the most basic option in the Send To menu. When you use this option, you send the recipient a copy of the open document. This copy is included in the body of the message. It isn't an attachment that the recipient can save and treat as an independent file.

When you select Mail Recipient, Word displays a toolbar and the text entry fields necessary to send an e-mail message with Outlook. In addition, it displays an Introduction field where you can describe the material included in the body of the message. The following illustration shows what the main Word window looks like after clicking Mail Recipient.

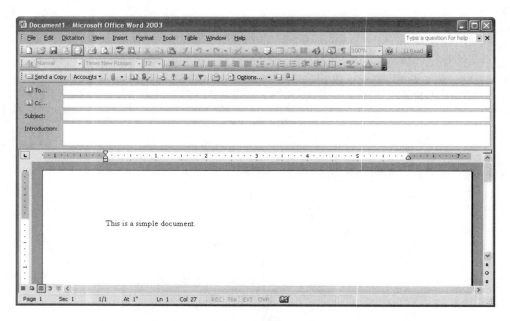

Once you fill in the To, Subject, Introduction, and any other fields, click Send Copy to e-mail a copy of the document to the recipient or recipients.

Use the Mail Recipient For Review Option

The Mail Recipient For Review menu option sounds as if it should be similar to the Mail Recipient option. However, things are significantly different when you send out a document for review. A copy of the document you are sending is included as an attachment in a Review message like the one in Figure 25-3.

 *Your reviewers should be using Office Outlook 2003 and Office Word 2003 to review documents sent with the Mail Recipient For Review option.*

The recipients can review the document, suggest changes, then return the document with their comments. The details of the review process vary slightly depending on which application the document originates in. See the Sending for Review topic in the help system of the application for more information.

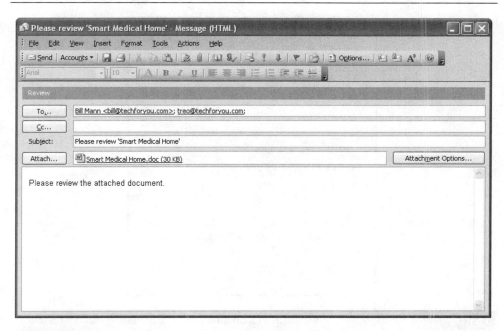

FIGURE 25-3   The Mail Recipient For Review option generates a Review message with the document attached to it.

Use the Routing Recipient Option

While the two Mail Recipient options allow you to send a copy of the document to one or more recipients simultaneously, the Routing Recipient option is fundamentally different. With this option, by default a single attached copy of the document goes to each recipient in turn. This method enables each recipient to make changes to the same document and to see what changes previous recipients have made.

In addition to the benefit of having everyone work on the same document, the Routing Recipient option allows you to track the status of the document as it travels among recipients. You can also set up the routing so that the document is automatically returned to you after the last recipient finishes with it.

The key to using the Routing Recipient option is the Routing Slip dialog box (Figure 25-4) that appears when you select this option. In this dialog box, you create an ordered list of recipients who will receive the message, and set any other options you would like to apply to the routed message.

FIGURE 25-4 Attaching a routing slip to a document you are sending out for review causes it to be routed to all the recipients in order.

When each recipient finishes reviewing the document, that recipient goes to the File | Send To menu and selects Next Routing Recipient to speed the message on its way.

Appendix

Outlook 2003 Keyboard Shortcuts

How to...

■ Use Outlook 2003 keyboard shortcuts

While using the mouse to navigate and control Outlook is the easiest way to go, it isn't the fastest. Many of the functions and commands in Outlook have associated keyboard shortcuts, or combinations of keystrokes that replace pointing and clicking. Using keyboard shortcuts is faster than pointing and clicking, assuming there's a shortcut for what you want to do, and you remember it.

Microsoft took care of the first part of the equation by providing dozens of keyboard shortcuts for Outlook 2003. To help with the remembering part, I've covered popular keyboard shortcuts in the relevant chapters. As an additional aid, I've gathered a pretty comprehensive list of Outlook 2003 keyboard shortcuts in this appendix. Use it as a reference guide and as a tool to help you learn important keyboard shortcuts. This is not a comprehensive list of all the keyboard shortcuts in Outlook 2003. For a comprehensive list, search the help system for the topic Keyboard Shortcut.

 *Many of the keyboard shortcuts described here are common across Office System 2003 applications.*

Help System Keyboard Shortcuts

Help system keyboard shortcuts work across all the applications in Office System 2003. Some of them are specific to the Help pane, while others work in the Help window.

Help Pane Keyboard Shortcuts

The keyboard shortcuts in Table A-1 are effective when you are working in the Help pane.

Help Window Keyboard Shortcuts

The keyboard shortcuts in Table A-2 are effective when you are working in the Help window.

Action	Keyboard Shortcut
Select the next item in the Help pane	TAB
Select the preceding item in the Help pane	SHIFT-TAB
Perform the action for the selected item	ENTER
Scroll forward through the Help pane	DOWN ARROW
Scroll backward through the Help pane	UP ARROW
Open the preceding Task pane	ALT-LEFT ARROW
Open the next Task pane	ALT-RIGHT ARROW
Open the Pane Options menu	CTRL-SPACE
Open or close the current Task pane	CTRL-F1

TABLE A-1   Keyboard Shortcuts That Work in the Help Pane

A

General Menu and Toolbar Keyboard Shortcuts

The keyboard shortcuts in Table A-3 apply across the applications in Microsoft Office System 2003. That is, they should work in Word, Excel, and other Office System applications as well as in Outlook.

Basic Outlook Navigation Keyboard Shortcuts

The keyboard shortcuts in Table A-4 help you quickly navigate between the sections of Outlook.

Action	Keyboard Shortcut
Select the next hidden text or hyperlink	TAB
Select the preceding hidden text or hyperlink	SHIFT-TAB
Perform the action for the selected item	ENTER
Open the next Help topic	ALT-RIGHT ARROW
Open the preceding Help topic	ALT-LEFT ARROW
Print the current Help topic	CTRL-P
Switch between tiled and untiled mode for the Help window	ALT-U

TABLE A-2   Keyboard Shortcuts That Work in the Help Window

Action	Keyboard Shortcut
Select or deselect the menu bar	F10
Move to the next item in the selected toolbar	TAB
Move to the preceding item in the selected toolbar	SHIFT-TAB
Select the next toolbar	CTRL-TAB
Select the preceding toolbar	CTRL-SHIFT-TAB
Open the selected menu or perform the selected action	ENTER
Display a shortcut menu for the selected item	SHIFT-F10
Display the window shortcut menu	ALT-SPACE
Select the first item in a menu	HOME
Select the last item in a menu	END
Close an open menu	ESC
Display all the commands in a menu	CTRL-DOWN ARROW
Display the Start menu	CTRL-ESC

TABLE A-3   Keyboard Shortcuts That Work for any Office System 2003 Application

Item and File Keyboard Shortcuts

These shortcuts speed your work with items and files. Many of them are Outlook-specific, while some will also work in other applications.

Action	Keyboard Shortcut
Switch to the Mail pane	CTRL-1
Switch to the Calendar pane	CTRL-2
Switch to the Contacts pane	CTRL-3
Switch to the Tasks pane	CTRL-4
Switch to the Notes pane	CTRL-5
Switch to the Navigation pane Folder list	CTRL-6
Switch to the Navigation pane Shortcuts list	CTRL-7
Switch between panes	F6
Switch between the Outlook window, the Navigation pane, and the Reading pane	TAB
Select an Outlook folder to open	CTRL-Y

TABLE A-4   Keyboard Shortcuts That Help You Navigate Outlook Sections

Action	Keyboard Shortcut
Create a new Appointment	CTRL-SHIFT-A
Create a new Contact	CTRL-SHIFT-C
Create a new Distribution List	CTRL-SHIFT-L
Create a new Fax	CTRL-SHIFT-X
Create a new Folder (within Outlook)	CTRL-SHIFT-E
Create a new Journal Entry	CTRL-SHIFT-J
Create a new Meeting Request	CTRL-SHIFT-Q
Create a new Message	CTRL-SHIFT-M
Create a new Note	CTRL-SHIFT-N
Create a new Office document	CTRL-SHIFT-H
Post an item to the selected folder	CTRL-SHIFT-S
Create a new Task	CTRL-SHIFT-K
Create a new Task Request	CTRL-SHIFT-U

TABLE A-5   Keyboard Shortcuts the Create New Outlook Items and Files

Item and File Creation Keyboard Shortcuts

The keyboard shortcuts in Table A-5 let you create new Outlook items or files instantly.

Other Item and File Keyboard Shortcuts

The keyboard shortcuts in Table A-6 perform functions on items and files other than creating them.

Action	Keyboard Shortcut
Save the open item	CTRL-S
Save and Close	ALT-S
Save As	F12
Show the ScreenTip for the active item	SHIFT-F1
Undo the last action	CTRL-Z
Delete the selected item	CTRL-D
Print the selected item	CTRL-P
Copy the selected item	CTRL-SHIFT-Y

TABLE A-6   Keyboard Shortcuts That Work for any Office System 2003 Application

Action	Keyboard Shortcut
Move the selected item	CTRL-SHIFT-V
Open the Search toolbar to find particular items	F3
Open the Advanced Find dialog box	CTRL-SHIFT-F
Create a new Search folder	CTRL-SHIFT-P

TABLE A-6 Keyboard Shortcuts That Work for any Office System 2003 Application *(continued)*

Keyboard Shortcuts for Working with E-Mail

The keyboard shortcuts in Table A-7 can be quite useful and efficient when you're working with your e-mail.

Action	Keyboard Shortcut
Check for valid names in the recipients fields when Word is your e-mail editor	ALT-K
Check for valid names in the recipients fields when Outlook is your e-mail editor	CTRL-K
Check the spelling of the message body	F7
Open the Flag For Follow Up dialog box	CTRL-SHIFT-G
Add a Quick Flag to the selected message	INSERT
Forward a message	CTRL-F
Send a message	ALT-S
Switch to the Inbox	CTRL-SHIFT-I
Switch to the Outbox	CTRL-SHIFT-O
Reply to a Message	CTRL-R
Reply to all recipients of a Message	CTRL-SHIFT-R
Show blocked external message content	CTRL-SHIFT-I
Post to the selected folder	CTRL-SHIFT-S
Check for new mail	F9
Scroll down through a list of messages	DOWN ARROW
Scroll up through a list of messages	UP ARROW
Open the Address Book	CTRL-SHIFT-B
Mark a message as having been read	CTRL-Q

TABLE A-7 Keyboard Shortcuts for Working with E-mail

Action	Keyboard Shortcut
Accept a meeting or task request	ALT-C
Decline a meeting or task request	ALT-D

TABLE A-8   Keyboard Shortcuts for Working with Appointments and Tasks

Keyboard Shortcuts for Working with Appointments and Tasks

The keyboard shortcuts in Table A-8 will improve your efficiency when you are working with Appointments (including Meeting Requests) and Tasks.

Keyboard Shortcuts for Working with Contacts

The keyboard shortcuts in Table A-9 are useful when working with Contacts.

Keyboard Shortcuts for Working with Tasks

The keyboard shortcuts in Table A-10 are useful when working with Contacts.

Keyboard Shortcuts for Formatting Text

The keyboard shortcuts in Table A-11 are useful when formatting text in Outlook items and also work in other Office System 2003 applications.

Action	Keyboard Shortcut
Search for a Contact	F11
Dial the phone number of the selected Contact	CTRL-SHIFT-D

TABLE A-9   Keyboard Shortcuts for Working with Contacts

Action	Keyboard Shortcut
Search for a Contact	F11
Dial the phone number of the selected Contact	CTRL-SHIFT-D

TABLE A-10 Keyboard Shortcuts for Working with Tasks

Keyboard Shortcuts for Working with Views

There are quite a few keyboard shortcuts that affect views. In some cases, the same shortcut has different effects, depending on the type of view that's active and whether or not a group is selected.

Keyboard Shortcuts for Working in a Table View

The keyboard shortcuts in Table A-12 work when you are in a Table view.

Action	Keyboard Shortcut
Open the Format menu	ALT-O
Change the case of selected text	SHIFT-F3
Make the selected text bold	CTRL-B
Turn the selected line of text into a bullet item	CTRL-SHIFT-L
Italicize the selected text	CTRL-I
Increase the indentation of the current line	CTRL-T
Decrease the indentation of the current line	CTRL-SHIFT-T
Left-align the selected text	CTRL-L
Center the selected text	CTRL-E
Right-align the selected text	CTRL-R
Underline the selected text	CTRL-U
Increase the font size of the selected text	CTRL-]
Decrease the font size of the selected text	CTRL-[
Cut the selected text	CTRL-X
Copy the selected text	CTRL-C
Paste the selected text	CTRL-V
Remove all formatting from the selected text	CTRL-SHIFT-Z
Edit a URL that's included in the body of an item	CTRL-left click

TABLE A-11 Keyboard Shortcuts for Formatting Text

Action	Keyboard Shortcut
Open an item	ENTER
Select all the items in the view	CTRL-A
Select the item at the bottom of the View pane (not necessarily the last item in the view)	PAGE DOWN
Select the item at the top of the View pane (not necessarily the first item in the view)	PAGE UP
Extend the group of selected items by one	SHIFT-DOWN ARROW
Shorten the group of selected items by one	SHIFT-UP ARROW
Go to the next item without extending the list of selected items	CTRL-DOWN ARROW
Go to the preceding item without shortening the list of selected items	CTRL-UP ARROW
Select or deselect the active item	CTRL-SPACE
Open or expand the items in a selected group	ENTER

TABLE A-12   Keyboard Shortcuts for Working in a Table View

Keyboard Shortcuts for Working in the Day/Week/ Month Views

The keyboard shortcuts in Table A-13 are useful when you are working in the Day, Week, and Month views.

Action	Keyboard Shortcut
View multiple days, starting with the selected day	ALT-1 through 9
View 10 days, starting with the selected day	ALT-0
Switch to Weeks view	ALT-HYPHEN
Switch to Months view	ALT-EQUALS
Switch between the Calendar, TaskPad, and Folder lists	F6
Select the next Appointment	TAB
Select the preceding Appointment	SHIFT-TAB
In Day view, select the time slot that corresponds to the start of your work day	HOME
In Day view, select the time slot that corresponds to the end of your work day	END
In Day view, select the next time block	DOWN ARROW
In Day view, select the preceding time block	UP ARROW
In Day view, extend the selected block of time	SHIFT-DOWN ARROW
In Day view, shorten the selected block of time	SHIFT-UP ARROW

TABLE A-13   Keyboard Shortcuts for Working with Day/Week/Month Views

Action	Keyboard Shortcut
In Day view, move the selected item to the same day and time next week	ALT-DOWN ARROW
In Day view, move the selected item to the same day and time in the preceding week	ALT-UP ARROW
In Week or Month view, go to the first day of the week	HOME
In Week or Month views, go to the last day of the week	END
In Week view, go to the same day in the preceding week	PAGE UP
In Week view, go to the same day in the next week	PAGE DOWN
In Month view, go to the same day five weeks in the past	PAGE UP
In Month view, go to the same day five weeks in the future	PAGE DOWN
In the Date Navigator, go to the first day of the current week	ALT-HOME
In the Date Navigator, go to the last day of the current week	ALT-END
In the Date Navigator, go to the same day in the preceding week	ALT-UP ARROW
In the Date Navigator, go to the same day in the next week	ALT-DOWN ARROW
In the Date Navigator, go to the first day of the month	ALT-PAGE UP
In the Date Navigator, go to the last day of the month	ALT-PAGE DOWN

TABLE A-13 Keyboard Shortcuts for Working with Day/Week/Month Views *(continued)*

Keyboard Shortcuts for Address Card Views

The keyboard shortcuts in Table A-14 are helpful for working in Address Card views.

Action	Keyboard Shortcut
Select the preceding Address card	UP ARROW
Select the next Address card	DOWN ARROW
Select the first Address card in the list	HOME
Select the last Address card in the list	END
Select the first Address card on this page	PAGE UP
Select the last Address card on this page	PAGE DOWN
Select or deselect the active Address card	CTRL-SPACE
Extend the list of selected Address cards to the first card in the Contacts list	SHIFT-HOME
Extend the list of selected Address cards to the first card in the Contacts list	SHIFT-END
Select the first field in the selected Address card	F2
Move to the next field in an Address card (or from the last field of the card to the first field of the next card)	TAB
Move to the preceding field in an Address card (or from the first field of the card to the last field of the preceding card)	SHIFT-TAB

TABLE A-14 Keyboard Shortcuts for Address Card Views

Index

activating in an Office System application, 415–416

how Smart Tags work, 414

Schedule A Meeting option, 415

Show My Calendar option, 415

Smart Tag action in Word, 415

Smart Tag button, function of, 414

spam

See also junk e-mail filter

antivirus software, importance of, 307

tips for avoiding, 304–305

web beacons, 306, 307, 308–309

speech recognition

introduction to, 352

accuracy, improving, 359

Add or Remove Programs dialog box, 356

Asian languages, 352–353

best use of, 364

Dictation mode, working in, 361–362

Dictation *vs.* Voice Command modes in, 353

dictionary, adding words to, 363

error correction in, 362–363

installing Windows speech recognition system, 356–358

Language Bar, configuring to appear, 350–360

microphone, turning on, 360

Speech properties dialog box, 365

third-party speech recognition software, 355

training process for, 358

user profiles, creating/using, 364–366

verifying installation of, 354–355

Voice Command mode, working in, 363–364

spell-checker

See also e-mail messages

launching, 55

starting Outlook. *See* Outlook, starting/initializing

T

Table view

keyboard shortcuts for, 429

Tablet PCs

digital ink support on, 4–5

handwriting tools on, 8–9, 343

improved connection management on, 10

Journal view on, 228

notes on, 219

tasks

See also Calendar

assigning a task, 205–207

automatic tracking/updating of, 212–213

e-mails, turning into tasks, 210

Outlook Help system resource for, 214

receiving a task, 207–208

recurring tasks, 208–210

task creation from existing task, 204–205

task creation from scratch, 203

Task view, introduction to, 190–191, 202–203

TaskPad, activating, 191

TaskPad, use in scheduling tasks, 192, 211–212

teams. *See* SharePoint Team Services

Through the Specified Account option

upgrade problems with, 29

toolbars. *See* menus and toolbars

transforming Outlook items (into other Outlook items), 210

U

upgrading Outlook. *See* Outlook, upgrading

V

vCards

and corporate firewalls, 113

creating/sending, 112–113

as part of e-mail signature, 113–114

views

See also specific views; dialog boxes

introduction to, 268–269

arrangements, use of, 272–273

basic view types, 269

Calendar View, configuration of, 173, 174

By Company view (in Contacts), 104, 105

custom view, defining from existing view, 276–277

custom view, defining from scratch, 274–276

custom view, renaming, 277

Customize View: Sample New View dialog box, 275

filtering a view (view filter), 269–270

grouping items in a view, 271–272

Mail view, changing arrangements in, 273

sorting a view (ascending/descending order), 270–271

INTERNATIONAL CONTACT INFORMATION

AUSTRALIA
McGraw-Hill Book Company
Australia Pty. Ltd.
TEL +61-2-9900-1800
FAX +61-2-9878-8881
http://www.mcgraw-hill.com.au
books-it_sydney@mcgraw-hill.com

CANADA
McGraw-Hill Ryerson Ltd.
TEL +905-430-5000
FAX +905-430-5020
http://www.mcgraw-hill.ca

GREECE, MIDDLE EAST, & AFRICA
(Excluding South Africa)
McGraw-Hill Hellas
TEL +30-210-6560-990
TEL +30-210-6560-993
TEL +30-210-6560-994
FAX +30-210-6545-525

MEXICO (Also serving Latin America)
McGraw-Hill Interamericana Editores
S.A. de C.V.
TEL +525-1500-5108
FAX +525-117-1589
http://www.mcgraw-hill.com.mx
carlos_ruiz@mcgraw-hill.com

SINGAPORE (Serving Asia)
McGraw-Hill Book Company
TEL +65-6863-1580
FAX +65-6862-3354
http://www.mcgraw-hill.com.sg
mghasia@mcgraw-hill.com

SOUTH AFRICA
McGraw-Hill South Africa
TEL +27-11-622-7512
FAX +27-11-622-9045
robyn_swanepoel@mcgraw-hill.com

SPAIN
McGraw-Hill/
Interamericana de España, S.A.U.
TEL +34-91-180-3000
FAX +34-91-372-8513
http://www.mcgraw-hill.es
professional@mcgraw-hill.es

UNITED KINGDOM, NORTHERN,
EASTERN, & CENTRAL EUROPE
McGraw-Hill Education Europe
TEL +44-1-628-502500
FAX +44-1-628-770224
http://www.mcgraw-hill.co.uk
emea_queries@mcgraw-hill.com

ALL OTHER INQUIRIES Contact:
McGraw-Hill/Osborne
TEL +1-510-420-7700
FAX +1-510-420-7703
http://www.osborne.com
omg_international@mcgraw-hill.com

Sound Off!

Visit us at **www.osborne.com/bookregistration** and let us know what you thought of this book. While you're online you'll have the opportunity to register for newsletters and special offers from McGraw-Hill/Osborne.

We want to hear from you!

Sneak Peek

Visit us today at **www.betabooks.com** and see what's coming from McGraw-Hill/Osborne tomorrow!

Based on the successful software paradigm, Bet@Books™ allows computing professionals to view partial and sometimes complete text versions of selected titles online. Bet@Books™ viewing is free, invites comments and feedback, and allows you to "test drive" books in progress on the subjects that interest you the most.

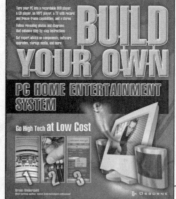
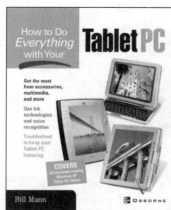

Microsoft
Office 2003
Answers for Everyone

Make the most of the entire Office system with help from these other books from Osborne

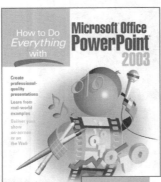

**Microsoft Office 2003:
The Complete Reference**
0-07-222995-0

**How to Do
Everything with
Microsoft Office
PowerPoint 2003**
0-07-222972-1

**How to Do
Everything with
Microsoft Office
FrontPage 2003**
0-07-222973-X

**Microsoft Access 2003
Professional Results**
0-07-222965-9

Available at Bookstores everywhere